A PLUME BOOK

TOP SECRET RESTAURANT RECIPES 2

TODD WILBUR is the top-selling QVC cookbook author. He's appeared on *The Oprah Winfrey Show, Today,* and *Live with Regis and Kathie Lee,* among others. He lives in Las Vegas

---

PRESENTS

TOP SECRET
RESTAURANT RECIPES 2

More Amazing Clones of Famous Dishes
from America's Favorite Restaurant Chains

BY
TODD WILBUR

Illustrated by the author

A PLUME BOOK

Visit us on the Web at: www.TopSecretRecipes.com.

Previously published as *Super Secret Restaurant Collection*

PLUME
Published by Penguin Group
Penguin Group (USA) Inc., 375 Hudson Street, New York, New York 10014, U.S.A. • Penguin Group (Canada), 90 Eglinton Avenue East, Suite 700, Toronto, Ontario, Canada M4P 2Y3 (a division of Pearson Penguin Canada Inc.) • Penguin Books Ltd., 80 Strand, London WC2R 0RL, England • Penguin Ireland, 25 St. Stephen's Green, Dublin 2, Ireland (a division of Penguin Books Ltd.) • Penguin Group (Australia), 250 Camberwell Road, Camberwell, Victoria 3124, Australia (a division of Pearson Australia Group Pty. Ltd.) • Penguin Books India Pvt. Ltd., 11 Community Centre, Panchsheel Park, New Delhi – 110 017, India • Penguin Books (NZ) cnr Airborne and Rosedale Roads, Albany, Auckland 1310, New Zealand (a division of Pearson New Zealand Ltd.) • Penguin Books (South Africa) (Pty.) Ltd., 24 Sturdee Avenue, Rosebank, Johannesburg 2196, South Africa

Penguin Books Ltd., Registered Offices: 80 Strand, London WC2R 0RL, England

First published by Plume, a member of Penguin Group (USA) Inc. Previously published under the title *Super Secret Restaurant Collection*.

First Printing, January 2007
10 9 8 7 6 5 4 3 2

Some of the recipes in this edition are selected from *Top Secret Restaurant Recipes*, published by Plume.

CIP data is available.

ISBN: 978-0-452-28901-7

Manufactured in China

For Ajay and Roxie

CONTENTS

MANY THANKS . . .

Cloning these famous recipes requires thousands of hours of work locked up alone in a kitchen with only the sounds of the dishwasher and Howard 101 to keep me company. However, a book like this could never have been made without the support and efforts of many others on the outside whom I must now thank.

I feel privileged to have hooked up with Plume in the early 1990s for the very first *Top Secret Recipes* cookbook. Since then we have published seven more trade paperbacks together, plus two special QVC editions and several other special market volumes. Plume has made this culinary publishing journey a pleasure every step of the way, and I want to thank everyone there for your contributions, opinions and collaborations through the years. Specifically I must thank Barbara O'Shea, Clare Ferraro, Trena Keating, Emily Haynes, Sandra Dear, Cherisse Dike, Kimberly Cagle, and Marie Coolman from the bottom of my heart for all of your hard work and support on this book.

Thanks to everyone behind the scenes at QVC and all the great on-air hosts for making these books the top-selling cookbook series on the shopping network. To Anthony Corrado, my man in the kitchen at QVC who always makes the food look so good on TV: Thanks, bud. You're not only an awesome food stylist, but also a great friend.

Thanks to Robert Wortham of W&A Marketing and his assistant, John Lowry, for the great cover photos. It's more like a party than work, really. And I'm happy to see that you didn't leave hungry.

Thank you to all of the waiters, waitresses and bartenders who take the time to answer my annoying questions when I'm on a cloning mission. Creating these recipes wouldn't be possible without the little tidbits of information and clues that you provide regarding ingredients and/or preparation techniques of these famous dishes.

Thanks to my family and friends for your anxious and helpful taste-testing of many of these recipes. As always, if you've got taste buds and an opinion, I've got free food.

Thanks to Nobu the Akita for taking over where Zebu the Wonder Dog left off. Those are some big paw prints to fill, but you're doing great so far.

And last, thank you to Pamela, the love of my life. When I'm stuck, you yank me out. When I'm down, you lift me up. No matter what life dishes out, I know it's going to be much better with you sharing my plate.

INTRODUCTION

I feel out of place at the ritzy Stirling Club in Las Vegas—like a Macho Nacho Burrito at a caviar tasting. But there I am attending an invite-only shindig where impressionist Rich Little speaks in his own voice, and *Lifestyles of the Rich and Famous* host Robin Leach works the room. It's a very Vegas moment.

Then someone drags singer Clint Holmes over to our group. He's the Tom Jones–esque crooner headlining at Harrah's who was voted "Best All Around Entertainer in Las Vegas." I mention that I saw him perform in Atlantic City at the 1990 Miss America Pageant I was covering as a TV news reporter. When he ignores my comment I wonder, "Did I just insult the man?" Now I'm not sure what to say.

Thankfully, a friend cuts through the awkwardness to tell Clint what I do for a living, "Todd writes cookbooks."

She looks back my way, expecting me to elaborate. "The books are called *Top Secret Recipes*," I tell him. "They show people how to make famous food at home with common ingredients."

From past experience I realize that at this point I haven't provided enough information to make Clint understand my strange career path, so here's where I open up my stance and bend forward as though I'm carefully studying a piece of food. "I reverse-engineer brand-name foods, like a Big Mac or a Twinkie or Red Lobster Cheddar Bay Biscuits, and then create clone recipes that instruct you how to easily duplicate the taste of these foods in your own kitchen using ingredients you can find in any supermarket."

Now I wait to see if the ball will fall on red or black. About half of the people appreciate the unusual cookbook concept, and many of them have used the recipes before, either from the books or off the website. But the other half—and these are usually people who don't like to cook—shoot me a blank, puzzled stare followed by a cordial nod of fake acknowledgment. It's a look that says, "Why the heck would I want to duplicate food that I can just go out and buy?" It seems like the Best All Around Entertainer of the Year is in the latter category. Let's just say the roulette ball fell on green that night, since Clint was whisked away before I could continue with my explanation.

If I'd had the chance to explain in more detail why so many people enjoy cloning famous foods, I think I could have won Clint over. I'd tell him how cool it is making America's most popular food in our own kitchens and then watching people freak out when they take a bite. I would suggest that we can save money by making these dishes at home, and that with these formulas we have the freedom to customize our favorite brand-name foods for special tastes and dietary requirements. I'd remark that unlike any other cookbook, when you cook for the first time from a *Top Secret Recipes* cookbook, you know in advance what the finished product will taste like.

By this time, I'm sure I'd see the huge lightbulb over Clint's head pop on. And then he would ask the next inevitable question: "How do you get away with this?"

Now I would explain to Clint that these are original, personally copyrighted recipes that I create from scratch in my own laboratory (I know, ha ha; it's really my kitchen, Clint). I'd describe to him the time-consuming process of dissecting multiple samples, of sniffing out ingredients, of straining sauces and calculating measurements. And then I'd finish by explaining that I never represent these recipes as the actual recipes for the brand-name foods, because I respect the success and trademarks of the companies, and that I imitate as a compliment to the corporate chefs. It's flattery in its sincerest form, I'd say.

By now Clint would be ignoring everyone else. As he starts to understand the multiple benefits of this niche concept of culinary deconstruction/reconstruction, he would refuse to sing a song for the crowd, because he wants to hear more. "How exactly do you get these recipes? Do you get a job at the restaurants and steal them?" When he still doesn't completely grasp what I'm saying, I'd spend more time with him, and I would make sure to talk very slowly.

I would tell Clint that creating these recipes is a game. Each *Top Secret Recipe* is a little mystery to be unraveled without full knowledge of the original formula. I'd tell him that I have never worked at any of these chains, nor have I ever obtained corporate recipes. I would explain how the game must be played using certain kitchen sleuthing techniques that I have developed over the past 20 years. I will, for example, order the food to go, but ask that all of the elements of the dish be packed up separately (sauces, garnishes, etc.) so that back in the lab I can copy each component of the dish one at a time. I'd also describe my extensive research in cookbooks and on the Internet to understand ways that similar recipes are crafted. I'd tell him that only then do I write out the recipe and make my first attempt. After that, it's like sculpting, I'd say. I add a little of this, take out a little of that, until many, many batches later a good clone is formed.

Clint and I would really hit it off as we went on and on about cloning America's favorite brand-name foods. Eventually he'd realize that he has fallen way behind on his schmoozing, and say that, regretfully, he has to go. He'd offer me front-row tickets to his next show and then he'd ask when the new book is coming out. I'd tell him it's called *Top Secret Restaurant Recipes 2*, it'll be out very soon, and I'm writing the introduction right now. I'd also tell him that it's my best work.

He'd shake my hand and move into the crowd, and I'd feel like I just made a new friend. Before he's too far away, he'd turn back and offer me an enlightening Clint Holmes nugget of wisdom: "Hey, Todd," he'd say. "Don't spend too much time on that introduction. It sounds to me like it's those clone recipes people really want."

I'd promise to take his advice, because, deep down, I know Mr. Clint Holmes gets it. And he's right.

If you're new to *Top Secret Recipes*, you are about to experience a cookbook concept unlike any other. This book is a collection of

150 original recipes to clone signature items from America's largest casual restaurant chains. All the recipes have been created from a process of reverse-engineering, using common ingredients and simplified steps.

In the 10 years since *Top Secret Restaurant Recipes* was released, I have received thousands of e-mails and letters filled with cloning requests for chain restaurant appetizers and entrees and desserts that I hadn't thought about before, or that I never got around to dissecting for the first book. I'm happy to say that this latest collection is assembled with replica recipes from those mouthwatering suggestions. There are more full-service restaurant clone recipes included in this book than in any previous *Top Secret Recipes* volume.

In a full house, where the kitchen is the hub of activity, the process of preparing tasty meals can be a rewarding event in which all can participate. The reason I first created these *Top Secret Recipes* is that I found cooking home duplicates of favorite famous dishes adds an extra sprinkling of joy to the process. It's a real kick digging into a dish you made at home that comes out tasting just like a menu item from a famous restaurant chain. And now, with these clone recipes to assist you, a combination of taste-alike versions of your favorite courses from different chains can be served in one meal creating a dining experience you couldn't have in any one restaurant.

These days we spend nearly half of the money designated for food on dining outside of our homes. Emeril Lagasse, Rachael Ray and Martha Stewart are more popular than ever, but on any given day 44 percent of adults are filling their bellies in a diner, cafe, coffeehouse, bistro, sub shop, dinnerhouse, pizza joint, cafeteria or buffet somewhere in America rather than preparing food in their own shiny home kitchens. Speed and convenience are obviously major factors that play into our decision to pay someone to make food for us, but what about the cost? Out of curiosity, I priced each ingredient for a dozen recipes in this book and then broke those totals down by serving. If you're into saving a little coin, you'll see from this list how making food at home will usually cost much less than dining out:

Dish	Original	Clone
Applebee's Honey Grilled Salmon	$10.99	$6.38
Applebee's White Chocolate & Walnut Blondie	$4.99	$2.05
Cheesecake Factory Chicken Madeira	$14.95	$9.69
Claim Jumper Meatloaf	$12.95	$3.84
IHOP Country Griddle Cakes	$5.99	$1.15
Margaritaville Key Lime Pie	$5.25	$1.47
Olive Garden Sicilian Scampi	$8.95	$5.98
Olive Garden Chicken Scampi	$12.50	$5.01
Outback Steakhouse Grilled Shrimp on the Barbie	$8.49	$5.12
P. F. Chang's Chocolate Torte	$4.50	$2.70
P. F. Chang's Mai Tai	$6.50	$2.07
Romano's Macaroni Grill Penne Rustica	$11.99	$5.59

I first started hammering out these recipes immediately following the release of *Top Secret Restaurant Recipes*, so what you have here is the culmination of work that spans a decade. The process is time-consuming and tedious, and I resisted releasing this book before it contained the very best collection of clone recipes I could muster. Within the mix are many recipes that required repeated tooling over 6 months or more before I finally struck gold. If a recipe doesn't pierce the bull's-eye, I keep shooting until I score. If the final product isn't a direct hit, that recipe doesn't make the cut. Because of this strict process, I believe in my formulas, and I'm confident that you will find the results rewarding.

If you'd like additional input on these recipes, check out the *Top Secret Recipes* website (www.TopSecretRecipes.com), where fellow clone rangers have added their comments and suggestions for many of these formulas. The important thing is to enjoy the creative freedom you now have with this collection. Cooking at home means having the liberty to experiment with a variety of ingredients, and the ability to customize recipes to suit varying tastes and dietary requirements. I encourage you to make these recipes uniquely yours.

Until next time, I'll be down here in the top secret underground lab, dissecting away, to come up with another big batch of recipes that helps you create kitchen clones of America's favorite brand-name foods. Happy cloning!

APPLEBEE'S MUD SLIDE

MENU DESCRIPTION: *"Bury your sweet tooth with smooth Kahlua, creamy vanilla ice cream, whipped cream and rich Hershey's chocolate syrup."*

Sure, there's a little Kahlua in there, but this famous Applebee's drink is more dessert than cocktail, really. And the presentation will make you look like a pro because you spiral the chocolate syrup around the inside the glass before adding the drink. It looks cool and it's easy to do . . . even after you've had a couple. Grab a straw and prepare to crave another when this one's gone. No wonder this drink also comes in a larger size.

2 cups vanilla ice cream
2 ounces Kahlua coffee liqueur
Hershey's chocolate syrup (in a
    squirt bottle)

canned whipped cream

1. Measure 2 cups of ice cream into your blender. Add the Kahlua and blend until smooth.
2. Prepare a 16-ounce wine glass by swirling chocolate syrup around the inside of the glass. Hold the wine glass by the stem with one hand and twirl the wine glass as you squeeze the chocolate. Slowly move the chocolate up toward the rim of the glass so that the chocolate makes a continuous spiral around the inside of the glass.

3. Pour the drink from the blender into the glass. Add a pile of whipped cream to the top of the drink and drizzle additional chocolate syrup over the whipped cream. Add a straw and serve.

- MAKES 1 DRINK.

• • • •

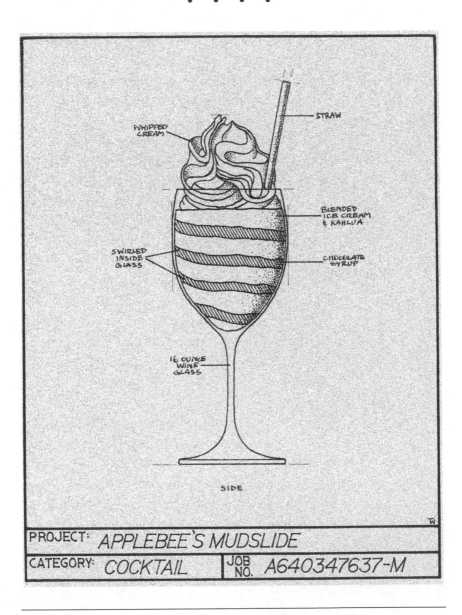

WHIPPED CREAM

STRAW

SWIRLED INSIDE GLASS

BLENDED ICE CREAM & KAHLUA

CHOCOLATE SYRUP

16 OUNCE WINE GLASS

SIDE

PROJECT:	*APPLEBEE'S MUDSLIDE*		
CATEGORY:	*COCKTAIL*	JOB NO.	*A640347637-M*

APPLEBEE'S
PERFECT APPLE MARGARITA

Here's a great twist on the traditional margarita. Sour apple schnapps and apple juice join forces with tequila and sweet and sour mix in a martini glass that's rimmed with cinnamon sugar. Hey, it's like drinking apple pie! This recipe makes one drink, but it's easy to double up. That's a good thing, since it seems like one is never enough.

2 tablespoons granulated sugar
¼ teaspoon ground cinnamon
1 ounce Sauza Hornitos tequila
1 ounce DeKuyper Sour Apple
    Pucker schnapps

2 ounces sweet-and-sour mix
2 ounces cold apple juice

GARNISH
olive
lime wedge

1. Mix sugar and cinnamon together in a small bowl, then pour the mixture onto a saucer or small plate. Moisten a napkin or clean towel with water. Run the wet napkin around the rim of the martini glass. Invert the glass and dip the moistened rim into the cinnamon/sugar. Set the glass aside for now.
2. Drop a handful of ice into a cocktail shaker.

3. Add the tequila, schnapps, sweet-and-sour, and apple juice. Shake vigorously.
4. Strain drink into the prepared martini glass, spear an olive and small lime wedge on a toothpick and drop it in the drink, and serve it up along with the shaker if there's any left over.

• SERVES 1.

• • • •

APPLEBEE'S PERFECT SUNRISE

Applebee's latest cocktail creation is a tasty warm-weather companion. The combination of tequilas, juices and syrups is served up in a chilled martini glass as the perfect re-creation of the classic tequila sunrise.

1 ¼ ounces 1800 Silver tequila
¼ ounce 1800 Reposado tequila
½ ounce simple syrup (see Tidbits)

½ ounce lime juice
1 ½ ounces sweet-and-sour mix
4 ounces orange juice
½ ounce grenadine

GARNISH
maraschino cherry

1. Fill a 10-ounce martini glass with ice and add cold water to chill the glass.
2. Drop a handful of ice into a shaker. Add tequilas, simple syrup, lime juice, sweet-and-sour and orange juice. Shake well.
3. Dump ice water out of the glass and strain the drink into it.
4. Drop a maraschino cherry into the drink and serve it up with the grenadine on the side in a shot glass.

- MAKES 1 DRINK.

TIDBITS

Make simple syrup by combining equal parts hot water and granulated sugar. Stir until sugar is dissolved. Allow syrup to cool before using. Simple.

•　•　•　•

APPLEBEE'S ONION PEELS

MENU DESCRIPTION: *"Crisp-fried tender onion strips served with a creamy horseradish dipping sauce."*

This signature appetizer from Applebee's is the chain's reaction to overwhelming success of Outback's Bloomin' Onion and Chili's Awesome Blossom. But, while accurate kitchen cloning of a Bloomin' Onion requires a special slicing device, cloning Onion Peels requires only the most basic kitchen prep and tools: Slice the onion, separate the slices, dip the slices in batter and fry. Just remember to make the essential horseradish dipping sauce in advance so that the ingredients can mingle and really get to know one another as they chill out in the fridge.

CREAMY HORSERADISH DIPPING SAUCE

½ cup mayonnaise
1 tablespoon prepared
   horseradish
2 teaspoons white vinegar
1 teaspoon water
1 teaspoon paprika
1 teaspoon ketchup
¼ teaspoon medium grind black
   pepper

⅛ teaspoon dried oregano
⅛ teaspoon cayenne pepper
dash garlic powder
dash onion powder

6 to 10 cups vegetable shortening
   (as required by fryer)
1 large white onion

BATTER

½ cup all-purpose flour
½ cup Progresso plain
   breadcrumbs

½ teaspoon salt
½ teaspoon ground black pepper
1 ½ cups milk

1. Make horseradish dipping sauce by combining ingredients in a medium bowl with a whisk. Mix until creamy then cover and chill the sauce.
2. Heat the shortening to 350 degrees in a deep fryer.
3. Slice the stem end and the root end off onion, then, with the onion resting on a flat side, cut down through the onion, slicing it in half. Slice each half 4 to 5 more times in a spoke fashion to create wedges of onion. Separate the onion pieces.
4. Create batter by combining all dry ingredients in a medium bowl. Whisk in milk until batter is smooth then let the batter sit for 5 minutes. It should thicken. Whisk batter again.
5. When the oil is hot dip each onion piece in the batter, let some of the batter drip off then drop the coated onion piece carefully into the hot oil. Fry 8 to 12 peels at a time for 1 to 2 minutes or until light brown. Drain on a rack or paper towels. Repeat until the onion is used up, stacking the newer batches on top of the old ones to keep them warm. When they're all done, serve the fried onion slices on a plate or in a paper-lined basket with horseradish dipping sauce on the side.

• SERVES 4 TO 6.

TIDBITS

While shortening works best for this recipe, you may also fry these with vegetable oil or canola oil.

• • • •

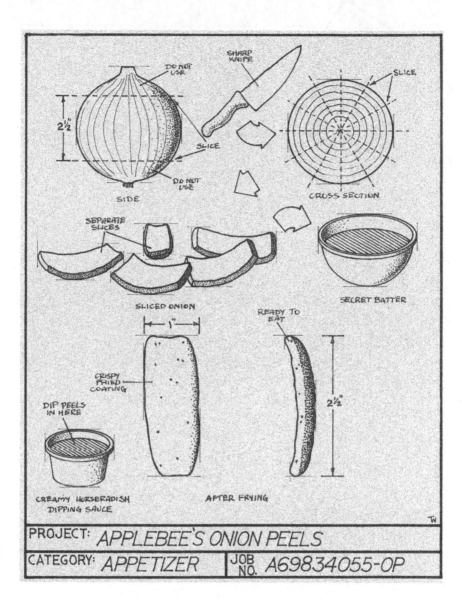

DO NOT USE

SHARP KNIFE

SLICE

2½"

SLICE

DO NOT USE

SIDE

CROSS SECTION

SEPARATE SLICES

SLICED ONION

SECRET BATTER

READY TO EAT

1"

CRISPY FRIED COATING

2½"

DIP PEELS IN HERE

CREAMY HORSERADISH DIPPING SAUCE

AFTER FRYING

PROJECT: *APPLEBEE'S ONION PEELS*

CATEGORY: *APPETIZER*   JOB NO. *A69834055-OP*

APPLEBEE'S BAKED FRENCH ONION SOUP

It may not be listed on the menu, but this is Applebee's most la-dled soup each and every day. Just be sure you have some oven-safe soup bowls on hand before you jump into this clone, since you're going to pop the dish under the broiler to brown and melt the cheese on top. Under the gooey melted provolone of the original version you get from Applebee's is a unique round crouton that's made from bread that looks like a hamburger bun. In fact, that's exactly what we'll use for our clone. The round shape of the buns is perfect for topping the soup.

3 tablespoons vegetable oil
6 medium white onions, sliced
8 cups beef broth (Swanson is best)
1 cup water
2½ teaspoons salt

½ teaspoon garlic powder
¼ teaspoon ground black pepper
5 plain hamburger buns
10 slices provolone cheese
10 teaspoons shredded Parmesan cheese

1. Add 3 tablespoons oil to a large soup pot or saucepan over medium/high heat. Add the sliced onions and sauté for 20 minutes until the onions begin to soften and start to become translucent. You don't want them to brown.
2. Add the beef broth, water, salt, garlic powder and black

pepper to the pan and bring mixture to a boil. When soup begins to boil, reduce heat and simmer for 45 minutes.

3. To make the croutons cut off the top half of each top of the hamburger bun so that the bread is the same thickness as the bottom half of each bun. Throw the top crusts away. Now you should have 10 round pieces of bread—5 bottom buns, and 5 top buns with the tops cut off. Preheat oven to 325 degrees. Place the bread in the oven directly on the rack and bake for 15 to 20 minutes or until each piece is golden brown and crispy. Set these croutons aside until you need them.

4. When the soup is done, spoon about 1 cup into an oven-safe bowl. Float a crouton on top of the soup, then place a slice of provolone cheese on top of the crouton. Sprinkle ½ teaspoon of shredded parmesan cheese over the provolone.

5. Place the bowl into your oven set to high broil. Broil the soup for 5 to 6 minutes or until the cheese is melted and starting to brown (you may need to broil longer if you are making more than one bowl at a time). Sprinkle an additional ½ teaspoon of shredded parmesan cheese over the top of the soup and serve. Repeat process to prepare remaining servings.

• MAKES 10 SERVINGS.

•   •   •   •

APPLEBEE'S
SANTA FE CHICKEN SALAD

MENU DESCRIPTION: *"Grilled chipotle chicken breast with gua-camole and sour cream on a bed of greens tossed with two cheeses, pico de gallo, tortilla strips and our Mexi-ranch dressing."*

Create a robust chipotle marinade that fills your chicken fillets with flavor. As you wait for the chicken to marinate you have plenty of time to throw together clones of the Mexi-ranch dressing and fresh pico de gallo. Now most of the work is done, and you're standing in front of the gate to salad heaven. When you're ready to enter, simply grill the chicken, assemble your salads and open wide.

You should know that if you don't have buttermilk for the dressing, and don't want to buy a whole carton to use just a single tablespoon, simply substitute regular milk. You'll find ground chipotle pepper where all the spices are in the market (I use Mc-Cormick). If you can't track down ground chipotle, use ground cayenne pepper. Just be sure to measure roughly half the amount, since cayenne packs more heat than chipotle.

MARINADE

2 cups water
⅓ cup soy sauce
3 tablespoons granulated sugar
2 tablespoons salt
2 tablespoons apple cider vinegar

1 tablespoon ground chipotle
 pepper (or 1 ½ teaspoons
 ground cayenne pepper)
2 teaspoons hickory smoke
 flavoring

2 teaspoons paprika
2 teaspoon garlic powder
1 teaspoon onion powder

1 teaspoon ground black pepper

4 skinless chicken breast fillets

MEXI-RANCH DRESSING

½ cup mayonnaise
2 tablespoons minced onion
2 tablespoons diced tomato
1 tablespoon buttermilk
1 tablespoon white vinegar
2 teaspoons minced fresh cilantro
1 teaspoon canned chopped mild
   green chiles

¾ teaspoon paprika
½ teaspoon granulated sugar
¼ teaspoon salt
pinch dried dill weed
pinch ground cumin
pinch cayenne pepper

PICO DE GALLO

2 medium tomatoes, diced
⅓ cup diced red onion
1 jalapeno, seeded and diced
2 teaspoons lime juice

2 teaspoons minced fresh cilantro
¼ teaspoon salt
¼ teaspoon ground black
   pepper

8 cups chopped iceberg lettuce
8 cups chopped romaine lettuce
1 cup chopped red cabbage
1 cup fancy shredded Cheddar
   cheese

1 cup fancy shredded Monterey
   Jack cheese
4 handfuls tortilla strips or chips
½ cup sour cream
½ cup guacamole

1. You want to marinate the chicken for 2 hours in advance, so make the marinade first by combing all the ingredients for the marinade in a medium bowl. Stir well until the sugar has dissolved. Drop the chicken breasts into the marinade, then cover and chill for 2 hours. You don't want to marinate for much more than 2 hours or the chicken could get tough.
2. While the chicken marinates, make the Mexi-ranch dressing by combining the ingredients in a medium bowl. Cover and chill so the flavors will develop as the chicken marinates.

3. You'll also make the pico de gallo in advance so that it can rest a bit in the fridge. Combine all the ingredients in a medium bowl, then cover and chill this as well.
4. When the chicken has marinated for 2 hours, fire up the grill to medium/high heat. Grill the chicken breasts for 4 to 7 minutes per side or until chicken is done. Take the chicken off the grill then let it rest for a bit while you prepare the salads.
5. Build each salad in a large bowl by first tossing 2 cups chopped iceberg lettuce and 2 cups chopped romaine lettuce with ¼ cup chopped red cabbage and about ¼ cup of the dressing.
6. Combine the shredded cheeses then add, about ½ cup to each salad on the lettuce. Sprinkle a handful of tortilla strips or crumbled chips on next.
7. Slice each chicken breast into strips and arrange each one on each of the salads. Sprinkle about ¼ cup of pico de gallo over the top.
8. Finish off each salad by adding a 2-tablespoon scoop of sour cream on one side of each salad, then a 2-tablespoon scoop of guacamole on the other side of the salad.

• SERVES 4.

•   •   •   •

APPLEBEE'S
ALMOND RICE PILAF

You're grilling some steaks or baking some chicken and don't know what to serve on the side? Try out this simple clone for a dish that's served along with several of Applebee's entrees. Since the recipe requires converted rice (because instant rice is gross) you have to plan ahead about 25 minutes to give the rice time to cook. It's worth the wait. The secret to an authentic, great-tasting rice pilaf is sautéing the uncooked rice kernels in butter first, before adding the liquid—in this case chicken broth. Then, as the rice is cooking, you have plenty of time to sauté the almonds, celery, and onions that are tossed into the rice at the end.

3 tablespoons butter
1 cup uncooked converted rice
2¼ cups chicken broth
⅛ teaspoon salt

⅓ cup sliced or slivered almonds
¼ cup diced celery
¼ cup diced onion
1 teaspoon dried parsley

1. Melt 2 tablespoons butter over medium heat in a medium saucepan. Be sure to use a saucepan with a lid. Add 1 cup uncooked converted rice and sauté rice for 2 to 4 minutes in the butter or until some of the rice begins to turn light brown. As the rice is cooking heat chicken broth on high in microwave for 3 to 4 minutes or until the broth begins to bubble. When the rice begins to brown, quickly add the hot stock and salt to the pan. Cover the pan, reduce heat to low and simmer rice for 20 minutes.

2. As rice cooks, melt remaining 1 tablespoon butter in a medium skillet over medium heat. Add almonds and sauté for 1 to 2 minutes or until the almonds begin to brown. Add celery and onion and sauté for another couple of minutes or until the onion begins to turn translucent.
3. When the rice has cooked for 20 minutes, remove it from the heat. Add almonds, celery, onion and parsley to the rice, then let it sit, covered, for 5 minutes or until the remaining liquid is absorbed.

- SERVES 4.

•　•　•　•

APPLEBEE'S
BOURBON STREET STEAK

MENU DESCRIPTION: *"This succulent 10 oz. steak is jazzed up with Cajun spices and served with sautéed onions, mushrooms, garlic mashed potatoes and garlic toast."*

This Cajun-style dish is named after the famous street in the French Quarter in New Orleans. No bourbon is needed to re-create the secret taste of this signature steak entree from America's largest casual dining chain. Plan to make this dish approximately 24 hours in advance, so the steaks have time to soak up the goodness. This long marinating time will also give the meat tenderizer a chance to do its thing, but don't go longer than 24 hours, or the protein fibers may become so tender that they turn mushy. I used Mc-Cormick brand tenderizer, which uses bromelian, a pineapple extract, to tenderize the meat. Lawry's (Adolph's) meat tenderizer, uses papain, from papayas, to tenderize the proteins, but this brand also brings other spices into the mix and will alter the flavor of your finished product. Both of these tenderizers include a lot of salt, so we won't need to include salt as part of the marinade formula.

2 10-ounce top sirloin steaks

MARINADE

2 tablespoons Worcestershire sauce
2 tablespoons soy sauce
4 teaspoons chili powder
4 teaspoons minced garlic
1½ teaspoons meat tenderizer
  (McCormick is best)

2 teaspoons paprika
2 teaspoons ground black pepper
1 teaspoon ground cayenne pepper
1 teaspoon onion powder
½ teaspoon ground oregano
2 cups water

GARLIC BUTTER

3 tablespoons salted butter
⅛ teaspoon garlic powder
pinch salt

ON THE SIDE

1 tablespoon olive oil
1 tablespoon salted butter
2 cups thinly sliced white onion
    (about ½ onion)
2 cups sliced white mushrooms
⅛ teaspoon salt
⅛ teaspoon ground black pepper

1. Combine all marinade ingredients in a medium bowl.
2. Pound steaks with a kitchen mallet until about ¾-inch thick.
3. Submerse steaks in marinade, cover and store overnight in the refrigerator.
4. When your steaks have marinated for approximately 24 hours, preheat a barbecue grill to medium/high heat and grill the steaks for 3 to 5 minutes per side or until cooked as desired.
5. Melt 3 tablespoons butter and combine with ⅛ teaspoon garlic powder and a pinch of salt.
6. Combine 1 tablespoon butter and 1 tablespoon olive oil in a medium skillet over medium/low heat. When the butter is melted, add 2 cups of sliced onion and sauté for 2 to 3 minutes or until onion begins to soften. Add sliced mushrooms, ⅛ teaspoon salt and ⅛ teaspoon black pepper to pan, and sauté for another 2 to 3 minute or until onion and mushrooms begin to lightly brown.
7. When the steaks are done, spoon a couple teaspoons of garlic butter over the top of each steak and serve with mushrooms and onion on the side.

• SERVES 2.

• • • •

APPLEBEE'S CHICKEN FAJITA ROLLUP

MENU DESCRIPTION: *"A large flour tortilla topped with melted Monterey Jack and Cheddar cheeses, grilled chipotle chicken, shredded lettuce and pico de gallo. Rolled, sliced and served with a Mexi-ranch dipping sauce"*

Take Applebee's delicious chicken chipotle fajita recipe, roll it up in a large flour tortilla with lettuce, cheeses and fresh pico de gallo and you've got a meal to wrap your hands around. The Mexi-ranch dipping sauce is the perfect creamy compliment for this recipe and you can use what's left over for a dressing on your next salad. The sauce is actually just a kicked-up ranch dressing recipe that includes a small amount of buttermilk in the ingredients list. But if you don't want to buy a whole carton of buttermilk to use just a tablespoon for this recipe, that's okay. Substitute the regular moo juice you've got sitting in the fridge. For the spicy marinade it's best to use ground chipotle pepper (dried smoked red jalapeno) made by McCormick. If you can't find that stuff, cut the amount in half and use cayenne pepper. For the cheeses, many major brands make a Cheddar/Jack blend that will work great here if you'd rather not buy the cheeses separately. That's helpful if you're about to tip the limit for the express lane checkout line.

MARINADE

2 cups water

⅓ cup soy sauce

3 tablespoons granulated sugar

2 tablespoons salt

2 tablespoons white vinegar
1 tablespoon ground chipotle
    pepper(or 1 ½ teaspoons
    ground cayenne pepper)
2 teaspoons hickory smoke
    flavoring

2 teaspoons paprika
2 teaspoon garlic powder
1 teaspoon onion powder
1 teaspoon ground black pepper

4 skinless chicken breast fillets

MEXI-RANCH DIPPING SAUCE

½ cup mayonnaise
2 tablespoons minced onion
2 tablespoons diced tomato
1 tablespoon buttermilk
1 tablespoon white vinegar
2 teaspoons minced fresh cilantro
1 teaspoon canned chopped mild
    green chiles

¾ teaspoon paprika
½ teaspoon granulated sugar
¼ teaspoon salt
pinch dried dill weed
pinch ground cumin
pinch cayenne pepper

PICO DE GALLO

2 medium tomatoes, diced
⅓ cup diced red onion
1 jalapeno, seeded and
    diced
2 teaspoons lime juice
2 teaspoons minced fresh
    cilantro
¼ teaspoon salt

¼ teaspoon ground black pepper

4 large flour tortillas
1 cup fancy shredded Cheddar
    cheese
1 cup fancy shredded Monterey
    Jack cheese
4 cups shredded iceberg lettuce

1. The chicken needs to marinate for 2 hours, so make the marinade first by combining the ingredients in a medium bowl. Stir well until the sugar has dissolved. Add four chicken breasts to the marinade, cover and chill for 2 hours. Don't let the chicken marinate for much more than that or it could get tough.
2. While the chicken marinates, prepare the dipping sauce by

combining the ingredients in a medium bowl. Stir well then cover and chill. This will allow all the flavors to develop nicely while parked in the fridge.

3. The pico de gallo will also develop nicely in the fridge. Combine all those ingredients, then cover and chill it as well.

4. When you're ready to make your roll-ups, preheat your grill to medium/high heat. Grill the chicken breast for 4 to 7 minutes per side or until done.

5. Build each roll-up by first laying a large flour tortilla in a large skillet over low-heat. Sprinkle about ½ cup of the combined cheeses over the surface of the tortilla while it heats up in the pan. When the cheese begins to melt, remove the tortilla from the pan. Sprinkle about 1 cup of shredded lettuce in a strip across the center of the tortilla, followed by about 3 tablespoons of pico de gallo. Slice one grilled chicken breast into bite-size chunks and arrange the chicken on the lettuce. Fold the ends of the tortilla over the filling, then roll the tortilla from the bottom. Make a diagonal cut across the center of the roll-up and serve with a small dish of the dipping sauce on the side.

• SERVES 4.

•　•　•　•

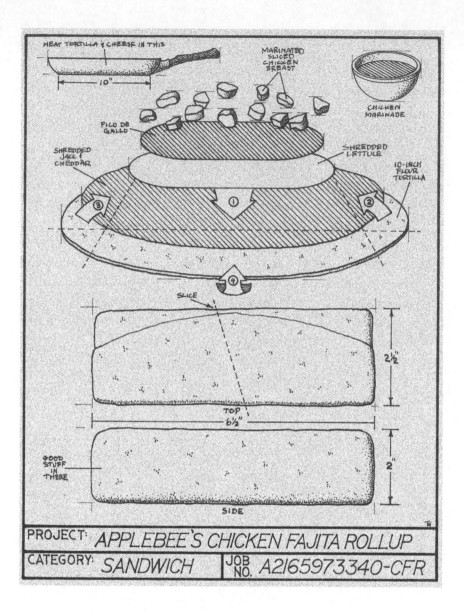

HEAT TORTILLA & CHEESE IN THIS

10"

MARINATED
SLICED
CHICKEN
BREAST

CHICKEN
MARINADE

PICO DE
GALLO

SHREDDED
JACK &
CHEDDAR

SHREDDED
LETTUCE

10-INCH
FLOUR
TORTILLA

①

②

③

④

SLICE

TOP

6½"

2½"

GOOD
STUFF
IN
THERE

SIDE

2"

PROJECT: *APPLEBEE'S CHICKEN FAJITA ROLLUP*

CATEGORY: *SANDWICH*   JOB NO. *A2165973340-CFR*

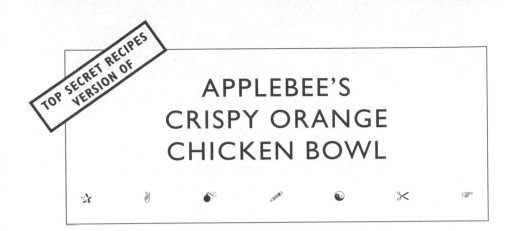

APPLEBEE'S
CRISPY ORANGE
CHICKEN BOWL

MENU DESCRIPTION: *"Breaded boneless chicken breast is delicately spiced and covered in a spicy-sweet orange glaze. Served in a big bowl over almond rice pilaf and a flavorful mixture of mushrooms, broccoli, red pepper, sugar snap peas and shredded carrots. Topped with toasted almonds and crispy noodles."*

Concoct a carbon copy of the delicious spicy orange glaze that's tossed over the crispy chicken and you're well on your way to re-creating this Applebee's signature meal-in-a-bowl. The sweet, tangy and spicy sauce is made easily from simmering a mixture of orange juice, brown sugar, marmalade and a few other secret ingredients. As for the crispy chicken, rather than going to the trouble of breading and frying the chicken from scratch, I've cut a lot of time off the prep by including frozen breaded chicken fingers that you simply bake in the oven just before you're ready to assemble the dish. I used Claim Jumper brand chicken tenderloins for this recipe, since one 20-ounce box was perfect for the two servings this recipe yields. These are mongo-huge restaurant-size portions, so you'll be able to divide this recipe up into four modest servings with ease.

SPICY ORANGE SAUCE

1 cup orange juice	3 tablespoons orange marmalade
½ cup light brown sugar	2 tablespoons soy sauce

1 tablespoon vegetable oil
1/2 teaspoon minced parsley
1/4 teaspoon chili flakes

1/4 teaspoon minced garlic
1/8 teaspoon dried thyme
1 tablespoon rice vinegar

4 cups almond rice pilaf (from
    recipe on page 15)
20 ounces breaded chicken
    fingers, baked
    (approx. 12 strips)
1 1/2 cups broccoli florets

1 cup sliced red bell pepper
1 cup sliced mushrooms
3/4 cup sugar snap peas
1/4 cup shredded carrot
1/2 cup crispy chow mein noodles
1/4 cup sliced or slivered almonds

1. Make the spicy orange sauce by combining all ingredients, except vinegar, in a medium saucepan. Simmer over medium/low heat for 15 minutes or until thick. Remove from heat and add vinegar.
2. If you haven't already baked your chicken fingers, now is the time to cook them following the directions on the package.
3. Steam the broccoli, red bell pepper, mushrooms, sugar snap peas and carrot in a steamer basket in a covered saucepan over simmering water for 10 minutes or until the broccoli is tender. Salt and pepper the veggies.
4. Prepare each dish by spooning 2 cups of the rice pilaf into two large bowls. Divide the steamed vegetables in half and spoon them over the rice. Cut each of the chicken fingers in half and slide them into a large bowl. Pour the orange sauce over the chicken and toss. Spoon the chicken and sauce onto the veggies in each bowl. Sprinkle 1/4 cup of chow mein noodles over each dish, followed by about 2 tablespoons of almonds, and serve.

• SERVES 2.

•   •   •   •

APPLEBEE'S HONEY GRILLED SALMON

☆ ✌ 💣 ✏ ☯ ✂ ☞

MENU DESCRIPTION: *"Flame-grilled Atlantic Salmon with Applebee's Honey Pepper Sauce served with a side of almond rice pilaf, seasoned vegetables and toasted garlic bread."*

It's all about the sauce. This sweet, tangy and slightly spicy sauce goes perfectly with salmon, but can also be used on chicken or ribs. Just be sure to watch the sauce closely as it cooks in case it starts to bubble over. If it sounds like I'm speaking from experience, you're right—oh, what a beautiful mess I made on one attempt. So cook the sauce slowly, and watch it closely as it thickens. If it gets too thick, you can always add a bit of water to thin it out. I suggest serving this salmon with almond rice pilaf as they do in the restaurant. You'll find that clone recipe on page 15.

HONEY PEPPER SAUCE

¾ cup honey
⅓ cup soy sauce
¼ cup dark brown sugar, packed
¼ cup pineapple juice
juice of 1 lemon (about 2 tablespoons)
2 tablespoons white vinegar
2 teaspoons olive oil

1 teaspoon ground black pepper
½ teaspoon cayenne pepper
½ teaspoon paprika
¼ teaspoon garlic powder

4 8-ounce salmon fillets (without skin)
vegetable oil

1. Make the sauce by combining all ingredients in a medium saucepan over medium/low heat. Stir occasionally until sauce begins to boil, then simmer uncovered for 15 minutes or until syrupy. Watch the sauce closely to be sure it doesn't bubble over.
2. Preheat barbecue grill to medium heat. Rub each salmon fillet with vegetable oil, then add a light sprinkling of salt and pepper. Grill the salmon for 4 to 7 minutes per side or until done. Serve salmon with a small cup of the honey pepper sauce on the side.

- SERVES 4.

•　•　•　•

APPLEBEE'S
TEQUILA LIME CHICKEN

MENU DESCRIPTION: *"A tender boneless chicken breast marinated with lime juice and tequila flavors and grilled. Served on a bed of crisp tortilla strips. Topped with a Mexi-ranch and Jack-Cheddar sauce. Served with Southwest rice and pico de gallo."*

Because of the huge success of this dish, Applebee's has recently changed the name to "Fiesta Lime Chicken," and trademarked the name. Most people still know this dish by its original title, so that's what I'm going with for this book. When making your clone, just be sure not to marinate the chicken for much longer than the 2 to 3 hours specified, or the acid in the lime juice may toughen your chicken. The bed of crispy corn tortilla strips can be easily made by simply crumbling store-bought tortilla chips, or, if you want strips more closely resembling those served at the restaurant, just follow the Tidbits below. Serve this dish with your choice of rice, and some salsa or pico de gallo on the side.

MARINADE

1 cup water
⅓ cup teriyaki sauce
2 tablespoons lime juice
2 teaspoons minced garlic
1 teaspoon liquid mesquite smoke

½ teaspoon salt
¼ teaspoon ground ginger
¼ teaspoon tequila

4 skinless chicken breast fillets

MEXI-RANCH SAUCE

¼ cup mayonnaise
¼ cup sour cream
1 tablespoon milk
2 teaspoons minced tomato
1 ½ teaspoons white vinegar
1 teaspoon minced canned
    jalapeno slices (nacho slices)
1 teaspoon minced onion
¼ teaspoon dried parsley
¼ teaspoon Tabasco pepper sauce
⅛ teaspoon salt
⅛ teaspoon dried dill weed

⅛ teaspoon paprika
⅛ teaspoon cayenne pepper
⅛ teaspoon ground cumin
⅛ teaspoon chili powder
dash garlic powder
dash ground black pepper

1 cup shredded Cheddar/
    Monterey Jack cheese blend
2 cups crumbled tortilla chips or
    fried tortilla strips (see Tidbits)

1. Prepare marinade by combining marinade ingredients in a medium bowl. Add the chicken to the bowl, cover and chill for 2 to 3 hours.
2. Make the Mexi-ranch dressing by combining all of the ingredients in a medium bowl. Mix well until smooth, then cover the dressing and chill it until it's needed.
3. When you are ready to prepare the entree, preheat the oven to high broil. Also, preheat your barbecue or indoor grill to high heat. When the grill is hot cook the marinated chicken breasts for 3 to 5 minutes per side, or until they're done.
4. Arrange the cooked chicken in a baking pan. Spread a layer of Mexi-ranch dressing over each piece of chicken (you'll have plenty left over), followed by ¼ cup of the shredded cheese blend. Broil the chicken for 2 to 3 minutes, or just until the cheese has melted.
5. Spread a bed of ½ cup of the tortilla strips or crumbled tortilla chips on each of four plates. Slide a chicken breast onto the chips on each plate and serve with your choice of rice, and pico de gallo or salsa.

• SERVES 4.

Crumbling store-bought tortilla chips is the easy way to make the bed of crunchy chips that the tequila lime chicken rests on. But, you can make tortilla strips like those served at the restaurant by cutting a stack of eight 6-inch corn tortillas in half. Stack the halves on top of each other and slice the tortillas into thin strips. Fry the tortilla strips in batches in 2 cups of preheated oil in a large skillet for 3 to 5 minutes or until crispy. Salt lightly and cool on paper towels.

•　•　•　•

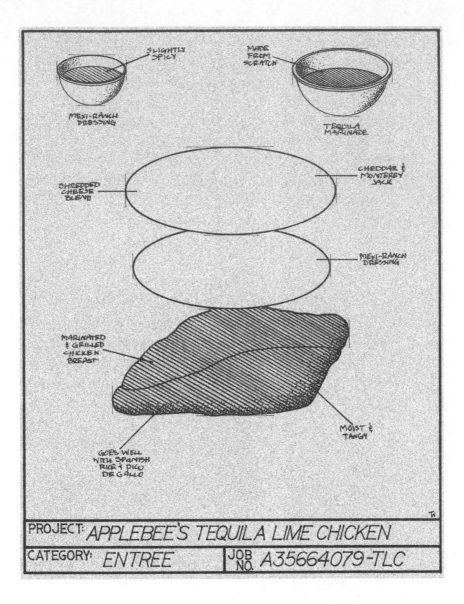

SLIGHTLY SPICY

MEXI-RANCH DRESSING

MADE FROM SCRATCH

TEQUILA MARINADE

SHREDDED CHEESE BLEND

CHEDDAR & MONTEREY JACK

MEXI-RANCH DRESSING

MARINATED & GRILLED CHICKEN BREAST

MOIST & TANGY

GOES WELL WITH SPANISH RICE & PICO DE GALLO

PROJECT: APPLEBEE'S TEQUILA LIME CHICKEN

CATEGORY: ENTREE

JOB NO. A35664079-TLC

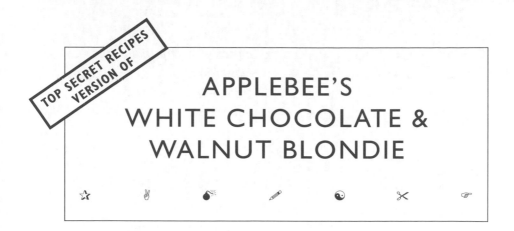

APPLEBEE'S WHITE CHOCOLATE & WALNUT BLONDIE

MENU DESCRIPTION: *"Dare to indulge with a white chocolate and walnut blondie under a scoop of ice cream and chopped walnuts. Served warm and topped at your table with a rich, sizzling maple butter sauce."*

For Applebee's regulars, this dessert is a hands-down favorite. In a hot skillet comes a delicious slice of white chocolate and walnut cake (it's similar to a brownie in texture) topped with a scoop of ice cream and warm maple butter sauce bubbling as it hits the pan. Commence with the salivating. To re-create this pile of pleasure at home you start by making the cake from scratch. For the white chocolate, get a couple of 1-ounce bars or one 8-ounce bar and chop it into chunks. White chocolate chunks work best in this recipe, but you can certainly use white chocolate chips in a pinch. While the blondie cake is baking, whip up the sauce—it will be fluffy at first. When you're ready to serve the dessert, zap the sauce in the microwave until it's hot and creamy. Arrange the decadence in a hot skillet and serve it sizzling to happy, drooling mouths.

BLONDIE

4 egg whites
½ cup butter, softened (1 stick)
½ cup light brown sugar, packed

¼ cup granulated sugar
1 teaspoon vanilla extract
2¼ cups all-purpose flour

1 teaspoon baking soda
½ teaspoon baking powder
¼ teaspoon salt
½ cup milk

8 ounces white chocolate (cut into
    chunks)
½ cup chopped walnuts

SAUCE

½ cup butter, softened (1 stick)
½ cup powdered sugar
¼ cup cream cheese, softened
2 tablespoons maple syrup

¼ teaspoon salt

8 scoops vanilla ice cream
½ cup chopped walnuts

1. Preheat oven to 325 degrees.
2. To make the blondie cake whip the egg whites until they are stiff and form peaks. Add softened butter, ½ cup packed brown sugar, ¼ cup granulated sugar, and vanilla and mix with an electric mixer until smooth. In a separate bowl sift together flour, baking soda, baking powder and ¼ teaspoon salt. Add the dry ingredients to the wet ingredients and mix well until smooth. Mix in milk, white chocolate chunks, and walnuts. Pour ingredients into a greased 9x13-inch baking pan and bake for 40 to 45 minutes or until cake is golden brown on top. Slice cake into 8 equal slices when cool.
3. While cake bakes, combine all ingredients for the sauce in a medium bowl with an electric mixer.
4. To prepare dessert, heat a small skillet on your stove over high heat for about 5 minutes. A cast-iron skillet is the best. (You can also serve the dessert on a plate, but you'll miss out on the showy sizzle.) Arrange the cake in the center of the skillet or plate. Heat up the sauce for 30 to 60 seconds in the microwave until hot. Place a scoop of vanilla ice cream on the cake, then drizzle some of the sauce over the top, followed by a tablespoon of chopped walnuts. Serve immediately.

• SERVES 8.

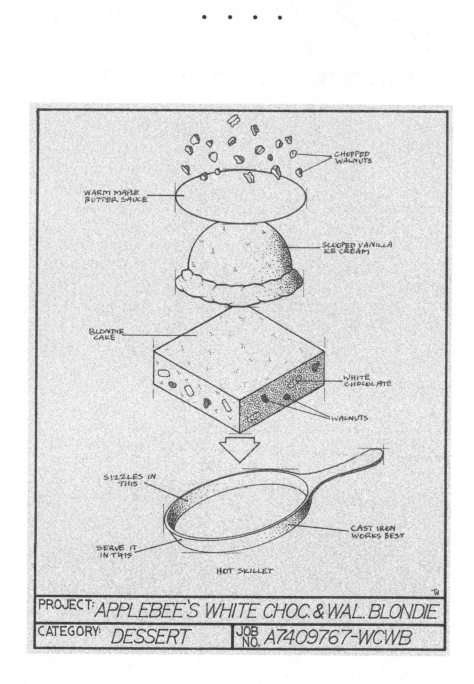

CHOPPED WALNUTS

WARM MAPLE BUTTER SAUCE

SCOOPED VANILLA ICE CREAM

BLONDIE CAKE

WHITE CHOCOLATE

WALNUTS

SIZZLES IN THIS

CAST IRON WORKS BEST

SERVE IT IN THIS

HOT SKILLET

PROJECT:	APPLEBEE'S WHITE CHOC. & WAL. BLONDIE
CATEGORY: DESSERT	JOB NO. A7409767-WCWB

BENIHANA
GINGER SALAD DRESSING

Before your meal at the Benihana chain of hibachi grill restaurants you are served a side salad doused in this tangy, slightly sweet, fresh ginger dressing. When spooned over a simple iceberg lettuce salad this easy clone transforms your bowl of greens into a great start for any meal. Making the dressing is as simple as dumping the ingredients into a blender, whizzing it up, and popping it into the cooler to chill. I've seen many attempts to duplicate this coveted formula, but I think the original clone recipe presented here comes closer to the real thing than any other recipe out there.

½ cup minced onion
½ cup peanut oil
⅓ cup rice vinegar
2 tablespoons water
2 tablespoons minced fresh ginger
2 tablespoons minced celery
2 tablespoons ketchup

4 teaspoons soy sauce
2 teaspoons granulated sugar
2 teaspoons lemon juice
½ teaspoon minced garlic
½ teaspoon salt
¼ teaspoon ground black pepper

Combine all ingredients in a blender. Blend on high speed for about 30 seconds or until all of the ginger is pureed. Chill.

• MAKES 1¾ CUPS.

• • • •

BENIHANA
JAPANESE ONION SOUP

MENU DESCRIPTION: *"It takes half a day to make this perfect combination of onion, celery, carrot and garlic."*

Before a skilled chef appears tableside to perform his culinary prestidigitation on the hot hibachi grill at Benihana, you're treated to a tasty bowl of chicken broth-based soup with fried onions, sliced mushrooms and green onions floating cheerfully on top. The restaurant menu claims this soup takes a half a day to make, but we can clone it in a fraction of that time using canned chicken broth (I use Swanson brand). This soup works great as a prelude to your favorite Asian dishes or other Benihana clones since it's so light and won't fill up anyone before the main course. I've included a simple technique here for making the breaded fried onions from scratch (for the most accurate clone), but you can skip that step by substituting French's canned French Fried Onions that are sold in most markets.

4 cups canned chicken broth
2 cups water
1 white onion (see Tidbits)
½ carrot, coarsely chopped (about
     ¼ cup)
½ celery stalk, coarsely chopped
     (about ¼ cup)
1 small clove garlic, sliced

½ teaspoon salt
1 cup vegetable oil
1 cup milk
1 cup all-purpose flour
6 medium mushrooms, thinly
     sliced
4 green onions, diced (green part
     only)

1. Combine chicken broth and water in a large saucepan over high heat. Slice the white onion in half, and then coarsely chop one half (save the other half for later). Add coarsely chopped onion, carrot, celery, garlic, and salt to the saucepan and bring to a boil. Reduce heat and simmer for 10 minutes, or until the onion starts to become translucent.
2. As the broth simmers, heat up 1 cup of vegetable oil in a small saucepan over medium heat. Slice the remaining white onion into very thin slices. Separate the slices, dip the slices into the milk, then into the flour. Fry the breaded onion, a handful at a time in the oil until golden brown. Drain on a paper towel.
3. When the soup has simmered for 10 minutes, strain the vegetables out of the broth and toss them out. Pour the broth back into the pan and keep it hot over low heat.
4. To serve soup, ladle about 1 cup of broth into a bowl. Drop a few pieces of fried onion into the soup, followed by 6 to 8 mushroom slices (about 1 mushroom each) and a couple pinches of diced green onion. When the fried onion sinks to the bottom of the bowl (a couple of minutes), serve the soup.

• MAKES 6 SERVINGS.

TIDBITS

You will only need ½ of a white onion if you opt to use the canned French's French Fried Onions for this recipe—the small can will be enough—rather than frying your own. You also won't need the vegetable oil, milk or flour listed in the ingredients.

•   •   •   •

BENIHANA
MANDARIN ORANGE
CHEESECAKE

This charismatic cheesecake is a specialty at the world's largest Benihana restaurant located in the Hilton hotel and casino in Las Vegas. But don't expect to find this amazing dessert on the menu at any of the other 69 Benihana eateries, since it's custom-made just for the Sin City location and probably unlike any cheesecake you've had. Check it out: The lightly orange-flavored, fluffed-up cream cheese sits on layer of soft white cake, the edge is frosted and coated with crunchy hazelnut crumbs, and the top is covered with wedges of mandarin oranges in an orange-flavored gelatin. Every element of this top secret kitchen clone is made from scratch, and the finished product is well worth the work you put in. For the cake layer, we whip up just enough of a simple white cake batter to fit into the bottom of a 9-inch springform pan. The cheese layer in our clone is created with a special custom combination of gelatin, Dream Whip, and cream cheese so that no baking is required to firm it up. You could, of course, use a store-bought white frosting for the edge of the cake, but since you only need a small amount of frosting the clone recipe here makes it cheaper. The hazelnuts are candied with sugar and reduced to crumbs in a food processor (you can find a ½-cup bag of chopped hazelnuts in most supermarkets that is perfect for this). And two 15-ounce cans of mandarin orange wedges is just the right amount for garnishing the top. Just be sure to save ½-cup of the liquid from the cans of orange wedges to create the gel that holds the topping in place.

CAKE

¼ cup all-purpose flour
¼ teaspoon baking powder
pinch of salt
2 tablespoons butter, softened

¼ cup granulated sugar
2 tablespoons milk
⅛ teaspoon vanilla extract
1 egg

CREAM CHEESE LAYER

1 envelope unflavored gelatin
¾ cup granulated sugar
1 cup boiling water
1 envelope Dream Whip
½ cup low-fat milk
3 8-ounce pkgs. cream cheese,
    softened

1 teaspoon vanilla extract
¼ teaspoon orange extract
¼ teaspoon lemon juice
5 drops yellow food coloring
1 drop red food coloring

TOPPING

2 15-ounce cans mandarin
    oranges (in light syrup)
1 teaspoon unflavored gelatin

NUT CRUST

1 tablespoon water
2 tablespoons granulated sugar
½ cup chopped hazelnuts
    (2.25 ounce bag)

ICING

¼ cup vegetable shortening
½ cup powdered sugar
1 tablespoon milk
⅛ teaspoon vanilla extract

1. To make cake layer, combine flour, baking powder and salt in a small bowl. Cream together butter and sugar with an electric mixer in a medium bowl. Add dry ingredients to the butter and mix well. Mix in milk, vanilla and 1 egg. Pour into a well-greased 9-inch springform pan (or line it with parchment paper). Slam pan down on the counter a few times to

even out the batter. Bake in a preheated 350 degree oven for 15 minutes or until the cake is light brown on top.

2. For the cream cheese layer, combine gelatin with ¾ cup sugar in a medium bowl. Add boiling water and stir until gelatin is dissolved. Set this aside.

3. Prepare Dream Whip by whipping together 1 envelope of Dream Whip and ½ cup milk with an electric mixer in another medium bowl. Whip it good until the topping makes stiff peaks.

4. In another bowl, whip the cream cheese with vanilla, orange extract, lemon juice and food coloring in a large bowl until smooth. Slowly add the gelatin mixture while beating.

5. Add half (about 1 cup) of the Dream Whip to the cream cheese mixture and beat until smooth.

6. Pour this mixture over the cake layer in the springform pan. Chill for 2 hours or until firm.

7. Drain the liquid from the cans of mandarin oranges, saving ½ cup. Heat the ½ cup liquid in the microwave on high for 1 to 1½ minutes or until hot. Dissolve 1 teaspoon unflavored gelatin in the liquid. Combine liquid with orange wedges and pour over the top of the firmed-up cheesecake that's still in the springform pan. Chill the cake for at least 2 more hours.

8. For the crunchy nut crust, combine 1 tablespoon water with 2 tablespoons sugar in a small saucepan over medium heat. When sugar is dissolved and liquid begins to boil, add the hazelnuts and stir until nuts are coated. Stir often until the water has cooked off, then continue to stir until the sugar begins to caramelize and turn light brown. Be careful not to burn the nuts. The nuts are done when they are light brown and glazed with candied sugar. Pour the nuts onto a plate and let them cool completely. When the candied nuts are cool, chop them up in a food processor until they are the consistency of crumbs.

9. Make the icing by combining shortening with powdered sugar, milk and vanilla.

10. When the mandarin orange gelatin has firmed up on top of

the cake, remove the cake from the springform pan. Use a spatula to spread the icing around the edge of the cake. Press the hazelnut crumbs onto the icing around the edge of the cake (you've got more than enough hazelnut crumbs and much of it will fall off as you press it on the sides). Chill the cake for at least another hour before serving. To serve, cut cake into 12 slices.

• MAKES 12 SERVINGS.

•   •   •   •

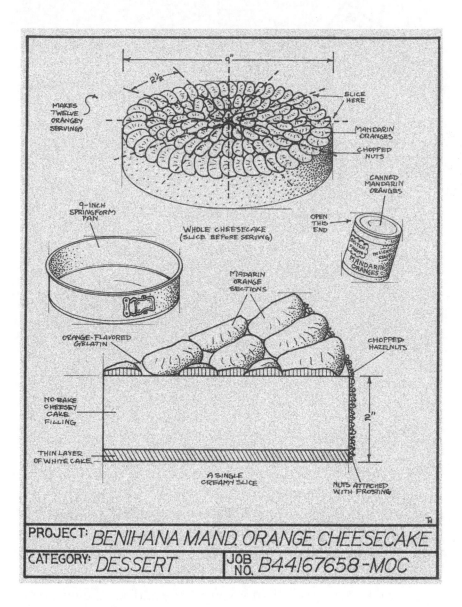

MAKES TWELVE ORANGEY SERVINGS

9"

2½"

SLICE HERE

MANDARIN ORANGES

CHOPPED NUTS

CANNED MANDARIN ORANGES

OPEN THIS END

MANDARIN ORANGES

9-INCH SPRINGFORM PAN

WHOLE CHEESECAKE (SLICE BEFORE SERVING)

MADARIN ORANGE SECTIONS

ORANGE-FLAVORED GELATIN

CHOPPED HAZELNUTS

2"

NO-BAKE CHEESEY CAKE FILLING

THIN LAYER OF WHITE CAKE

A SINGLE CREAMY SLICE

NUTS ATTACHED WITH FROSTING

PROJECT: *BENIHANA MAND. ORANGE CHEESECAKE*

CATEGORY: *DESSERT*

JOB NO. *B44/67658-MOC*

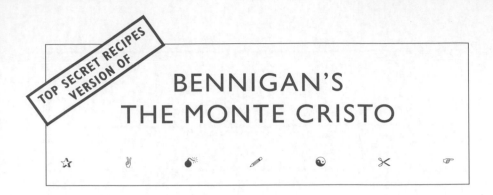

BENNIGAN'S
THE MONTE CRISTO

MENU DESCRIPTION: *"A delicious combination of ham and turkey, plus Swiss and American cheeses on wheat bread. Lightly battered and fried until golden. Dusted with powdered sugar and served with red raspberry preserves for dipping."*

It sounds crazy, but tastes great: A triple-decker ham, turkey, and cheese sandwich is dipped in a tempura-style batter; fried to a golden brown; then served with a dusting of powdered sugar and a side of raspberry preserves. For over ten years tons of cloning requests for this one have stacked up at *TSR* Central, so it was time for a road trip. There are no Bennigan's in Las Vegas, and since the Bennigan's chain made this sandwich famous, I headed out to the nearest Bennigan's in San Diego. Back home, with an ice chest full of original Monte Cristo sandwiches well-preserved and ready to work with, I was able to come up with this simple clone for a delicious sandwich that is crispy on the outside, and hot, but not greasy, on the inside (the batter prevents the shortening from penetrating). This recipe makes one sandwich, which may be enough for two. If you want to make more, you'll most likely have to make more batter so that any additional sandwiches get a real good dunking.

8 to 12 cups vegetable shortening

SANDWICH

3 slices whole wheat sandwich
    bread
1 slice Swiss cheese (deli-style)
3 ounces sliced turkey (deli-style)

1 slice American cheese
    (deli-style)
3 ounces sliced ham (deli-style)

BATTER

2 egg yolks
1 cup ice water

1 cup all purpose flour
1 teaspoon baking soda

ON TOP

powdered sugar

ON THE SIDE

raspberry preserves

1. Heat 8 to 12 cups of shortening in a deep fryer or large saucepan to 375 degrees. You will need the hot shortening to be at least 4 inches deep.
2. Make the sandwich by arranging the slice of Swiss cheese on a piece of wheat bread. Arrange the turkey breast on the Swiss cheese. Place a piece of wheat bread on the turkey. Place the slice of American cheese on the wheat bread. Arrange the ham slices on the American cheese. Top off the sandwich with the third slice of bread. Make sure the meat is not hanging over the edge of the sandwich. Press down on the sandwich with the palm of your hand to flatten it a bit.
3. Make the batter by beating the egg yolks. Stir in the ice water. Measure the flour and baking soda into a sifter, and sift the mixture into the ice water and egg yolk. Stir with a large spoon, but don't mix it too well. You should still have many visible lumps in the batter.
4. Slice the sandwich in half from corner to corner. Dip one half of the sandwich in the batter, while holding it together with your fingers (the batter will hold the sandwich together in the shortening). Coat the sandwich well, but let any excess

batter fall off. Drop the battered sandwich half into the oil. If your pan or fryer can fit the other half of the sandwich, batter that piece and drop it into the fryer as well. If your fryer is small, you may only be able to fry only one half at a time. Fry the sandwich for 6 to 8 minutes, turning it over halfway through cooking time. It should be golden brown when done.

5. Remove the sandwich halves to paper towels to drain. When you can touch the sandwich, slice each half in half making four pieces. Dust the sandwich with powdered sugar and serve it with a small bowl of raspberry preserves.

• Makes 1 sandwich.

• • • •

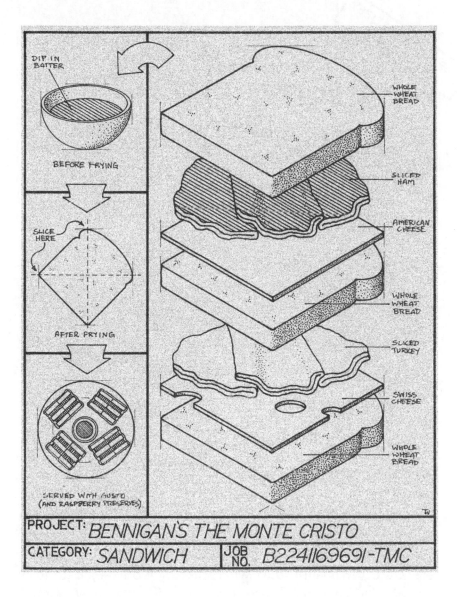

DIP IN BATTER

BEFORE FRYING

SLICE HERE

AFTER FRYING

SERVED WITH GUSTO
(AND RASPBERRY PRESERVES)

WHOLE WHEAT BREAD

SLICED HAM

AMERICAN CHEESE

WHOLE WHEAT BREAD

SLICED TURKEY

SWISS CHEESE

WHOLE WHEAT BREAD

PROJECT: *BENNIGAN'S THE MONTE CRISTO*

CATEGORY: *SANDWICH* **JOB NO.** *B224II69691-TMC*

BUFFALO WILD WINGS
BUFFALO WINGS
AND SAUCES

☆ ✌ 💣 ✏ ☯ ✂ ☞

MENU DESCRIPTION: *"Here they are in all their lip-smacking, award-winning glory: Buffalo, New York–style chicken wings spun in your favorite signature sauce."*

Since Buffalo, New York, was too far away, Jim Disbrow and Scott Lowery satisfied their overwhelming craving in 1981 by opening a spicy chicken wing restaurant close to home in Kent, Ohio. With signature sauces and a festive atmosphere, the chain has now evolved from a college campus sports bar with wings to a family restaurant with over 300 units. While frying chicken wings is no real secret—simply drop them in hot shortening for about 10 minutes—the delicious spicy sauces make the wings special. There are 12 varieties of sauce available to coat your crispy chicken parts at the chain, and three of the traditional hot sauces are cloned here. These sauces are very thick, almost like dressing or dip, so we'll use an emulsifying technique that will ensure a creamy final product where the oil won't separate from the other ingredients. These are clones for the most popular sauces: Spicy Garlic, Medium, and Hot. I've also added another big seller, Caribbean Jerk, to the list, followed by the cooking and coating technique for the wings. The first three sauce recipes might look the same at first glance, but each has slight variations. The bottom line is that you can make your sauce hotter or milder by adjusting the level of cayenne pepper. You can find Frank's pepper sauce by the other hot sauces at the market. If you can't find that brand, you can also use Crystal brand Louisiana hot sauce.

SPICY GARLIC WING SAUCE

1 cup Frank's cayenne pepper
  sauce
⅓ cup vegetable oil
1 teaspoon granulated sugar
1 teaspoon garlic powder
½ teaspoon coarse ground black
  pepper

½ teaspoon cayenne pepper
½ teaspoon Worcestershire sauce
1 egg yolk
2 teaspoons water
2 teaspoons cornstarch

MEDIUM WING SAUCE

1 cup Frank's cayenne pepper
  sauce
⅓ cup vegetable oil
1 teaspoon granulated sugar
½ teaspoon cayenne pepper
½ teaspoon garlic powder

½ teaspoon Worcestershire sauce
⅛ teaspoon coarse ground black
  pepper
1 egg yolk
2 teaspoons water
2 teaspoons cornstarch

HOT WING SAUCE

1 cup Frank's cayenne pepper
  sauce
⅓ cup vegetable oil
1 teaspoon granulated sugar
1½ teaspoons cayenne pepper
½ teaspoon garlic powder

½ teaspoon Worcestershire sauce
⅛ teaspoon coarse ground black
  pepper
1 egg yolk
2 teaspoons water
2 teaspoons cornstarch

1. Combine all ingredients except egg yolk, water and cornstarch for the sauce of your choice in a small saucepan. Heat sauce over medium heat until boiling, then reduce heat and simmer for 5 minutes. Remove pan from the heat and allow it to cool, uncovered, for 10 minutes.

2. While the sauce cools, vigorously whisk egg yolk with 2 teaspoons water in a medium bowl for about 2 minutes or until color is pale yellow. Whisk in cornstarch until dissolved.
3. Drizzle the hot sauce mixture into the egg yolk mixture in a steady stream while rapidly whisking. This will create a thick, creamy emulsion that will prevent the oil from separating. Cover the sauce and chill it until it's needed.

- MAKES 1½ CUPS.

CARIBBEAN JERK SAUCE

The chain sells each of its 12 signature sauces in the restaurant because many of them work great as a baste or side sauce for a variety of home cooked masterpieces. This sauce is a favorite for that reason (ranking at the top of the list with Spicy Garlic as the chain's best-seller), so I thought it would be a useful clone that doesn't require you to fill up the fryer to make chicken wings. You can use this sauce on grilled chicken, pork, ribs, salmon or anything you can think of that would benefit from the sweet, sour and spicy flavors that come from an island-style baste.

3 tablespoons margarine
2 tablespoons minced green onion (white and light green parts only)
1 cup water
¾ cup ketchup
½ cup plus 2 tablespoons dark brown sugar
¼ cup apple cider vinegar
2 tablespoons white vinegar
2 tablespoons Frank's cayenne pepper sauce
2 teaspoons ground black pepper

2 teaspoons Worcestershire sauce
2 teaspoons lemon juice
1½ teaspoons cayenne pepper
1 teaspoon dried parsley flakes
1 teaspoon cornstarch
½ teaspoon salt
½ teaspoon garlic powder
½ teaspoon dried thyme
¼ teaspoon onion powder
⅛ teaspoon ground cloves
⅛ teaspoon ground nutmeg
⅛ teaspoon ground allspice
⅛ teaspoon rubbed sage

1. Melt margarine over medium/low heat. Add minced green onions and cook for 5 minutes. You just want to sweat the onions to soften them up. You're not looking to brown them.
2. Remove the pan from the heat, and whisk in the remaining ingredients. Put the pan back on the stove and bring the mixture to a boil over medium heat. Reduce heat and simmer for 45 minutes or until the sauce darkens and thickens. Cover sauce, then cool and chill until it's needed.

- MAKES 2 CUPS.

WINGS   **ON THE SIDE**
20 chicken wing pieces   celery sticks
6 to 12 cups vegetable shortening

1. Heat shortening in your fryer to 350 degrees.
2. Drop the wings into the shortening and fry for 10 to 12 minutes, or until the wings are turning light brown. Remove wings to a rack or paper towels to drain for 1 minute.
3. Put the wings into a plastic container with a lid. Add ¼ cup to ⅓ cup of your sauce of choice to the container, put the lid on and give it a good shake. Pour wings out onto a plate and add celery on the side. Oh, and get the napkins ready.

- SERVES 2 TO 4 AS AN APPETIZER.

• • • •

CALIFORNIA
PIZZA KITCHEN
CALIFORNIA COSMO

MENU DESCRIPTION: *"Our Original! Featuring Ciroc Snap Frost vodka, an all grape vodka, combined with red grape juice and accented with the sweet orange flavor of Cointreau and frozen red seedless grapes."*

While other vodkas are made from potatoes, wheat, molasses, corn, or rye, Ciroc is the first vodka to be distilled from late harvest French grapes. These super sweet grapes and the 5-step distilling process makes this vodka unique and extra smooth, with a subtle fruity flavor that goes great with grape juice and the orange flavor of Cointreau. Plan ahead for this drink by piercing three red seedless grapes on a toothpick and popping them into the freezer for at least an hour. Or, if you're like me, you'll have a dozen or so of these garnishes sitting in a small bag in the freezer ready to go when guests show up for happy hour.

1 ¼ ounces Ciroc Vodka
½ ounce Cointreau
2 ounces red grape juice

GARNISH
3 red seedless grapes on a
toothpick, frozen

1. Fill an 8-ounce martini glass with ice to chill the glass.
2. Fill a cocktail shaker with ice.

3. Measure Ciroc Vodka, Cointreau and grape juice into the shaker. Cover and shake vigorously.
4. Dump the ice out of the martini glass, and strain the cocktail into the glass.
5. Garnish with three grapes that have been pierced onto a toothpick and frozen. Serve it up, or sip it yourself.

•   MAKES 1 COCKTAIL.

•   •   •   •

CALIFORNIA PIZZA KITCHEN THAI CRUNCH SALAD

MENU DESCRIPTION: *"Shredded napa cabbage, chilled grilled chicken breast, julienne cucumbers, edamame, crispy wontons, peanuts, cilantro, julienne carrots, red cabbage and scallions tossed with a lime-cilantro dressing. Topped with crispy rice sticks and Thai peanut dressing."*

Plan ahead for this amazing salad clone by first grilling the chicken, then chilling it, and preparing the cilantro-lime dressing and the peanut sauce in advance. The menu description says that the salad is topped with "crispy rice sticks," but upon close inspection I determined they are actually crispy bean threads, cooked in a flash when dropped into hot oil for a few seconds. The crispy wontons are made from frying thinly sliced wonton wrappers in the same hot oil. For the edamame (soybeans), look in the frozen food section, and if they're still in their pods, be sure to take them out before measuring and tossing them into the salad. Once you've got everything chilled and chopped, building each dish is a breeze, and you'll have four huge dinner-size salads that will each be enough for a meal.

LIME-CILANTRO DRESSING

½ cup vegetable oil

¼ cup rice vinegar

½ cup coarsely chopped cilantro

¼ cup minced red bell pepper

¼ cup honey
4 teaspoons Dijon mustard
2 teaspoons sesame oil
2 teaspoons lime juice

2 cloves garlic
dash salt
dash ground black pepper

SPICY PEANUT SAUCE

½ cup crunchy peanut butter
6 tablespoons hoisin sauce
2 tablespoons soy sauce
2 tablespoons rice vinegar
2 tablespoons light brown sugar
1 tablespoon chili sauce
   (or chili-garlic sauce)
1 teaspoon sesame oil
½ teaspoon minced ginger
½ cup water
2 to 3 cups vegetable oil or
   vegetable shortening
8 wonton wrappers

1 handful bean threads
4 small skinless chicken breast
   fillets
1 cup cooked edamame
1 cup unsalted peanuts
12 cups chopped napa cabbage,
   chopped (1 large head)
2 cups thinly sliced red cabbage
2 cups shredded or julienned
   carrot
1 cup julienned cucumber
4 green onions, chopped
   (green part only)

1. Make lime-cilantro dressing by combining all ingredients in a blender on high speed for 20 seconds, or until cilantro is chopped fine but not entirely pureed. Cover and chill.
2. Make spicy peanut sauce by combining all ingredients in a small saucepan over medium/low heat. Heat until sauce is hot, but not boiling, and sugar is dissolved. Pour mixture into a blender and blend for about 20 seconds. Cover and chill.
3. Flatten chicken breasts by covering them with plastic wrap and pounding them thin with a kitchen mallet. Rub oil on each breast, sprinkle each with a little salt and pepper, and grill for 3 to 4 minutes per side or until done. Wrap and chill the cooked chicken.
4. Make crispy wontons by heating 2 cups of vegetable shortening or oil in a medium saucepan to 375 degrees. Slice a stack of 8 wonton wrappers into ¼-inch wide strips. Slice those strips in half. Fry them in hot oil for about 30 seconds or until light brown. Drain on paper towels.

5. Fry a big handful of beans threads in hot oil for about 10 seconds or until they float to the top of the oil. Drain on paper towels.

6. Cook edamame following the directions on the package. If the soybeans are in the pods, remove them and chill the beans after they have cooked.

7. Toast the peanuts by heating them up in a skillet over medium/ low heat for 3 to 4 minutes or just until they start to brown. Immediately remove them from the heat so that they don't burn.

8. Now you're ready to build the salads. For each serving, combine 3 cups napa cabbage, ½ cup red cabbage, ½ cup carrot, ¼ cup cucumber, ¼ cup edamame, ¼ cup toasted peanuts, ¼ cup crispy wontons, and a couple tablespoons of chopped green onion in a large bowl. Thinly slice a cold chicken breast into bite-size pieces and add it to the salad. Pour 4 to 5 tablespoons of cilantro-lime dressing over the salad and toss well.

9. Carefully pour tossed salad onto a serving plate. Sprinkle about ½ cup crispy bean threads on top of the salad.

10. Spoon spicy peanut sauce into a squirt bottle and squirt the sauce in a sweeping motion over the top of the salad. Repeat for remaining servings.

• MAKES 4 LARGE SALADS.

• • • •

CALIFORNIA PIZZA KITCHEN CALIFORNIA CLUB PIZZA

MENU DESCRIPTION: *"Applewood smoked bacon, grilled chicken and Mozzarella cheese, hearth baked, then topped with Roma tomatoes, chilled chopped lettuce tossed in mayonnaise and fresh sliced avocados."*

There's no better way to clone the great pizzas from this creative chain than to start with dough made from scratch. And since the only way to re-create commercial-style pizza dough is to use the same slow-rising technique the pros use, you're going to have to plan ahead at least 24 hours. This is the length of time it will take for the gluten in the flour to work its magic while resting comfortably in your refrigerator. And, if you've got the patience, I think 48 hours is even better. Once the dough is ready to go, you should bake your pizzas—this recipe makes two—on a preheated pizza stone in your oven. If you don't already have one, you can find one of the round or rectangular stones in just about any houseware store. This cooking method is the absolute best way to produce an evenly baked finished product with a texture and taste that mirrors the amazing pies CPK whips out of rocket-hot brick pizza ovens.

PIZZA DOUGH

¾ cup warm water
   (105 to 115 degrees)

1½ teaspoons yeast
2 teaspoons granulated sugar

1 ¾ cups bread flour

1 teaspoon salt

2 chicken breasts, pounded thin

olive oil cooking spray

2 cups shredded mozzarella
    cheese

½ cup cooked thick bacon,
    crumbled (about 6 slices)

2 tablespoons olive oil

3 cups chopped iceberg lettuce

1 cup chopped romaine lettuce

4 tablespoons mayonnaise

2 large roma tomatoes, sliced into
    8 slices each

1 avocado, sliced into 16 slices

1. Make the pizza dough by dissolving yeast and granulated sugar in ¾ cup warm water in a small bowl or glass measuring cup. Let the mixture sit for 5 minutes or until it gets foamy on top.

2. Combine flour and salt in a large bowl. Make a depression in the flour and pour the yeast mixture and oil into it. Stir the liquid gradually drawing more flour into it, until you can form the dough into a ball. Use your hands to knead the dough on a lightly floured surface for 10 minutes, or until the texture of the dough is smooth. Coat dough with oil, cover it and let it sit in a warm spot for 1 to 2 hours or until it doubles in size. Punch down the dough, cover it again and let it sit for 24 to 48 hours in your fridge.

3. Cover chicken breasts and pound them to about ½-inch thick with a kitchen mallet. Spray chicken liberally with olive oil cooking spray (or rub with olive oil), then sprinkle on some salt and pepper. Grill the chicken on a preheated grill for 3 to 4 minutes per side or until it's done. You can also sauté chicken in a skillet on your stove for 4 to 5 minutes per side or until done. Cool and chop chicken into ½-inch cubes.

4. When it gets close to pizza time, remove the dough from the refrigerator. It needs to warm up for about 2 hours before you use it. Also, place a pizza stone in your oven and crank the temperature up to 500 degrees.

5. Assemble each pizza by dividing the dough in half and rolling one half into a 10-inch circle on a lightly floured surface. Place the dough onto a pizza pan or a pizza peel that will be

used to slide the dough onto the hot pizza stone. Be sure to flour the pan or pizza peel liberally with flour so that the assembled pizza will slide off easily.

6. Spray the pizza dough with a generous amount of olive oil spray. Spread 1 cup of shredded mozzarella cheese on the dough. Sprinkle half of the bacon on next, followed by half of the chicken. Slide the pizza onto the pizza stone and bake for 9 to 10 minutes or until the cheese and crust begins to brown.

7. While pizza bakes, combine 1½ cups chopped iceberg lettuce with ½ cup of chopped romaine in a bowl. Stir in 2 tablespoons of mayonnaise and mix well until all of the lettuce is coated with mayo.

8. When the pizza comes out of the oven, slice it into 8 pieces. Spoon the lettuce mixture over the top, then place a roma tomato slice on each slice of pizza. Finish off your pie by placing an avocado slice on each slice of pizza. Repeat the process for the remaining pizza.

- MAKES 2 PIZZAS, 8 SLICES EACH.

• • • •

CALIFORNIA
PIZZA KITCHEN
JAMAICAN JERK
CHICKEN PIZZA

MENU DESCRIPTION: *"Grilled Jamaican Jerk spiced chicken breast with our spicy sweet Caribbean sauce, mozzarella cheese, applewood smoked bacon, mild onions, roasted red & yellow peppers and scallions."*

This CPK creation is a top pick at the 162-unit chain, most likely because chefs slather on a delicious sweet and spicy Caribbean sauce where tomato sauce usually sits on traditional Italian-style pies. Making the sauce from scratch is the way to go for true clone rangers, but if you'd like a shortcut, find Tiger Sauce in your local market where the bottled hot sauces are sold, and use that. If you want another shortcut, rather than mixing your own jerk seasoning from scratch, use any jerk blend you can find in the store or snag a bottle of our own Top Secret Island Rub at the *TopSecret Recipes* website (www.TopSecretRecipes.com). I do recommend making the pizza dough from scratch rather than buying prepared dough, however. You'll need to plan ahead on this part of the recipe so that the dough has a chance to slowly rise in your fridge overnight. I also recommend that you use a pizza stone to bake the two pizzas this recipes makes to re-create the baking results of CPK's stone ovens.

PIZZA DOUGH

¾ cup warm water
  (105 to 115 degrees)
1½ teaspoons yeast
2 teaspoons granulated sugar

1¾ cups bread flour
1 teaspoon salt
2 tablespoons olive oil

CARIBBEAN SAUCE

½ cup light brown sugar
¼ cup water
¼ cup ketchup
¼ cup light corn syrup
¼ cup minced white onion
2 tablespoons red wine vinegar
1 teaspoon minced garlic

1 teaspoon lemon juice
½ teaspoon salt
½ teaspoon crushed red pepper
  flakes
¼ teaspoon ground black pepper
⅛ teaspoon dried thyme
⅛ teaspoon ground allspice

JERK SEASONING

2 tablespoons light brown sugar
1½ teaspoons salt
½ teaspoon ground black pepper
½ teaspoon ground paprika
½ teaspoon ground allspice

¼ teaspoon garlic powder
¼ teaspoon onion powder
⅛ teaspoon ground cayenne
  pepper
pinch ground cinnamon

2 chicken breasts, pounded thin
olive oil cooking spray
1 red bell pepper
1 yellow bell pepper
2 cups plus 4 tablespoons
  shredded mozzarella cheese

½ cup cooked thick bacon,
  crumbled (about 6 slices)
½ cup thinly sliced white onion
2 tablespoons chopped green
  onion (green part only)

1. Make the pizza dough by dissolving yeast and granulated sugar in ¾ cup warm water in a small bowl or glass measuring cup. Let the mixture sit for 5 minutes or until it gets foamy on top.
2. Combine flour and salt in a large bowl. Make a depression in the flour and pour the yeast mixture and oil into it. Stir the liquid gradually drawing more flour into it, until you can form

the dough into a ball. Use your hands to knead the dough on a lightly floured surface for 10 minutes, or until the texture of the dough is smooth. Coat dough with oil, cover it and let it sit in a warm spot for 1 to 2 hours or until it doubles in size. Punch down the dough, cover it again and let it sit overnight in your fridge.

3. You can also make the sauce a day ahead by combining all ingredients in a medium saucepan. Simmer over medium/low heat for 7 minutes. Puree cooled sauce in a blender for 10 seconds, then cover it and let it chill out in the fridge.

4. When it gets close to pizza time, remove the dough from the refrigerator. It needs to warm up for about 2 hours before you use it. Also, place a pizza stone in your oven and crank the temperature up to 500 degrees.

5. Combine all of the ingredients for the jerk seasoning. Cover chicken breasts and pound them to about ½-inch thick with a kitchen mallet. Spray chicken liberally with olive oil cooking spray (or rub with olive oil), then sprinkle on some seasoning. Grill chicken on a preheated grill for 3 to 4 minutes per side or until done. You can also sauté chicken in a skillet on your stove for 4 to 5 minutes per side or until done. Cool and chop into ½-inch cubes.

6. Roast red bell peppers by setting them directly over a high flame on a gas stove. Turn the peppers as the skin chars black, then plunge them into ice water and remove the blackened skin. If you don't have a gas stove, you can also roast the peppers on a baking sheet in a 450-degree preheated oven for 45 minutes or until skin is charred, then peel the skin off in cold water. Dice about 2 tablespoons of each pepper for each pizza. Seal the rest of the roasted pepper and refrigerate. It will keep for about two days.

7. Assemble each pizza by dividing the dough in half and rolling one half into a 10-inch circle on a lightly floured surface. Place the dough onto a pizza pan or a pizza peel that will be used to slide the dough onto the hot pizza stone. Be sure to flour the pan or pizza peel liberally with flour so that the assembled pizza will slide off easily.

8. Spray the pizza dough with a generous amount of olive oil spray. Spoon 3 to 4 tablespoons of sauce onto the dough, followed by 1 cup of shredded mozzarella. Sprinkle 1 cup of diced chicken on next, followed by ¼ cup of the cooked bacon. Sprinkle 2 tablespoons of diced roasted red bell pepper and 2 tablespoons of diced roasted yellow bell pepper on the pizza. Sprinkle ¼ cup of thinly sliced onion on next, followed by just a couple tablespoons of additional mozzarella. Slide the pizza onto the pizza stone and bake for 9 to 10 minutes or until the cheese and crust begins to brown. Remove from the oven and sprinkle with 1 table-spoon chopped green onion.

9. Slice pizza into 8 pieces and serve. Repeat for remaining pizza.

- MAKES 2 PIZZAS, 8 SLICES EACH.

•   •   •   •

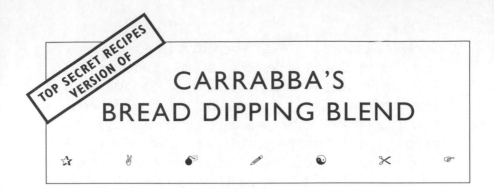

CARRABBA'S
BREAD DIPPING BLEND

When you sit down for Italian-style grub at one of the more than 168 nationwide Carrabba's restaurants, you're first served a small plate with a little pile of herbs and spices in the middle to which the waiter adds olive oil. Now you're set up to dip your sliced bread in the freshly flavored oil. To craft a version of this tasty blend at home you'll need a coffee bean grinder or a small food processor to finely chop the ingredients.

1 tablespoon minced fresh basil
1 tablespoon chopped fresh parsley
1 tablespoon minced fresh garlic
1 teaspoon dried thyme
1 teaspoon dried oregano
1 teaspoon ground black pepper
   (freshly ground is best)

½ teaspoon minced fresh rosemary
½ teaspoon ground sea salt or
   kosher salt
¼ teaspoon crushed red pepper

½ teaspoon olive oil
⅛ teaspoon fresh lemon juice

1. Combine all the ingredients, except oil and lemon juice in a small food processor or coffee bean grinder. Chop briefly until all ingredients are about the same size.
2. Stir in oil and lemon juice.
3. To serve, combine about 1 teaspoon blend to 3 to 4 table-spoons extra virgin olive oil on a small dish. Dip sliced bread in mixture.

• Makes about ¼ cup blend.

• • • •

CARRABBA'S HOUSE SALAD DRESSING (CREAMY PARMESAN)

When Johnny Carrabba and his uncle Damian Mandola opened the first Carrabba's restaurant in 1986, they used a collection of their own traditional family recipes to craft a terrific Italian menu. You'll even find the names of friends and family in several of those dishes including Pollo Rosa Maria, Chicken Bryan, Scampi Damian and Insalata Johnny Rocco. Now we can easily re-create the taste of the delicious dressing that's tossed into the salad served before each Carrabba's entree. And we need only six ingredients. For the grated Parmesan cheese, go ahead and use the stuff made by Kraft that comes in the green shaker canisters. And if you don't have any buttermilk, you can substitute regular milk. Since it's so thick, this dressing is best when tossed into your salad before serving it, just like the real thing.

½ cup mayonnaise
¼ cup grated Parmesan cheese
¼ cup buttermilk

1 ½ teaspoons minced garlic
½ teaspoon minced fresh parsley
½ teaspoon lemon juice

Whisk together all ingredients in a small bowl.

• MAKES 1 CUP.

• • • •

CARRABBA'S CHICKEN MARSALA

MENU DESCRIPTION: *"Fire-roasted chicken breast topped with mushrooms, prosciutto and our Florio Marsala wine sauce."*

To reverse-engineer this big-time favorite entree, I ordered the dish to go, with the sauce on the side, so that I could separately analyze each component. After some trial and error in the underground lab, I found that recreating the secret sauce from scratch is easy enough with a couple small cans of sliced mushrooms, a bit of prosciutto, some Marsala wine, shallots, garlic and a few other good things. Cooking the chicken requires a very hot grill. The restaurant chain grills chicken breasts over a blazing real wood fire, so crank your grill up high enough to get the flames nipping at your cluckers (no, that's not an euphemism). If your grill has a lid, keep it open so you can watch for nasty flare-ups.

MARSALA SAUCE

⅓ cup butter

1 slice prosciutto, diced

2 teaspoons minced shallots

2 teaspoons minced garlic

2 4-ounce cans sliced mushrooms (drained)

¼ cup Marsala wine

¼ teaspoon ground black pepper

1 cup chicken broth

2 teaspoons cornstarch

1 teaspoon minced fresh parsley

2 tablespoons heavy cream

CHICKEN SEASONING

1 ¼ teaspoons salt
1 teaspoon ground black pepper
½ teaspoon dried oregano
½ teaspoon dried thyme
½ teaspoon dried parsley
¼ teaspoon marjoram

¼ teaspoon garlic powder
¼ teaspoon onion powder

4 skinless chicken breasts fillets
olive oil

1. Melt butter over low heat in a medium saucepan.
2. Turn heat up to medium/high to sauté the prosciutto in the melted butter for about 2 to 3 minutes (be careful not to burn the butter). Add shallots and garlic and sauté for about 30 seconds. Add Marsala wine, simmer for another 30 seconds or so, then add drained mushrooms and black pepper. Simmer over medium/high heat for 5 minutes.
3. Dissolve cornstarch in chicken broth. Add broth to the saucepan and simmer for an additional 5 minutes.
4. Add parsley and cream to the sauce and simmer for 3 to 4 minutes or until thick. Remove pan from the heat, then cover it until needed.
5. Preheat barbecue grill on high heat. Combine ingredients for chicken seasoning in a small bowl. Use your thumb and fingers to crush the herbs and spices in the bowl to make a finer blend.
6. Wrap each chicken breast in plastic wrap and pound with a kitchen mallet until uniform in thickness. Brush each chicken breast generously with olive oil. Sprinkle seasoning blend over both sides of each chicken breast and grill for 6 to 8 minutes per side or until done. Give chicken a one-quarter turn on each side while cooking to make criss-cross grill marks.
7. Serve entree by arranging each chicken breast on a plate. Spoon one quarter of the Marsala sauce over each serving of chicken and dig in.

• SERVES 4.

•   •   •   •

THE
CHEESECAKE FACTORY
MINI CRABCAKES

MENU DESCRIPTION: *"Served with remoulade sauce."*

The secret to great crab cakes starts with great crab. Freshly cooked blue crab is the crab of choice for these crustacean cakes, but you can often find high quality canned backfin blue crab in some stores. One such brand comes in 16-ounce cans from Phillips Seafood and is sold at Costco, Sam's Club, Wal-Mart and Von's stores. Once you've got the crab grabbed you need to pick up some panko. Panko is Japanese-style breadcrumbs usually found near the other Asian foods in your market. The Factory uses a little bit of panko to coat each of these small crab cakes for a great, lightly crunchy texture. One order of this appetizer at the restaurant gets you 3 crab cakes; this recipe makes 6 cakes from ½-pound of crab. If you have a 1-pound can of crabmeat, you can save the leftover ½-pound for another recipe or double-up on this one. Any surplus crab cakes will keep for 24 hours in the fridge before you need to get them in a pan. Oh, and one other thing to remember when making crab cakes: Be gentle. Don't stir the crab too much into the other ingredients. Rather, fold the mixture gingerly with a spatula to combine. You want any big chunks of tasty crab to stay as big chunks of tasty crab in the finished product.

2 tablespoons mayonnaise

2 tablespoons minced green onion
(green part only)

2 tablespoons minced red bell
pepper

½ beaten egg

1 teaspoon minced fresh parsley

1 teaspoon Old Bay seasoning

½ teaspoon yellow prepared
mustard

½ pound lump crab meat

3 tablespoons plain breadcrumbs
(such as Progresso)

¼ cup panko (Japanese
breadcrumbs)

vegetable oil

REMOULADE SAUCE

½ cup mayonnaise

2 teaspoons capers

2 teaspoons chopped dill pickle
slices (hamburger pickles)

1 teaspoon lemon juice

½ teaspoon minced fresh parsley

½ teaspoon paprika

½ teaspoon chili powder

¼ teaspoon cayenne pepper

¼ teaspoon ground cumin

⅛ teaspoon salt

1. Measure all the ingredients for the crab cakes—except the breadcrumbs, crab, panko and vegetable oil—into a large bowl. Use a whisk to blend ingredients together. Carefully fold the crab and breadcrumbs into the whisked ingredients. Be sure not to over stir the mixture or those tasty lumps of crab will fall apart. The best crab cakes have nice big chunks of crab in 'em.

2. Rub a light coating of oil in six cups of a nonstick standard size muffin tin, then use your hands or a spoon to fill the cups with equal amounts of the crab mixture. Press down a bit on each crab cake so that the top is flat. Don't press too hard or the crab cakes may be hard to get out. Cover the muffin tin with plastic wrap and pop it in the fridge for an hour or so. This step will help the cakes stay together when they're browned in the oil.

3. Make the remoulade sauce by combining all the ingredients in a small bowl. Cover and chill the sauce until you're ready to serve up the crab cakes.

4. After the crab cakes have chilled through, heat up about ¼-inch of vegetable oil in large skillet over medium/low heat. Fill a shallow bowl with the panko breadcrumbs.
5. Carefully turn the crab cakes out onto a plate. Gently roll each crab cake around in the panko breadcrumbs. Each crab cake should be wearing a light coating of panko.
6. Test the oil by dropping a pinch of panko into the pan. It should sizzle. Sauté the crab cakes in the hot oil for 1½ to 3 minutes on each side or until the cakes are golden brown.
7. Drain crab cakes on paper towels or a rack very briefly, then serve them up hot with the remoulade sauce alongside in a little dish.

• MAKES 6 SMALL CRAB CAKES.

• • • •

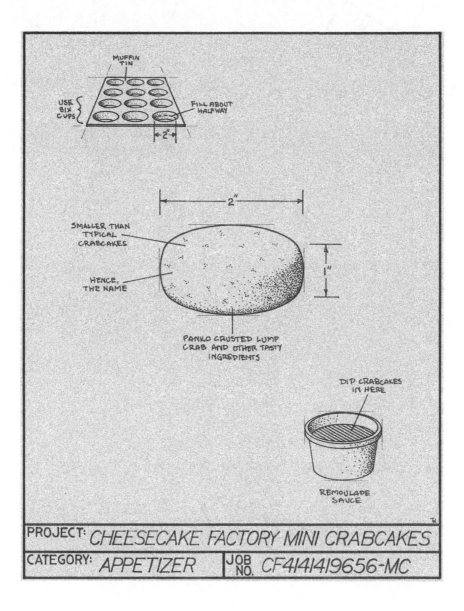

MUFFIN
TIN

USE
SIX
CUPS

FILL ABOUT
HALFWAY

2"

2"

SMALLER THAN
TYPICAL
CRABCAKES

HENCE,
THE NAME

1"

PANKO CRUSTED LUMP
CRAB AND OTHER TASTY
INGREDIENTS

DIP CRABCAKES
IN HERE

REMOULADE
SAUCE

PROJECT: CHEESECAKE FACTORY MINI CRABCAKES

CATEGORY: APPETIZER   JOB NO. CF4141419656-MC

THE
CHEESECAKE FACTORY
SWEET CORN TAMALE CAKES

MENU DESCRIPTION: *"Topped with sour cream, salsa, avocado and salsa verde."*

Nestled between slick full-page ads on page 7 of the huge 19-page spiral-bound menu from The Cheesecake Factory, is a long list of fabulous appetizers that includes this Southwestern-style crowd pleaser. Hand-formed tamale cakes are arranged on fresh salsa verde, topped with sour cream and a creamy Southwestern sauce, with a fresh avocado and cilantro garnish. It's happiness on a plate. And, while the ingredients list below may seem intimidating at first, the three sauces are very simple to make, and your crew will be rewarded and impressed by your effort. (The flavors in the sauces develop after sitting for a bit so you can prepare them all in advance and let them chill in the fridge until chow time.) If you get anything short of a standing ovation for this dish, it's important to encourage kudos by waving the pages of this recipe in front of your diners while casually wiping your brow. Sometimes you have to milk it.

SALSA VERDE

2 tomatillos, chopped (remove papery skin)

1 4-ounce can mild green chilies

1 green onion, chopped

2 tablespoons fresh cilantro

1 ¼ teaspoons granulated sugar

¼ teaspoon ground cumin
¼ teaspoon salt

⅛ teaspoon ground
   black pepper

TOMATO SALSA

1 medium tomato, diced
1 tablespoon minced Spanish
   onion
1 tablespoon minced, fresh
   cilantro

¼ teaspoon lime juice
½ small fresh jalapeno, minced
dash salt
dash ground black pepper

SOUTHWESTERN SAUCE

½ cup mayonnaise
1 teaspoon white vinegar
1 teaspoon water
¾ teaspoon granulated sugar
½ teaspoon chili powder

¼ teaspoon paprika
⅛ teaspoon cayenne pepper
⅛ teaspoon onion powder
dash salt
dash garlic powder

CAKES

1½ cups frozen sweet corn
½ cup butter, softened (1 stick)
3 tablespoons granulated sugar

⅛ teaspoon salt
½ cup masa harina (corn flour)
2 tablespoons all-purpose flour

GARNISH

¼ cup sour cream
½ avocado, chopped

2 tablespoons coarsely chopped,
   fresh cilantro

1. Prepare salsa verde by combining all ingredients (tomatillos, green chilies, green onion, cilantro, sugar, cumin, salt, and pepper) in a food processor on high speed. Cover and chill.
2. Prepare tomato salsa by combining all ingredients (diced tomato, onion, cilantro, lime juice, jalapeno, salt, and pepper) in a small bowl. Cover and chill.

3. Prepare Southwestern sauce by combining all ingredients (mayonnaise, vinegar, water, sugar, chili powder, paprika, cayenne, onion powder, salt, and garlic powder) in a small bowl. Cover and chill.
4. Preheat oven to 400 degrees.
5. Prepare the tamale cakes by chopping 1 cup of the frozen corn in a food processor until it's coarsely pureed. Combine pureed corn with softened butter, sugar, and salt. Blend well with electric mixer until smooth.
6. Add masa and flour and blend well. Mix in the remaining ½ cup of frozen corn kernels by hand.
7. Measure ½ cup portions of the mixture and form it into 3-inch wide patties with your hands. Arrange the patties on a baking sheet and bake for 25 to 30 minutes or until the cakes are browned on the bottom. Carefully flip all cakes with a spatula and bake for an additional 5 to 7 minutes or until other side is browned.
8. While the cakes are baking, spoon a portion of the salsa verde onto a plate or platter (you may want to heat up your plate in the oven for a bit to help warm the sauce). You'll need to use enough salsa verde to coat the entire plate—it should be about ¼-inch deep. Arrange the tamale cakes side-by-side on the salsa verde. Spoon a dollop of sour cream onto each tamale cake. Drizzle the Southwestern sauce over the cakes in a criss-cross pattern (use a squirt bottle if you've got one—see Tidbits). Spoon some tomato salsa over the cakes, followed by the chopped avocado. Finish off the plate by sprinkling the coarsely chopped cilantro leaves over the top.

TIDBITS

Save your empty plastic mustard or ketchup bottles to use in recipes such as this one. Use the squirt bottle to drizzle the southwestern sauce over your dish to give it that slick professional look. And if you want to cut out some of the fat in the sauce, you can easily substitute light mayo for the regular stuff.

You'll find tomatillos in the produce section, usually near the tomatoes or peppers. Be sure to remove the papery skin before using them.

Masa harina, or corn flour, is found in the baking aisle by the other flours or where the Mexican foods are stocked.

- SERVES 4.

• • • •

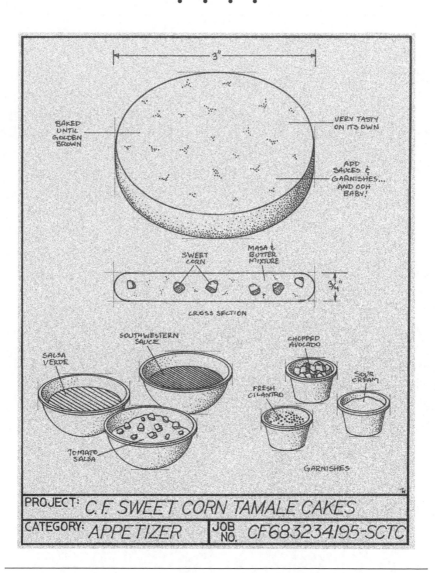

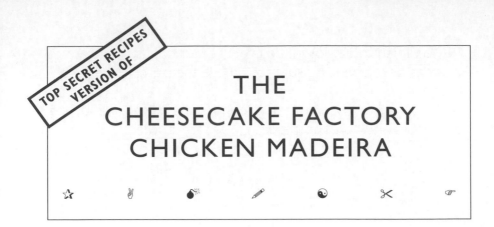

THE
CHEESECAKE FACTORY
CHICKEN MADEIRA

MENU DESCRIPTION: *"Our most popular chicken dish! Sautéed chicken breast topped with fresh asparagus and melted mozzarella cheese, covered with fresh mushroom madeira sauce. Served with mashed potatoes."*

What makes this chicken dish The Cheesecake Factory's "most popular" is the sweet and tangy madeira wine reduction sauce spooned over the top. Man, I could slurp that rich nectar straight from a glass (mushrooms might clog up a straw). It's that good. And—get this—it's easy. Even though the real stuff appears to include veal stock, we can concoct a great knockoff using canned beef broth. Get sliced mozzarella cheese from your deli section and be sure to pound the chicken breasts very thin using plastic wrap to cover each one before you whack on it. Also, in typical Cheesecake Factory style, their entree is huge, including two chicken fillets and a giant pile of mashed potatoes on the side. This recipe makes a total of four chicken fillets, which divides into two servings if you're at the restaurant. At home though, this is probably the perfect amount for a gaggle of four.

1 tablespoon olive oil	8 asparagus spears
4 skinless chicken breast fillets	4 mozzarella cheese slices

MADEIRA SAUCE

2 tablespoons olive oil
2 cups sliced fresh
   white mushrooms
3 cups madeira wine

2 cups beef broth
1 tablespoon butter
¼ teaspoon ground
   black pepper

1. Heat up 1 tablespoon olive oil in a large skillet over medium heat. Cover each chicken breast with plastic wrap then use a mallet to flatten the chicken to about ¼-inch thick. Sprinkle each fillet with salt and pepper.
2. Sauté the chicken fillets for 4 to 6 minutes per side, or until the chicken has browned just a bit. Remove chicken fillets from the pan and wrap them together in foil to keep the fillets warm while you make the sauce. Don't clean the pan. You want all that cooked-on goodness to stay in the skillet to help make the sauce.
3. With the heat still on medium, add two tablespoons of oil to the skillet. Add the sliced mushrooms and sauté for about two minutes. Add the madeira wine, beef broth, butter and pepper. Bring sauce to a boil, then reduce heat and simmer for about 20 minutes or until sauce reduces to about one-quarter of its original volume. When the sauce is done it will have thickened and turned a dark brown color.
4. As the sauce is simmering, bring a medium saucepan filled about halfway with water to a boil. Add a little salt to the water. Toss the asparagus into the water and boil for 3 to 5 minutes, depending on the thickness of your asparagus spears. Drop the asparagus in a bowl of ice water to halt the cooking. The asparagus should be slightly tender when done, not mushy.
5. Set oven to broil. Prepare the dish by arranging the cooked chicken fillets on a baking pan. Cross two asparagus spears over each fillet, then cover each with a slice of mozzarella cheese. Broil the fillets for 3 to 4 minutes or until light brown spots begin to appear on the cheese.

6. To serve, arrange one or two chicken breasts on each plate, then spoon 3 or 4 tablespoons of madeira sauce over the chicken.

• MAKES 2 TO 4 SERVINGS.

•   •   •   •

THE CHEESECAKE FACTORY BANG-BANG CHICKEN & SHRIMP

MENU DESCRIPTION: *"A spicy Thai dish with the flavors of curry, peanut, chile, and coconut. Sautéed with vegetables and served over rice."*

This dish ranks very high among the most frequent entree clone requests from this growing chain's huge menu, and anyone who is a fan of Thai dishes falls in love with it. I dig recipes that include scratch sauces that can be used with other dishes. The curry and peanut sauces here are good like that. They can, for example, be used to sauce up grilled skewers of chicken or other meats, or as a flavorful drizzle onto lettuce wraps. But even though I've included the peanut sauce recipe from scratch here, you can take the quick route and save a little prep time by picking up a pre-made peanut sauce found near the other Asian foods at the market. Since the sauce is used sparingly in a drizzle over the top of this dish it won't make a big difference which way you go. This recipe produces two Cheesecake Factory–size servings—anyone who's been there knows that means "off-the-hook big." If your diners aren't prepared to process the gargantuan gastronomy and you're all out of doggie bags, you can easily split this recipe into four more sensible portions.

CURRY SAUCE

2 teaspoons chili oil
1/4 cup minced onion
2 tablespoons minced garlic
2 teaspoons minced ginger
1 cup chicken broth
1/2 teaspoon ground cumin
1/2 teaspoon ground coriander
1/2 teaspoon paprika
1/4 teaspoon salt

1/4 teaspoon ground black
    pepper
1/4 teaspoon ground mace
1/4 teaspoon turmeric
3 cups coconut milk
2 medium carrots, julienned
1 small zucchini, julienned
1/2 cup frozen peas

PEANUT SAUCE

1/4 cup creamy peanut butter
2 tablespoons water
4 teaspoons granulated sugar
1 tablespoon soy sauce
1/2 teaspoon chili oil
1 teaspoon rice vinegar
1 teaspoon lime juice

2 skinless chicken breast fillets
16 large raw shrimp, shelled
1/4 cup cornstarch
1/2 cup vegetable oil

4 cups cooked white rice

GARNISH

1 1/2 cups flaked coconut
1/2 teaspoon dried parsley,
    crumbled

2 tablespoons chopped peanuts
2 green onions, julienned

1. Make the curry sauce by heating the chili oil in a large saucepan over medium heat. When the oil is hot add the onion, garlic, and ginger. Sauté for about 30 seconds then add the chicken broth. Add the spices (cumin, coriander, paprika, salt, black pepper, mace, and turmeric) and stir well. Simmer for 5 minutes then add the coconut milk. Bring mixture back up to a boil, then reduce heat and simmer for 20 minutes or until sauce begins to thicken. Add the julienned carrots and zucchini, and the frozen peas. Simmer mixture for 10 minutes or until carrots become tender.

2. Make peanut sauce by combining peanut butter, water, sugar,

soy sauce, rice vinegar, lime juice, and chili oil in a small saucepan over medium heat. Heat just until mixture begins to
bubble, then cover the pan and remove it from the heat.

3. Toast the flaked coconut by preheating your oven to 300 degrees. Spread coconut on a baking sheet and toast it in the
oven. Stir the coconut around every 10 minutes so that it
browns evenly, but watch it closely in the last 5 minutes so it
doesn't get too dark. After 25 to 30 minutes the coconut
should be light brown. Take it out of the oven and let it cool.

4. Cut the chicken breasts into bite-size pieces. Coat the
chicken and shrimp with cornstarch. Heat the vegetable oil in
a wok or large skillet over medium heat. Add the coated
chicken to the pan and sauté it for a couple minutes, turning
as it cooks. Add the shrimp to the pan. Cook the shrimp and
chicken for a couple minutes, until it's done, then remove
everything to a rack or towel to drain.

5. Build the two plates (or you can divide the meal into four
portions) by filling a soup bowl with 1 or 2 cups of white
rice. Press down on the rice. Invert the bowl onto the center
of a plate, tap it a bit, and then lift off the bowl leaving a
formed pile of rice in the center of each plate. Arrange an
equal portion of chicken and shrimp around the rice. Spoon
the curry sauce and vegetables over the chicken and shrimp,
being careful not to get any sauce on top of the rice.

6. Drizzle peanut sauce over the dish concentrating most of it
on the rice. Sprinkle ½ teaspoon of crumbled, dried parsley
over the center of the rice. Add a tablespoon of chopped
peanuts on the parsley, and then place a pile of julienned
green onions on top. Sprinkle ½ cup to ¾ cup of toasted coconut over the chicken and shrimp and serve it up.

- MAKES 2 TO 4 SERVINGS.

• • • •

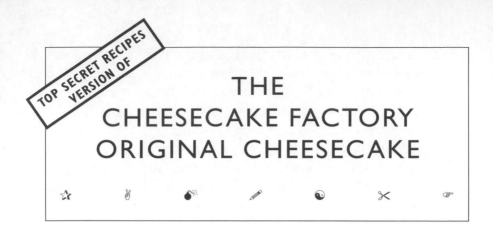

THE
CHEESECAKE FACTORY
ORIGINAL CHEESECAKE

MENU DESCRIPTION: *"Our famous Original cheesecake recipe! Creamy and light, baked in a graham cracker crust. Our most popular cheesecake!"*

Oscar and Evelyn Overton's wholesale cheesecake company was successful quickly after it first started selling creamy cheesecakes like this clone to restaurant chains in the early 1970s. When some restaurants balked at the prices the company was charging for high-end desserts, Oscar and Evelyn's son David decided it was time to open his own restaurant, offering a wide variety of quality meal choices in huge portions, and, of course, the famous cheesecakes for dessert. Today the chain has over 87 stores across the country, and consistently ranks number one on the list of highest grossing single stores for a U.S. restaurant chain.

Baking your cheesecakes in a water bath is part of the secret to producing beautiful cheesecakes at home with a texture similar to those sold in the restaurant. The water surrounds your cheesecake to keep it moist as it cooks, and the moisture helps prevent ugly cracking. You'll also start the oven very hot for just a short time, then crank it down to finish. I also suggest lining your cheesecake pan with parchment paper to help get the thing out of the pan when it's done without a hassle.

CRUST

1 ½ cups graham cracker crumbs
¼ teaspoon ground cinnamon
⅓ cup melted margarine

4 8-ounce pkgs. cream cheese

1 ¼ cups granulated sugar
½ cup sour cream
2 teaspoons vanilla extract
5 eggs

TOPPING

½ cup sour cream
2 teaspoons granulated sugar

OPTIONAL GARNISH

canned whipped cream

1. Preheat oven to 475 degrees. Place a large pan or oven-safe skillet (that the cheesecake pan will fit inside) filled with about ½-inch of water into the oven while it preheats. This will be your water bath.
2. Combine 1 ½ cups graham cracker crumbs and ¼ teaspoon cinnamon into a medium bowl. Mix in ⅓ cup melted margarine. Press the crumb into a 9-inch spring form pan that has been lined on the bottom and side with parchment paper. Use the bottom of a drinking glass to press the crumb mixture flat into the bottom of the pan and about ⅔ the way up the side. Wrap a large piece of foil around the bottom of the pan to keep the cheesecake dry when placed in the water bath in the oven. Put the crust in your freezer until the filling is done.
3. Use an electric mixer to combine the cream cheese with the sugar, sour cream, and vanilla. Blend mixture for a couple minutes or until the ingredients are smooth and creamy. Be sure to scrape down the sides of the bowl. Whisk the eggs in a medium bowl and then add them to the cream cheese mixture. Blend the mixture just enough to integrate the eggs.
4. Remove the crust from the freezer and pour the filling into it.
5. Carefully place the cheesecake into the preheated water bath. Bake for 12 minutes at 475 degrees, then turn the oven

down to 350 degrees and bake for 50 to 60 minutes or until the top of the cheesecake turns a light brown or tan color. Remove the cheesecake from the oven to cool.

6. When the cheesecake has cooled, combine ½ cup sour cream and 2 teaspoons sugar. Spread the sweetened sour cream over the entire top surface of the cheesecake. Cover and chill the cheesecake in the refrigerator for at least 4 hours. To serve, slice the cheesecake into 12 equal portions. Apply a pile of canned whipped cream to the top of each slice and serve.

• MAKES 12 SERVINGS.

• • • •

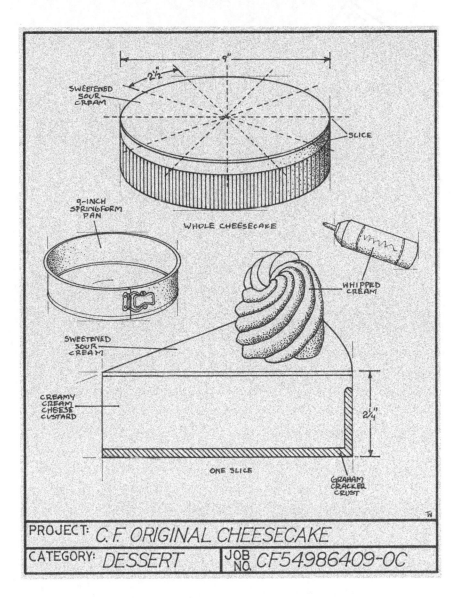

9"

2½"

SWEETENED
SOUR
CREAM

SLICE

WHOLE CHEESECAKE

9-INCH
SPRINGFORM
PAN

WHIPPED
CREAM

SWEETENED
SOUR
CREAM

CREAMY
CREAM
CHEESE
CUSTARD

2¼"

ONE SLICE

GRAHAM
CRACKER
CRUST

TW

PROJECT: *C.F. ORIGINAL CHEESECAKE*

CATEGORY: *DESSERT*

JOB NO. *CF54986409-OC*

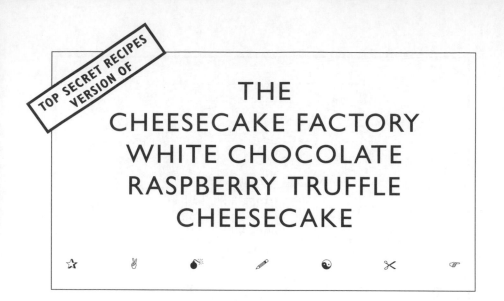

THE CHEESECAKE FACTORY WHITE CHOCOLATE RASPBERRY TRUFFLE CHEESECAKE

MENU DESCRIPTION: *"Our creamy cheesecake with chunks of white chocolate and swirls of imported seedless raspberries throughout. Baked in a chocolate crust and finished with white chocolate shavings and whipped cream."*

I'm not sure why "truffle" is in the name of this great dessert, but who cares when you've got raspberry preserves swirled throughout the cream cheese filling upon a layer of white chocolate chunks and crumbled chocolate cookie wafer crust. Yum. No wonder this cheesecake is the number one pick from the chain's massive list of flavored cheesecake choices.

CRUST

1 ½ cups chocolate cookie
    crumbs or 20 crumbled Oreo
    cookies (with filling removed)
⅓ cup margarine, melted

½ cup raspberry preserves
¼ cup water

4 8-ounce pkgs. cream cheese
1 ¼ cups granulated sugar
½ cup sour cream
2 teaspoons vanilla extract
5 eggs
4 ounces white chocolate,
    chopped into chunks

OPTIONAL GARNISH
2 ounces shaved white chocolate
canned whipped cream

1. Preheat oven to 475 degrees. Place a large pan or oven-safe skillet filled with about ½-inch of water into the oven while it preheats. This will be your water bath.

2. Combine the raspberry preserves with ¼ cup water in a medium microwave-safe bowl. Heat for 1½ minutes on high in your microwave. Stir until smooth. Strain to remove the raspberry seeds (toss 'em out), then let the strained preserves sit to cool, then put the bowl in the refrigerator until later.

3. Measure 1½ cups chocolate cookie crumbs (or crush 20 Oreo cookie wafers—with the filling scraped out—in a resealable plastic bag) into a medium bowl. Mix in ⅓ cup melted margarine. Press the crumb into a 9-inch spring form pan that has been lined on the bottom and side with parchment paper. Use the bottom of a drinking glass to press the crumb mixture flat into the bottom of the pan and about ⅔ the way up the side. Wrap a large piece of foil around the bottom of the pan to keep the cheesecake dry when placed in the water bath. Put the crust in your freezer until the filling is done.

4. Use an electric mixer to combine the cream cheese with the sugar, sour cream, and vanilla. Mix on medium speed for a couple minutes or until the ingredients are smooth and creamy. Be sure to scrape down the sides of the bowl. Whisk the eggs in a medium bowl and then add them to the cream cheese mixture. Blend the mixture just enough to integrate the eggs.

5. Remove the crust from the freezer and sprinkle 4 ounces of white chocolate chunks onto the bottom of the crust. Pour half of the cream cheese filling into the crust. Drizzle the raspberry preserves over the entire surface of the filling. Use a butter knife to swirl the raspberry into the cream cheese.

Just a couple passes is fine, you don't want to blend the raspberry and cream cheese together too much. Pour the other half of the filling into the crust.

6. Carefully place the cheesecake into the water bath in the oven. Bake for 12 minutes at 475 degrees, then turn the oven down to 350 degrees and bake for 50 to 60 minutes or until the top of the cheesecake turns a light brown or tan color. Remove the cheesecake from the oven to cool. When the cheesecake is cool, use the foil from the bottom to cover the cheesecake and chill it in the refrigerator for at least 4 hours.

7. Before serving, sprinkle the entire top surface of cheesecake with 2 ounces of shaved white chocolate. To serve, slice the cheesecake into 12 equal portions. Apply a pile of canned whipped cream to the top of each slice and serve.

- MAKES 12 SERVINGS.

• • • •

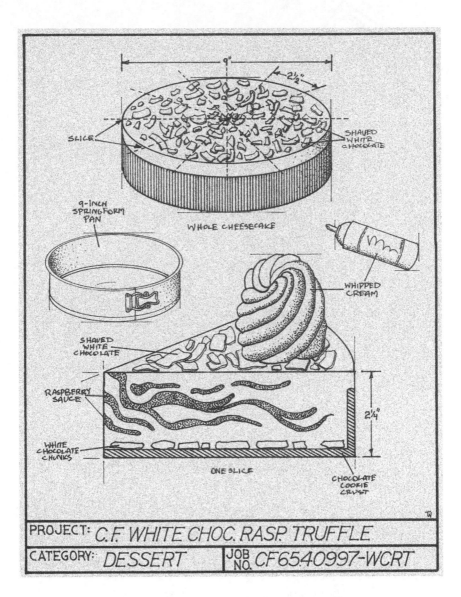

9"

2½"

SLICE

SHAVED
WHITE
CHOCOLATE

9-INCH
SPRINGFORM
PAN

WHOLE CHEESECAKE

WHIPPED
CREAM

SHAVED
WHITE
CHOCOLATE

RASPBERRY
SAUCE

2¼"

WHITE
CHOCOLATE
CHUNKS

ONE SLICE

CHOCOLATE
COOKIE
CRUST

TW

PROJECT: *C.F. WHITE CHOC. RASP. TRUFFLE*

CATEGORY: *DESSERT* JOB NO. *CF6540997-WCRT*

CHEVYS
FRESH SALSA

☆ ✌ 💣 ✎ ☯ ✂ ☞

Whip out the food processor and fire up the grill because you'll need these essential tools to clone one of the best restaurant salsas in the business. The key to recreating the flavor of the real deal is to fire roast the tomatoes and the jalapenos, and to add a little mesquite-flavored liquid smoke. The restaurant chain uses a mesquite grill, so these steps are crucial to getting the same smoky flavor as the addictive restaurant version. Chevys uses chipotle peppers, which are smoked red jalapenos. But unless you grow your own jalapenos, it may be difficult to find the riper red variety in your local supermarket. For this recipe, the green jalapeno peppers will work fine if you can't find the red ones. Adjust the number of jalapenos you use based on the size of the peppers that are available: If you have big jalapenos you need only 6, and you'll need around 10 if your peppers are small.

6 medium tomatoes
6 to 10 jalapenos (use more if
    small, fewer if large)
¼ of a medium Spanish onion
2 cloves garlic
2 tablespoons chopped fresh
    cilantro

2 tablespoons white vinegar
2 teaspoons salt
1½ teaspoons liquid mesquite
    smoke

1. Preheat your barbecue grill to high temperature.
2. Remove any stems from the tomatoes, then rub some oil

over each tomato. Leave the stems on the jalapenos and rub some oil on them, too.

3. Place the tomatoes on the grill when it's hot. After about 10 minutes, place all of the jalapenos onto the grill. In about 10 minutes you can turn the tomatoes and the peppers. When almost the entire surface of the peppers has charred black you can remove them from the grill. The tomatoes will turn partially black, but when the skin begins to come off they are done. Put the peppers and tomatoes on a plate and let them cool.

4. When the tomatoes and peppers have cooled, remove most of the skin from the tomatoes and place them into a food processor. Pinch the stem end from each of the peppers remove any skin that has burned, and place the peppers into the food processor with the tomatoes.

5. Add the remaining ingredients to the food processor and puree on high speed for 5 to 10 seconds or until the mixture has a smooth consistency.

6. Place the salsa into a covered container and chill for several hours or overnight so that the flavors develop.

• MAKES APPROXIMATELY 2 CUPS.

•   •   •   •

CHEVY'S
MANGO SALSA

This zippy mango salsa clone from America's "Fresh Mex" chain is great sprinkled over fajitas, burritos, tacos, salads, sandwiches ... you name it. The salsa is so good on its own you may be tempted to eat it straight from the bowl with a spoon. A little bit of fresh habanero pepper brings the heat to this concoction, but if you can't track down fresh peppers use a couple drops of your favorite bottled habanero sauce.

1 peeled mango, seeded and diced (about 2 cups)	1 teaspoon minced fresh cilantro
¼ cup minced white onion	1 teaspoon fresh lime juice
2 tablespoons minced red bell pepper	½ teaspoon finely minced habanero pepper
	⅛ teaspoon salt

Combine all ingredients in a medium bowl. Cover and chill before serving.

• MAKES 2⅓ CUPS.

• • • •

CHEVYS CHILE CON QUESO

This top secret clone of the cheesy appetizer from this 107-unit Mexican food chain is perfect to whip out for your festive fiestas. This recipe will make enough of the spicy cheese concoction for plenty of party-time double dipping. The Anaheim chile has a mild spiciness, so we'll toss a jalapeno in there for an extra spicy kick. If you can't find an Anaheim pepper, use any mild green chilies that are available, as long as you get about ½ cup of diced pepper in the mix.

one 16-ounce box Velveeta, diced
¾ cup whole milk
1 green Anaheim pepper, seeded and diced (about ½ cup)
¼ cup diced white onion
1 jalapeno pepper, seeded and diced
2 teaspoons minced cilantro

juice of 1 lime
¼ teaspoon dried oregano
¼ teaspoon ground black pepper (freshly ground is best)
pinch of salt
pinch of dried thyme
2 medium tomatoes, seeded and diced (about ⅔ cup)

GARNISH
¼ cup ranchero cheese, crumbled

tortilla chips for dipping

1. Combine Velveeta and milk in a medium saucepan over medium/low heat. Stir often as cheese melts. Be careful not to burn it.
2. When cheese is melted add all remaining ingredients except the tomatoes. Continue to cook over medium/low heat for 7 minutes, stirring often to prevent burning. Stir in tomatoes and remove the queso from the heat.
3. Pour queso into a serving dish, top with crumbled ranchero cheese and serve with tortilla chips for dipping.

• MAKES ABOUT 2 CUPS.

TIDBITS

Ranchero cheese is a crumbly Mexican cheese that can be found near the cream cheese in your supermarket.

• • • •

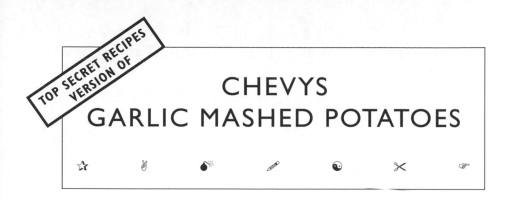

CHEVYS
GARLIC MASHED POTATOES

This easy-to-clone dish comes alongside many of the tasty entrees at this Mexican restaurant chain, or it can be ordered up, pronto, on the side. It's a nice clone to have around since it goes well with so many of your homemade dishes, Mexican or otherwise. Get yourself four large russet potatoes and start peeling, but you don't need to peel all the skin off. Leave a little skin on there for texture. And when you boil the potatoes, toss the whole garlic cloves right in the pot. That way the garlic begins to flavor the potatoes as they boil, and when you mash the potatoes the cooked garlic gets mashed up too. Cool, eh?

6 to 7 cups water
4 medium/large russet potatoes
6 cloves garlic
6 tablespoons butter (¾ stick)

½ cup heavy cream
¾ teaspoon salt
¼ teaspoon ground black pepper

1. Peel potatoes, but leave some skin on. Slice the potatoes into quarters.
2. Boil the potatoes and garlic for 30 minutes in the water in a large saucepan or pot. Make sure the water completely covers the potatoes. When potatoes are tender drain them. Don't lose the garlic—keep it with the potatoes.
3. Pour potatoes and garlic back into the pan. Commence with the thorough mashing. Mashing is fun. Stir in butter,

cream, salt and pepper and reheat over medium/low heat
until hot.

• SERVES 6 TO 8.

• • • •

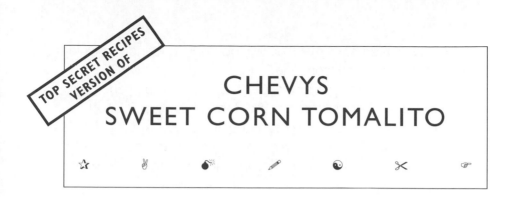

CHEVYS
SWEET CORN TOMALITO

Other Mexican food chains such as Chi-Chi's and El Torito call it "Sweet Corn Cake." But at Chevy's, the corn-filled, pudding-like stuff that's served with most entrees is known as "Tomalito." That masa harina in there (corn flour) is what's used to make tamales, and it can be found in your supermarket either with the corn meal and flour, or wherever the other Mexican/Spanish items are stocked. Everything else here is basic stuff. While other corn cake recipes may require canned corn or canned cream-style corn, Chevys' "no cans in the kitchen" commandment requires that we use frozen corn for a proper clone. Of course, you may also use corn that's been cut fresh from the cob, if you're up for the task.

4 cups frozen corn, thawed
⅓ cup butter, softened (⅔ stick)
½ cup granulated sugar
¾ cup milk

½ cup masa harina
½ cup corn meal
½ teaspoon baking powder
½ teaspoon salt

1. Preheat oven to 325 degrees.
2. Cream softened butter together with sugar in a large bowl with an electric mixer until smooth. Add milk and masa and mix well.
3. Use a blender or food processor to puree 2 cups of corn until smooth. Add pureed corn to butter/masa mixture and

mix well. Add corn meal, baking powder, salt, and remaining corn and mix until combined.

4. Pour mixture into an ungreased 8x8-inch baking pan. Cover with foil and place it into a 9x13-inch baking pan. Add hot water to the larger baking pan until it's about ⅓ full. Bake for 1½ to 2 hours or until corn cake is firm in the center. Let it sit covered for 10 minutes before serving. To serve, scoop out ½ cup portions with a large spoon.

• MAKES 8 SERVINGS.

•   •   •   •

CHEVYS FLAN

☆　　✌　　💣　　✏　　☯　　✂　　☞

Abiding by this large Mexican food chain's "no cans in the kitchen" edict, we'll craft our clone of the delicious flan dessert with fresh whole milk, rather than canned sweetened condensed milk required by most flan recipes out there. The canned stuff has a bit of a funky taste to it, plus it's much too sweet to be an accurate Chevys knockoff. When you're ready to clone this one, be sure to get some parchment paper (it's near the wax paper in the supermarket). When laid over the top of the baking pan, the parchment paper helps the flan cook faster and more evenly than if left uncovered. Aluminum foil doesn't seem to work as well since it tends to reflect the heat away from your ramekins of sweet, creamy goodness.

2½ cups granulated sugar
½ teaspoon ground cinnamon
¼ cup hot water
3 cups whole milk

4 eggs
3 egg yolks
1 teaspoon vanilla extract

1. Preheat oven to 300 degrees.
2. Combine cinnamon with 2 cups granulated sugar in a medium saucepan over medium/low heat. When sugar begins to melt, stir often until all sugar has dissolved and solution is light brown. Add water to pan and stir until smooth. Pour about ¼ cup sugar solution into each of six 6-ounce ramekins (custard cups). Swirl the sugar around the inside

edge of each of the ramekins. Arrange the ramekins in a 9x13-inch baking pan.

3. Heat milk in another medium saucepan over medium heat until it starts to bubble.

4. As milk heats up whisk together eggs, egg yolks, vanilla and remaining ½ cup sugar in a large bowl. Mix until sugar has dissolved.

5. When milk starts to bubble remove it from the heat. Carefully pour about ¼ cup of hot milk into the egg mixture while stirring. This will temper the eggs so they don't cook while adding the rest of the hot milk. Slowly add the remaining milk while mixing.

6. Fill the ramekins to the top with the custard mixture. Remove any foam from the top of each ramekin. Add water to the pan so that it goes halfway up the sides of the ramekins. Place a piece of parchment paper over the ramekins and bake for 75 to 90 minutes or until custard is firm and a knife inserted into the middle of the custard comes out clean.

7. Cool flan and cover each one with plastic wrap. Chill thoroughly before serving. To serve, simply cut around the inside edge of the ramekin with a knife, then turn the flan over onto a plate. The golden, caramelized sugar will spill down over the edges of the flan. Forget about the leftover hardened sugar that stays inside the ramekin. Let the dishwasher deal with it.

• MAKES 6 SERVINGS.

•　•　•　•

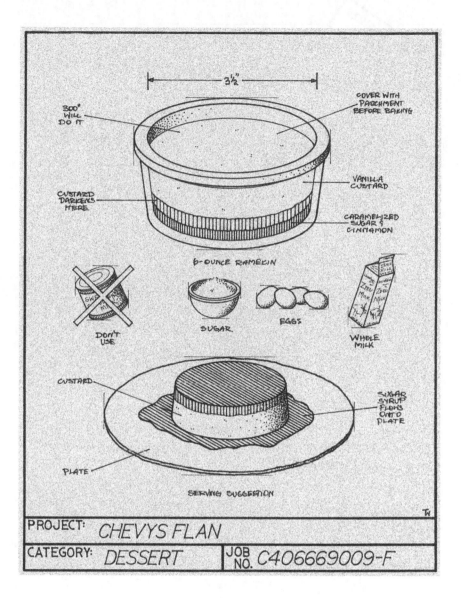

3½"

300° WILL DO IT

COVER WITH PARCHMENT BEFORE BAKING

VANILLA CUSTARD

CUSTARD DARKENS HERE

CARAMELIZED SUGAR & CINNAMON

6-OUNCE RAMEKIN

DON'T USE

SUGAR

EGGS

WHOLE MILK

CUSTARD

SUGAR SYRUP FLOWS ONTO PLATE

PLATE

SERVING SUGGESTION

TW

PROJECT:	*CHEVYS FLAN*	
CATEGORY: *DESSERT*	JOB NO.	*C406669009-F*

CHILI'S
SALSA

This super simple salsa can be made in a pinch with a can of diced tomatoes, some canned jalapenos, fresh lime juice, onion, spices and a food processor (or blender). Plus you can easily double the recipe by sending in a larger 28-ounce can of diced tomatoes, and simply doubling up on all the other ingredients. Use this versatile salsa as a dip for tortilla chips or plop it down onto any dish that needs flavor assistance—from eggs to taco salads to wraps to fish—for that extra special restaurant-style zing. You can adjust the heat level to suit your taste by tweaking the amount of canned jalapenos in the mix.

one 14.5-ounce can diced
    tomatoes
3 tablespoons canned diced
    jalapenos

1 tablespoon lime juice
1 teaspoon salt
¼ teaspoon ground cumin
½ cup diced Spanish onion

1. Combine diced tomatoes, jalapenos, lime juice and spices in a food processor. Run food processor on high speed for just a few moments until the tomatoes have been nearly pureed, yet still chunky. The jalapenos should be chopped into visible minced bits. Be careful not to over-process.

2. Pour the mixture into a bowl and add the sliced onion. Stir well, cover and store overnight for the flavors to properly develop.

• MAKES 2 CUPS.

•   •   •   •

CHILI'S BONELESS BUFFALO WINGS

MENU DESCRIPTION: *"Breaded chicken breast tossed in spicy wing sauce. Served with cool bleu cheese dressing."*

This clone gives us the zesty flavor of traditional Buffalo chicken wings, but the bones and skin are left back in Buffalo. That's because these "wings" are actually nuggets sliced from chicken breast fillets, then breaded and fried, and smothered with the same type of spicy wing sauce used on traditional wings. If you like the flavor of Buffalo wings, but wish you could use a fork, your spicy dreams have come true. Serve up these puppies with some celery sticks and bleu cheese dressing on the side for dipping.

1 cup all-purpose flour
2 teaspoons salt
½ teaspoon ground black pepper
¼ teaspoon cayenne pepper
¼ teaspoon paprika
1 egg
1 cup milk

2 skinless chicken breast fillets
6 to 10 cups vegetable or canola
    oil (amount required by your
    fryer)
¼ cup Frank's or Crystal hot
    sauce
1 tablespoon margarine

ON THE SIDE
bleu cheese dressing (for dipping)
celery sticks

102

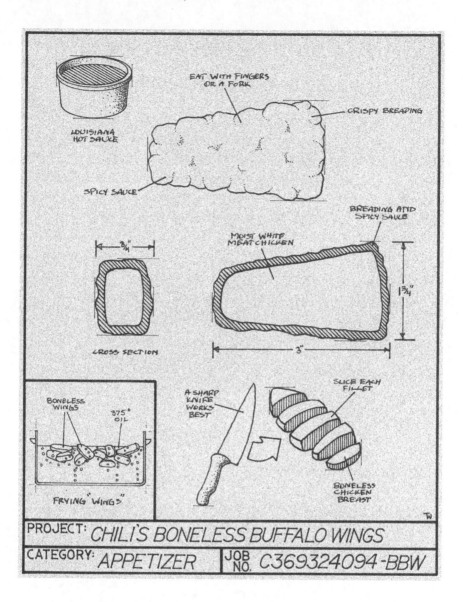

LOUISIANA HOT SAUCE

EAT WITH FINGERS OR A FORK

CRISPY BREADING

SPICY SAUCE

BREADING AND SPICY SAUCE

MOIST WHITE MEAT CHICKEN

$\frac{3}{4}$"

CROSS SECTION

$1\frac{3}{4}$"

3"

BONELESS WINGS

375° OIL

FRYING "WINGS"

A SHARP KNIFE WORKS BEST

SLICE EACH FILLET

BONELESS CHICKEN BREAST

TW

PROJECT: *CHILI'S BONELESS BUFFALO WINGS*

CATEGORY: *APPETIZER*   JOB NO. *C369324094-BBW*

1. Combine flour, salt, peppers and paprika in a medium bowl.
2. In another small bowl, whisk together egg and milk.
3. Slice each chicken breast into 6 pieces. Preheat 6 to 10 cups of vegetable oil in a deep fryer to 375 degrees.
4. One or two at a time, dip each piece of chicken into the egg mixture, then into the breading blend; then repeat the process so that each piece of chicken is double-coated.
5. When all chicken pieces have been breaded, arrange them on a plate and chill for 15 minutes.
6. When the chicken is done resting, drop each piece into the hot oil and fry for 5 to 6 minutes or until breading is golden brown.
7. As chicken fries, combine the hot sauce and margarine in a small bowl. Microwave sauce for 20 to 30 seconds or just until the margarine is melted, then stir to combine. You can also use a small saucepan for this step. Just combine the hot sauce and margarine in the saucepan over low heat and stir until margarine is melted and ingredients are blended.
8. When chicken pieces are done frying, remove them to a plate lined with a couple paper towels.
9. Place the chicken pieces into a covered container such as a Tupperware bowl or large jar with a lid. Pour the sauce over the chicken in the container, cover, and then shake gently until each piece of chicken is coated with sauce. Pour the chicken onto a plate and serve the dish with bleu cheese dressing and celery sticks on the side.

• SERVES 2 TO 4 AS AN APPETIZER.

• • • •

CHILI'S BONELESS SHANGHAI WINGS

MENU DESCRIPTION: *"Crispy breaded chicken breast topped with sweet and spicy ginger-citrus sauce. Served with spicy-cool wasabi-ranch dressing for dipping."*

So you're into boneless wings but you need a break from the traditional cayenne flavor of the Buffalo style. If fresh ginger-laced sweet-and-sour sauce sounds seducing, here is a variation worth snacking on. Along with the secret sauce recipe is an easy way to fabricate a carbon copy of Chili's great wasabi-ranch dressing simply by adding a few ingredients to Hidden Valley Ranch dressing. I've even suggested a drop of green food coloring to give the dressing the exact same green tint of the original. The wasabi powder won't really add much color, so this is the trick. By the way, you can find the dry, powdered form of wasabi horseradish in the supermarket aisle with the other Asian foods.

GINGER-CITRUS SAUCE

1¼ cups water
1 tablespoon cornstarch
¾ cup dark brown sugar
¼ cup soy sauce
2 tablespoons minced fresh ginger

1 teaspoon minced garlic
2 tablespoons lime juice
1 tablespoon lemon juice
¼ teaspoon crushed red pepper
   flakes

WASABI-RANCH DRESSING

½ cup Hidden Valley Ranch
   bottled salad dressing
2 tablespoons buttermilk (or
   whole milk)
1 teaspoon prepared horseradish
½ teaspoon powdered wasabi
1 drop green food coloring

1 cup all-purpose flour
2 teaspoons salt
½ teaspoon ground black pepper
¼ teaspoon cayenne pepper
¼ teaspoon paprika
1 egg
1 cup milk
2 skinless chicken breast fillets
6 to 10 cups vegetable or canola
   oil (amount required by your
   fryer)

1. Combine flour, salt, peppers and paprika in a medium bowl.
2. In another small bowl, whisk together egg and milk.
3. Slice each chicken breast into 6 pieces. Preheat 6 to 10 cups of canola oil in a deep fryer to 375 degrees.
4. One or two at a time, dip each piece of chicken into the egg mixture, then into the breading blend; then repeat the process so that each piece of chicken is double-coated.
5. When all chicken pieces have been breaded, arrange them on a plate and chill for 15 minutes.
6. As the chicken is resting, make the ginger-citrus sauce by dissolving the cornstarch in the water. Pour the mixture into a medium saucepan along with the rest of the sauce ingredients and bring the mixture to a boil over medium heat. When the sauce begins to bubble, reduce heat and simmer for 10 to 15 minutes or until thick. Remove the sauce from the heat and let it cool a bit.
7. Make the wasabi-ranch dressing while your ginger-citrus sauce is simmering. Simply whisk together the ranch dressing, buttermilk, prepared horseradish, powdered wasabi, and green food coloring in a small bowl. Cover and chill this until the wings are done.
8. When the chicken has rested and you're ready to cook,

lower the boneless wings into the oil and fry for 5 to 6 minutes or until each piece is browned. Depending on the size of your fryer, you may want to fry the chicken in batches so that the chicken isn't too crowded in there.

9. When chicken pieces are done frying, remove them to a draining rack or a plate lined with a couple paper towels.

10. When all the chicken is fried, place the pieces into a covered container such as a large jar with a lid. Pour the ginger-citrus sauce over the chicken in the container, cover it up, and then gently shake everything around until each piece of chicken is coated with sauce. Pour the chicken onto a plate and serve the dish with wasabi-ranch dressing on the side.

• SERVES 2 TO 4 AS AN APPETIZER.

• • • •

CHILI'S
CHICKEN CRISPERS

MENU DESCRIPTION: *"Strips of hand-battered chicken fried to perfection. Served w/sweet corn on the cob, honey-mustard dressing and homestyle fries."*

When biting into Chili's delicious trademarked Chicken Crispers, I detect the distinct flavor of MSG, or monosodium glutamate. Although there is no English word for it, the Japanese call this flavor *umami,* and it delivers a taste sensation that is different from bitter, salty, sweet or sour flavors. This fifth flavor is created naturally by glutamic acid, an amino acid, and it can be found in mushrooms, ripe tomatoes, fish and dairy products. But rather than adding something like Accent Flavor Enhancer—which is pure MSG—to this recipe, I thought of another approach. To clone the flavorful batter for this Chili's entree, I decided to bring canned chicken broth into the mix. Most chicken broths, including Swanson brand, contain autolyzed yeast extract. These yeast enzymes release flavor-enhancing compounds that work just like MSG, amplifying flavors in much the same way. Plus, the chicken broth is made with other goodies such as carrot, onion and celery that will contribute to a tasty crunchy coating. As for the frying, Chili's has recently switched to a shortening that contains no trans fat. So, if you want the best clone, use shortening, but find the kind that has no trans fat. Crisco now makes a version, and so does Smart Balance. Shortening produces a superior clone, but you can also use vegetable or canola oil, if that's what you dig.

HONEY MUSTARD DRESSING

⅔ cup mayonnaise

¼ cup honey

2 tablespoons Dijon mustard

pinch paprika

pinch salt

BATTER

1 egg, beaten

¼ cup whole milk

¾ cup chicken broth (Swanson)

1 ½ teaspoons salt

½ teaspoon ground black pepper

1 cup self-rising flour

6 to 10 cups shortening or vegetable oil (amount required by fryer)

10 chicken tenderloins

½ cup flour

1. Make honey mustard sauce by combining ingredients in a small bowl. Cover and chill until needed.
2. Heat shortening or oil in fryer to 350 degrees.
3. Combine beaten egg, milk, chicken broth, salt and pepper in a medium bowl. Whisk for about 30 seconds to dissolve salt. Whisk in 1 cup self-rising flour. Let batter sit for 5 minutes.
4. When you are ready to fry the chicken, coat each piece with dry flour (½ cup in a medium bowl), then dunk the chicken into the batter. Let a little batter drip off the chicken and lower it into the hot oil and fry for 7 to 9 minutes or until it's golden brown. Depending on the size of your fryer, you should be able to fry 3 or 4 tenderloins at a time. Drain fried chicken strips on a rack or paper towels for a minute or so, and serve with the honey mustard dressing on the side for dipping.

• SERVES 4 AS AN APPETIZER OR 2 AS AN ENTREE.

•　•　•　•

CHILI'S
CHILI QUESO

MENU DESCRIPTION: *"Our appetizing cheese dip with seasoned beef. Served with warm tostada chips."*

Take your chips for a dip in this top secret take on Chili's Queso Dip that comes to your table in a small cast-iron skillet along with a big bowl of tortilla chips. A popular recipe that's been circulating calls for combining Velveeta with Hormel No-Beans chili. Sure, it's a good start, but there's more to Chili's spicy cheese dip than that. Toss a few other ingredients into the saucepan and after about 20 minutes you'll have a great dip for picnic, party, or game time.

1 16-ounce box Velveeta Cheese	2 teaspoons paprika
1 15-ounce can Hormel Chili	1 tablespoon lime juice
(No Beans)	½ teaspoon ground cayenne
1 cup milk	pepper
4 teaspoons chili powder	½ teaspoon ground cumin

1. Cut the Velveeta into cubes. Combine the cheese with the remaining ingredients in a medium saucepan over medium heat. Stir frequently until cheese melts, then reduce heat and simmer for 20 minutes. Serve hot with tortilla chips for dipping.

• • • •

CHILI'S LETTUCE WRAPS

MENU DESCRIPTION: *"Grilled Asian-spiced chicken w/carrots, water chestnuts, green onions & almonds. Served with crisp Bibb lettuce and sesame-ginger & peanut sauces for dipping."*

Chili's take on the appetizer made popular at P. F. Chang's Asian Bistro got diners across the country wrapping lettuce around chopped chicken. Now you can bring Chili's version of the Asian tacos home along with the mega-addictive sesame-ginger and peanut dipping sauces. After you make the sauces and prepare the chicken, assemble the wraps by arranging some sliced chicken into the center of a leaf of butter lettuce, sprinkle on some shredded carrot, perhaps a few crunchy bean threads, add a little dipping sauce and open wide.

STIR FRY SAUCE

¼ cup water

1 teaspoon arrowroot

⅓ cup soy sauce

¼ cup granulated sugar

¼ cup white vinegar

1 tablespoon dried chives

1 tablespoon vegetable oil

2 teaspoons sesame seeds

1 teaspoon red pepper flakes

1 teaspoon chili oil

1 teaspoon peanut butter

½ teaspoon finely minced ginger

SESAME-GINGER DIPPING SAUCE

¼ cup water
¾ teaspoon arrowroot
⅓ cup granulated sugar
⅓ cup white vinegar
¼ cup soy sauce
1 teaspoon finely minced ginger

1 teaspoon vegetable oil
½ teaspoon sesame seeds
¼ teaspoon garlic powder
dash red pepper flakes
dash parsley

PEANUT DIPPING SAUCE

½ cup peanut butter
⅓ cup water
2 tablespoons white vinegar
½ teaspoon finely minced ginger
⅛ teaspoon crushed red pepper

¼ cup granulated sugar
¼ teaspoon garlic powder
½ teaspoon chili oil
½ teaspoon vegetable oil
1 tablespoon brown sugar

1 tablespoon vegetable oil
4 skinless chicken breast fillets
4 green onions

¼ cup minced water chestnuts
¼ cup sliced almonds
1 head butter lettuce

GARNISH
fried bean threads (see Tidbits)
shredded carrots

1. To prepare the stir-fry sauce, combine the water and arrow-root in a small bowl and stir until arrowroot is dissolved. Add this solution to the other stir-fry sauce ingredients in a small saucepan over medium heat. Bring to a boil, and then reduce heat to low and simmer for 5 to 6 minutes, or until thick.
2. To make the sesame-ginger dipping sauce combine the water and arrowroot in a small bowl and mix until arrowroot is dissolved. Combine this solution with the other dipping sauce ingredients in small saucepan over medium heat. Bring to a boil, and then reduce heat to low and simmer for 2 minutes.

3. Combine all ingredients for the peanut dipping sauce in a small saucepan over medium/low heat. Heat while whisking until sauce becomes smooth. Remove from heat when done.
4. To prepare the chicken heat 1 tablespoon of vegetable oil in a large skillet over medium heat. Cook the chicken breasts until done—3 to 5 minutes per side—turning every couple of minutes. You can tell when the chicken is done by pressing down on the middle of each chicken breast. It should be firm.
5. Remove the cooked chicken breast to a cutting board and slice it into strips with a sharp knife. Keep the pan hot. Load the chicken back into the same pan over medium/high heat, and add the water chestnuts. Heat for 1 minute.
6. Add 5 tablespoons of the stir-fry sauce to the chicken and heat for 2 minutes, stirring often. The sauce should be bubbling.
7. Add the sliced green onions and stir. The chicken is done.
8. Prepare each serving plate with a bed of bean threads. Spoon one-fourth of the chicken onto the bean threads. Sprinkle the chicken with about a tablespoon of sliced almonds. Add three leaves of butter lettuce to the plate, along with a garnish of shredded carrots. Repeat for the remaining servings. Serve with the sesame-ginger dipping sauce and peanut dipping sauce on the side.

• MAKES 4 SERVINGS.

TIDBITS

Bean threads can be found in the Asian food section of your supermarket. Before using as a garnish the threads must be flash-fried in a skillet in 2 inches of hot vegetable oil. When the threads float to the top remove them to a towel to drain.

• • • •

CHILI'S SOUTHWESTERN EGGROLLS

MENU DESCRIPTION: *"Smoked chicken, black beans, corn, jalapeno Jack cheese, red peppers and spinach wrapped inside a crispy flour tortilla. We serve it with our avocado-ranch dipping sauce."*

Chili's was the first chain to popularize the Southwestern-style eggroll, but as with any successful menu item, clones have been popping up on other major chains' appetizer menus over the past several years. Even though it's more like a small chimichanga than an eggroll, this appetizer is a fabulous creation with monster flavor. A flour tortilla is stuffed with a spicy blend of corn, green onions, black beans, spinach, jalapeno peppers, Monterey Jack cheese and spices; then it's deep-fried. Slice the rolls diagonally, dunk the wedges into a creamy avocado ranch sauce, and you've done your taste buds a solid. Make these several hours before you plan to serve them so that they can freeze before frying (it's a great dish to make a day ahead of a party or event). This freezing step will help the outside fry to a golden brown, but the eggrolls will stay folded, and oil won't seep in. Assembling the eggrolls takes a little time, so if you like these, I suggest making a double batch. Since you'll be freezing them, you'll have extra on hand in the freezer ready to cook with just a little additional effort.

1 skinless chicken breast fillet
1 tablespoon vegetable oil
2 tablespoons minced red bell
   pepper
2 tablespoons minced green onion
1/3 cup frozen corn
1/4 cup canned black beans, rinsed
   and drained
2 tablespoons thawed and
   drained frozen spinach
2 tablespoons diced, canned
   jalapeno peppers

1/2 tablespoon minced fresh
   parsley
1/2 teaspoon ground cumin
1/2 teaspoon chili powder
1/4 teaspoon salt
dash cayenne pepper
3/4 cup shredded Monterey Jack
   cheese
five 7-inch flour tortillas
6 to 10 cups vegetable or
   canola oil

AVOCADO-RANCH DIPPING SAUCE

1/4 cup smashed, fresh avocado
   (about half of an avocado)
1/4 cup mayonnaise
1/4 cup sour cream
1 tablespoon buttermilk
1 1/2 teaspoons white vinegar

1/8 teaspoon salt
1/8 teaspoon dried parsley
1/8 teaspoon onion powder
dash dried dill weed
dash garlic powder
dash pepper

GARNISH

2 tablespoons chopped tomato
1 tablespoon chopped onion

1. Preheat barbecue grill to high heat.
2. Rub the chicken breast with some vegetable oil then grill it
   on the barbecue for 4 to 5 minutes per side or until done.
   Lightly salt and pepper each side of the chicken while it
   cooks. Set chicken aside until it cools down enough to handle.
3. Preheat 1 tablespoon of vegetable oil in a medium-size skillet
   over medium-high heat.
4. Add the red pepper and onion to the pan and sauté for a
   couple minutes until tender.

5. Dice the cooked chicken into small cubes and add it to the pan. Add the corn, black beans, spinach, jalapeno peppers, parsley, cumin, chili powder, salt, and cayenne pepper to the pan. Cook for another 4 minutes. Stir well so that the spinach separates and is incorporated into the mixture.
6. Remove the pan from the heat and add the cheese. Stir until the cheese is melted.
7. Wrap the tortillas in a moist cloth and microwave on high for 1½ minutes or until hot.
8. Spoon approximately one-fifth of the mixture into the center of a tortilla. Fold in the ends and then roll the tortilla over the mixture. Roll the tortilla very tight, then pierce it with a toothpick to hold it together. Repeat with the remaining ingredients until you have five eggrolls. Arrange the eggrolls on a plate, cover the plate with plastic wrap and freeze for at least 4 hours. Overnight is best.
9. While the eggrolls freeze prepare the avocado-ranch dipping sauce by combining all of the ingredients in a small bowl.
10. Preheat 6 to 10 cups oil (use the amount required by your fryer) to 375 degrees.
11. Deep fry the eggrolls in the hot oil for 12 to 15 minutes and remove to paper towels or a rack to drain for about 2 minutes.
12. Slice each eggroll diagonally lengthwise and arrange on a plate around a small bowl of the dipping sauce. Garnish the dipping sauce with the chopped tomato and onion.

• SERVES 3 TO 4 AS AN APPETIZER.

•   •   •   •

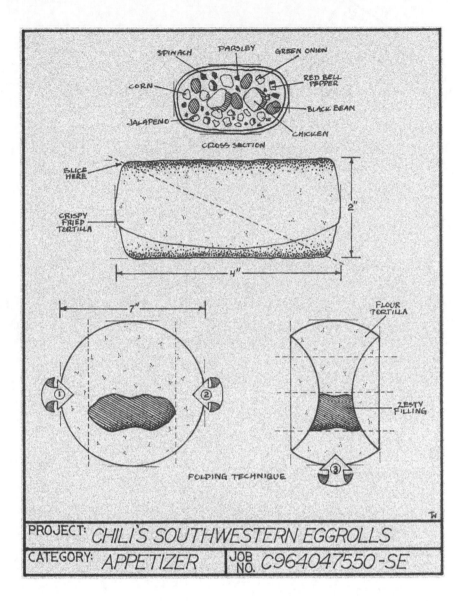

SPINACH
PARSLEY
GREEN ONION
CORN
RED BELL PEPPER
JALAPENO
BLACK BEAN
CHICKEN
CROSS SECTION

SLICE HERE
CRISPY FRIED TORTILLA
2"
4"

7"
①
②
FOLDING TECHNIQUE

FLOUR TORTILLA
ZESTY FILLING
③

PROJECT: *CHILI'S SOUTHWESTERN EGGROLLS*

CATEGORY: *APPETIZER*   JOB NO. *C964047550-SE*

CHILI'S CHICKEN ENCHILADA SOUP

It's an item that you won't find on the menu at this national restaurant chain, but ask your server about the soups du jour and you'll find this one is available every day of the week. This soup also happens to be one of Chili's most raved-about items, and the subject of many a recipe search on the *TSR* website (www.Top SecretRecipes.com). Part of the secret in crafting your clone is the addition of masa harina—a corn flour that you'll find in your supermarket near the other flours, or where all the Mexican foodstuffs are stashed.

1 tablespoon vegetable oil
1 lb. of skinless chicken breast
    fillets (approx. 3 fillets)
½ cup diced onion
1 clove garlic, pressed
4 cups chicken broth
1 cup masa harina

3 cups water
1 cup enchilada sauce
one 16-ounce box Velveeta, diced
1 teaspoon salt
1 teaspoon chili powder
½ teaspoon ground cumin

GARNISH
shredded Cheddar cheese
crumbled corn tortilla chips
salsa or pico de gallo

1. Add 1 tablespoon of oil to a large pot over medium heat. Add chicken breasts to pot and brown for 4 to 5 minutes per side. Set chicken aside.
2. Add onion and garlic to the pot and sauté over medium heat for about 2 minutes, or until onion begins to become translucent. Add chicken broth.
3. Combine masa harina with 2 cups of water in a medium bowl and whisk until blended. Add masa mixture to pot with onion, garlic and broth.
4. Add remaining water, enchilada sauce, cheese and spices to pot and bring mixture to a boil.
5. Shred the chicken into small, bite-size pieces and add it to the pot. Reduce heat and simmer soup for 30 to 40 minutes or until thick.
6. Serve soup in cups or bowls, and garnish with shredded Cheddar cheese, crumbled corn tortilla chips, and a spoonful of your favorite salsa or pico de gallo.

• MAKES APPROXIMATELY 12 SERVINGS.

•   •   •   •

CHILI'S SOUTHWESTERN VEGETABLE SOUP

If you like soup that's packed with veggies, that's low in fat, and has some of that Southwestern za-za-zing to it, this is the soup for you. Just toss all the ingredients in a pot and simmer. Garnish with some shredded cheese and crumbled tortillas, and prepare to take the chill off.

6 cups chicken broth (Swanson is best)

1 14.5-ounce can diced tomatoes, with juice

1 cup water

1 cup canned dark red kidney beans, with liquid

1 cup frozen yellow cut corn

1 cup frozen cut green beans

1 4-ounce can diced green chilies

½ cup diced Spanish onion

½ cup tomato sauce

6 corn tortillas, minced

1½ teaspoons chili powder

dash garlic powder

GARNISH

1 cup grated Cheddar/Jack cheese blend

1 cup crumbled corn tortilla chips

1. Combine all the soup ingredients in a large saucepan or soup pot over high heat. Be sure to mince the corn tortillas into

small pieces with a sharp knife before adding them to the soup.

2. Bring soup to a boil, then reduce the heat and simmer for 45 minutes to 1 hour, or until the soup has thickened and tortilla pieces have mostly dissolved.

3. To serve soup ladle 1 ½ cups into a bowl. Sprinkle a heaping tablespoon of the grated Cheddar/Jack cheese blend over the top of the soup, and then a heaping tablespoon of crumbled corn tortilla chips over the cheese.

• MAKES 6 SERVINGS.

• • • •

CHILI'S HONEY MUSTARD DRESSING

One of America's favorite casual chains brings us a popular salad dressing that you can't buy in stores. Instead, buy these six simple ingredients at a store and make your own version cheaply and quickly.

⅔ cup mayonnaise
¼ cup honey
2 tablespoons Grey Poupon Dijon
    mustard

1 teaspoon white vinegar
pinch paprika
pinch salt

Combine all ingredients in a medium bowl and whisk until combined.

- MAKES 1 CUP.

TIDBITS

Use low-fat mayo for a lighter version, but you already figured that out, huh?

• • • •

CHILI'S
GRILLED BABY BACK RIBS

MENU DESCRIPTION: *"Full rack of ribs 'double-basted' w/BBQ sauce. Served w/cinnamon apples & homestyle fries."*

One day the suits are sitting around a conference table taking in a pitch for TV ads filled with songs about baby back ribs and barbecue sauce. Soon after that Chili's launches its campaign featuring choreographed cooks in the back kitchen banging on pots and pans and belting out a jazzy ode to the meaty entrée. Silly as it may seem, the tune was catchy, and the baby back ribs racked up big sales. Now you can sing your own tune as you re-create the Chili's baby back experience without leaving the house. The flavor is found in the sauce, and the cooking secret is a slow-braising technique prior to grilling that will keep the meat juicy and tender like the original. And, hopefully, no one will see you dance.

SAUCE

1 ½ cups water
1 cup apple cider vinegar
½ cup tomato paste
1 tablespoon yellow mustard
⅔ cup dark brown sugar, packed
1 teaspoon liquid hickory smoke

1 ½ teaspoons salt
½ teaspoon onion powder
¼ teaspoon garlic powder
¼ teaspoon paprika

4 racks baby back ribs

1. Make the barbecue sauce by combining all of the ingredients for the sauce in a medium saucepan over medium heat. When it comes to a boil, reduce heat and simmer sauce, stirring often, for 45 to 60 minutes or until sauce is thick.
2. When you're ready to make the ribs, preheat the oven to 275 degrees.
3. Brush sauce over the entire surface of each rack of ribs. Wrap each rack tightly in aluminum foil and arrange the packets on a baking sheet with the seam of the foil facing up. Bake for 2 to 2½ hours or until the meat on the ribs has pulled back from the cut ends of the bones by about ½ inch. When the ribs are just about done, preheat your barbecue grill to medium heat.
4. Remove the ribs from the foil (careful not to burn yourself—the liquid inside will be hot!) and grill them on the barbecue for 4 to 8 minutes per side or until the surface of the ribs is beginning to char. Brush sauce on both sides of the ribs a few minutes before you remove them from the grill. Just be sure not to brush on the sauce too soon or it could burn.
5. Serve the ribs with extra sauce on the side and lots of napkins.

• MAKES 4 SERVINGS.

• • • •

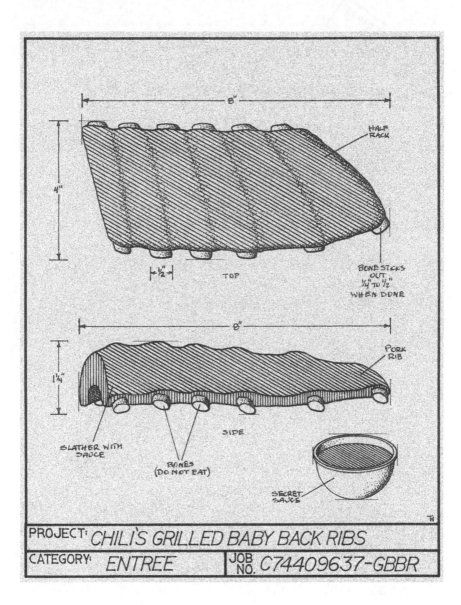

8"

4"

½"

TOP

HALF
RACK

BONE STICKS
OUT
¼" TO ½"
WHEN DONE

8"

1¼"

PORK
RIB

SLATHER WITH
SAUCE

BONES
(DO NOT EAT)

SIDE

SECRET
SAUCE

PROJECT: *CHILI'S GRILLED BABY BACK RIBS*

CATEGORY: *ENTREE*

JOB NO. *C74409637-GBBR*

CHILI'S
CHOCOLATE CHIP
PARADISE PIE

MENU DESCRIPTION: *"We start with a warm, chewy bar layered with chocolate chips, walnuts and coconut. Topped with vanilla ice cream and drizzled with hot fudge and caramel."*

One thing that makes this dessert special is the way it comes to your table sizzling in a cast-iron skillet—just like fajitas. The chocolate chip cookie and graham cracker crust "pie" sits in a hot skillet on top of bubbling cinnamon butter. It's topped with a scoop of vanilla ice cream, and then finished with walnuts, chocolate and caramel syrup. If you're a cloning perfectionist and want to present this dessert exactly like they do at the restaurant, you'll need a small skillet for each serving. Small cast-iron skillets are the best, but any 6 or 8-inch frying pan will do fine. You just have to be sure your pan is good and hot to get that authentic Chili's "sizzle" when you lay in the goodies. If you've got a big crew to feed and don't have enough skillets for each serving, you can add the cinnamon butter to individual serving plates, microwave the plates until the butter melts, then build each serving on the warm plates. It may not have the sizzle of the real thing, but it'll still taste like paradise.

COOKIE LAYER

1 cup all-purpose flour
½ teaspoon baking soda
¼ teaspoon baking powder
½ cup butter, softened (1 stick)
⅓ cup granulated sugar

1 egg
1 tablespoon milk
½ teaspoon vanilla extract
½ cup shredded coconut

CRUST LAYER

6 tablespoons butter (¾ stick)
¼ cup sugar
1½ cups graham cracker crumbs

1¼ cups semi-sweet chocolate
   chips
½ cup chopped walnuts

CINNAMON BUTTER

½ cup butter, softened (1 stick)
3 tablespoons granulated sugar
1½ teaspoons ground cinnamon

chocolate syrup
caramel syrup
6 tablespoons chopped walnuts

9 scoops vanilla ice cream

1. Preheat the oven to 325 degrees.
2. Combine the flour, baking soda and baking powder in a medium bowl.
3. In a separate large bowl, beat together the butter and sugar with an electric mixer. Continue beating for about 30 seconds or until mixture turns lighter in color. Add the egg, milk, and vanilla and beat until smooth.
4. Slowly mix the dry mixture into the wet mixture. Beat until combined and then mix in the coconut flakes. Set this cookie dough aside for now.
5. Melt 6 tablespoons of butter in a medium bowl in the microwave on high for about 30 seconds. Add the sugar and stir well for 30 seconds. Add the graham cracker crumbs and stir. Press this mixture into the bottom of a 9x9-inch baking dish or pan.

6. Sprinkle the cup of chocolate chips evenly over the graham cracker crust.
7. Press the cookie dough into the dish, covering the chocolate chips. Use flour on your fingers to keep the soft dough from sticking.
8. Sprinkle the chopped walnuts over the dough. Use your fingers to press the nuts into the dough.
9. Bake for 40 to 45 minutes or until the edges of the "pie" become light brown.
10. Prepare the cinnamon butter by creaming together the butter, sugar and cinnamon in a small bowl with an electric mixer on high speed.
11. When you are ready to make your dessert, heat up a small skillet over medium heat. When the skillet is hot, remove it from the heat then add about 1 tablespoon of the cinnamon butter to the pan. It should quickly melt and sizzle. Slice the "pie" into 9 pieces and place one into the hot skillet. If the "pie" has cooled, you can reheat each slice by zapping it in the microwave for 30 to 40 seconds.
12. Place a scoop of ice cream on top of the "pie." Drizzle chocolate and caramel syrup over the dessert and then sprinkle about 2 teaspoons of chopped walnuts over the top. Repeat for the remaining ingredients and serve sizzling in the skillet.

• MAKES 9 DESSERTS.

•   •   •   •

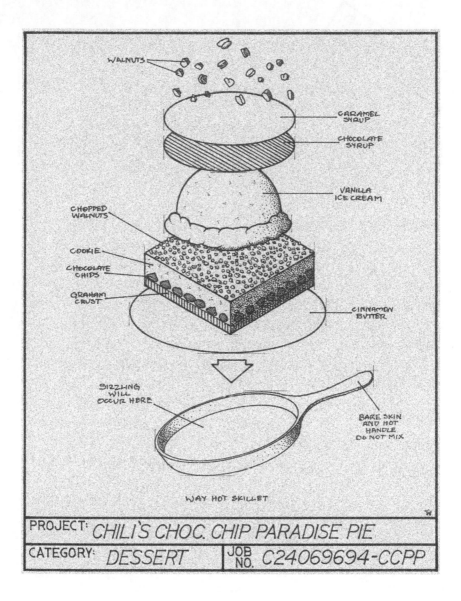

WALNUTS

CARAMEL SYRUP

CHOCOLATE SYRUP

VANILLA ICE CREAM

CHOPPED WALNUTS

COOKIE

CHOCOLATE CHIPS

GRAHAM CRUST

CINNAMON BUTTER

SIZZLING WILL OCCUR HERE

BARE SKIN AND HOT HANDLE DO NOT MIX

WAY HOT SKILLET

PROJECT:	CHILI'S CHOC. CHIP PARADISE PIE	
CATEGORY:	DESSERT	JOB NO. C24069694-CCPP

129

CHILI'S MOLTEN CHOCOLATE CAKE

MENU DESCRIPTION: *"Warm chocolate cake w/chocolate fudge filling. Topped w/vanilla ice cream under a crunchy chocolate shell."*

Get out your "easy" button for this one. While the clone recipe for this top-requested Chili's dessert is extremely simple to make—and can even be made days ahead of time—the resulting presentation is impressive. A chocolate fudge cake mix is all you need for the cake part of the recipe. The cake batter is poured into the large cups of a Texas-size muffin pan. When the cakes are done and cooled, invert them and cut a cylindrical chunk out of the bottom where the hot chocolate is loaded. Keep the cakes covered in the fridge until dessert time. To serve, nuke each cake for 45 seconds, plop a scoop of vanilla ice cream on top, thereby concealing the fudge compartment, and top it off with a little Smucker's Magic Shell (a chocolate topping that hardens on ice cream). When your diners dig into the cake, a delicious hot fudge center oozes out of the warm chocolate cake, and you're launched up to superhero status.

CAKE

1 18.25-ounce box chocolate fudge or dark chocolate cake mix
1 ⅓ cups water
½ cup vegetable oil
3 eggs

1 bottle Hershey hot fudge topping
8 scoops vanilla ice cream
Smucker's Magic Shell chocolate topping

GARNISH

whipped cream

1. Make cake batter following directions on the box and pour ½ cup of batter into the greased cups of a large (Texas-size) muffin pan. If your pan has six cups, bake the cakes in two batches of 4 cakes each. Bake for 30 to 40 minutes, or until a toothpick stuck into the center of one cake comes out clean. Turn all of the cakes out of the pan and let them cool.

2. The cakes will be served upside down, so you may have to slice a bit of the domed top off the cakes to help them lay flat when inverted. A serrated sandwich knife works best for this. After you've flipped over all of the cooled cakes, use a sharp paring knife to cut out a 1½-inch diameter cylindrical chunk in the center of the bottom (now the top) of each cake. The hole should be about 1½ inches deep. After slicing straight down into the cake in a circle, scoop out the chunk of cake with a teaspoon and discard the piece. Now you have a secret compartment to conceal the hot fudge pay-load.

3. Spoon about 2 tablespoons of fudge into each of the holes you've made in the cakes, then store the cakes in a sealed container in the refrigerator.

4. When you're ready to serve, heat one cake at a time in the microwave for 40 to 45 seconds on high, or until you see the fudge begin to bubble. Remove the cake from the microwave and let it rest for 30 seconds or so, then place a scoop of vanilla ice cream on top of the cake. Pour a coating of Magic Shell chocolate topping over the ice cream, add a little whipped cream, and serve.

• Makes 8 desserts.

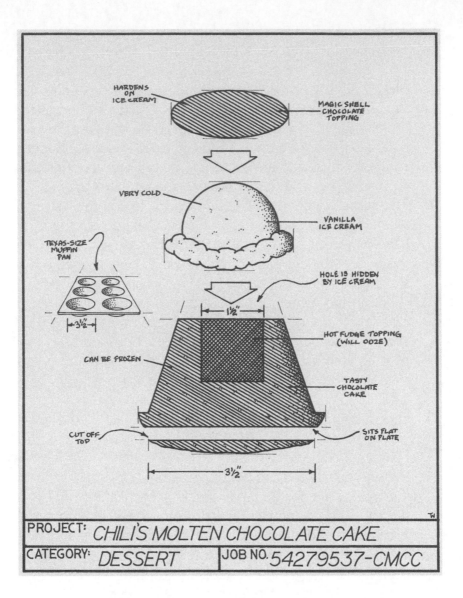

HARDENS ON ICE CREAM

MAGIC SHELL CHOCOLATE TOPPING

VERY COLD

VANILLA ICE CREAM

TEXAS-SIZE MUFFIN PAN

|← 3½" →|

HOLE IS HIDDEN BY ICE CREAM

1½"

HOT FUDGE TOPPING (WILL OOZE)

CAN BE FROZEN

TASTY CHOCOLATE CAKE

CUT OFF TOP

SITS FLAT ON PLATE

3½"

TW

PROJECT:	CHILI'S MOLTEN CHOCOLATE CAKE	
CATEGORY: DESSERT	JOB NO.	54279537-CMCC

CLAIM JUMPER
GARLIC CHEESE BREAD

Claim Jumper restaurants may only be found in the West, but the chain can claim national recognition for its delicious garlic cheese bread and toast. That's because you can find boxed loaves of the stuff ready for baking in the frozen food section of your well-stocked local supermarket. The recipe is such a simple one though, that it doesn't take much longer to make the cheesy goodness from scratch, and you save a few shekels to boot. Plus, it's nice to use fresh bread—your choice of either Texas toast or your favorite French loaf. (The restaurant serves the Texas toast version, and the supermarket version is a French loaf.) All you have to do for a clone is mix together a few basic ingredients, spread it generously on the bread of your choice, and pop it in the oven.

SPREAD

½ cup butter (1 stick)
¾ cup shredded Cheddar cheese
2 tablespoons grated Parmesan
    cheese
½ teaspoon garlic powder

¼ teaspoon Worcestershire sauce
¼ teaspoon salt
dash ground black pepper
dash paprika

BREAD

12 slices Texas toast (thick-sliced
  white bread) or 1 large
  French bread loaf, sliced
  through the middle

1. Preheat oven to 400 degrees.
2. Combine all ingredients for the spread in a small bowl.
3. Smear spread generously on one side of each slice of Texas toast or on the face of each half of French bread loaf.
4. Bake for 10 to 12 minutes or until cheese begins to brown and bubble. Cut each slice of Texas toast in half before serving, as they do in the restaurant. For the French bread, slice it as thick as you like.

• MAKES ABOUT 12 SLICES TOAST OR TWO LARGE HALVES OF FRENCH BREAD.

• • • •

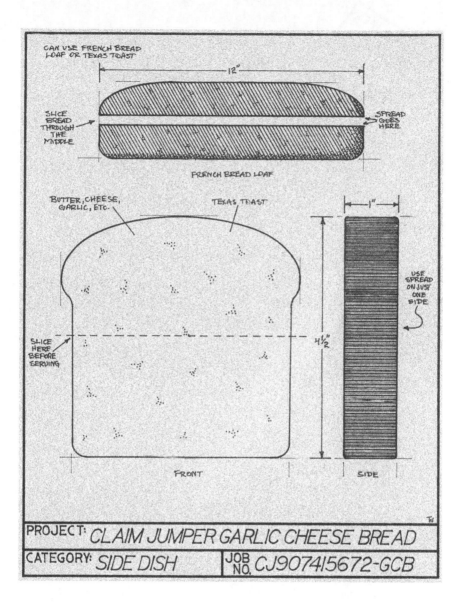

CAN USE FRENCH BREAD
LOAF OR TEXAS TOAST

12"

SLICE
BREAD
THROUGH
THE
MIDDLE

SPREAD
GOES
HERE

FRENCH BREAD LOAF

BUTTER, CHEESE,
GARLIC, ETC.

TEXAS TOAST

1"

USE
SPREAD
ON JUST
ONE
SIDE

SLICE
HERE
BEFORE
SERVING

4½"

FRONT

SIDE

PROJECT: *CLAIM JUMPER GARLIC CHEESE BREAD*

CATEGORY: *SIDE DISH*   **JOB NO.** *CJ907415672-GCB*

CLAIM JUMPER
FIRE-ROASTED ARTICHOKE

MENU DESCRIPTION: *"Marinated Fire-Roasted Split Artichokes Served with Tomato Relish and Garlic Mayo."*

I've been searching for the chain restaurant with the best recipe for roasted artichokes, and I think I've found it. With roasted garlic mayonnaise and a delicious tomato relish on the side, Claim Jumper takes the prize. This recipe is for just one artichoke, but feel free to add another if more than a couple hungry mouths are waiting. Just be sure to double up on the tomato relish.

1 large artichoke	juice of 2 lemons
8 cups water	4 cups ice
3 tablespoons salt	

ROASTED GARLIC MAYONNAISE

⅓ cup mayonnaise	¼ teaspoon lemon juice
1 head garlic	dash salt
1 tablespoon olive oil	

TOMATO RELISH

1 medium tomato, diced (about ½ cup)	1 clove garlic, minced (about 1 teaspoon)

1 teaspoon minced onion	¼ teaspoon salt
2 basil leaves, minced	dash ground black pepper
½ teaspoon olive oil	
½ teaspoon balsamic vinegar	1 tablespoon butter, melted

1. Prepare the artichoke by cutting about an inch off the top with a sharp knife. Use scissors to clip the thorny tips off of all the outer leaves so no one gets punctured. Cut the artichoke in half down through the middle. Dissolve 3 tablespoons salt in 8 cups of water in a large bowl. Add juice of 2 lemons and ice, then drop the artichoke halves in the cold brine to marinate for 2 to 3 hours.

2. While artichoke is marinating, roast the head of garlic by preheating your oven to 325 degrees. Cut the top off of a head of garlic and cut the bottom (the root end) so that the garlic will sit flat. Remove most of the papery skin from the garlic, but leave just enough to hold the garlic together. Drizzle 1 tablespoon of olive oil over the garlic, then place it in a small oven-safe casserole dish. Cover it with a lid or aluminum foil and bake for 1 hour or until the garlic begins to brown. When you can handle the garlic, squeeze about 1 tablespoon of roasted garlic from the head and combine it with the mayo, lemon juice and salt. Stir well.

3. While the garlic is roasting prepare the tomato relish by combining all of the ingredients in a small bowl. Stir well, then cover and refrigerate until needed.

4. When you are ready to cook the artichoke, bring some water to a boil in a large saucepan with a steamer basket. You don't want the water to touch the artichoke if you can help it. If you don't have a steamer basket, fill the pan with just an inch or so of water. When the water is simmering, add the artichoke halves, cover, and steam for 40 to 50 minutes or until the artichoke is tender. While artichoke halves are steaming, preheat your barbecue grill to high heat.

5. When the steamed artichokes are cool enough to handle,

use a spoon to scrape out the fuzzy choke inside each half. Brush melted butter over the entire surface of each steamed artichoke half and place each half, flat-side down on the pre-heated grill. Grill for 4 to 6 minutes or until dark charring marks appear on the face of each half. Serve grilled-side-up with tomato relish (strain the liquid from the relish before serving) and roasted garlic mayonnaise on the side.

- SERVES 2 AS AN APPETIZER.

• • • •

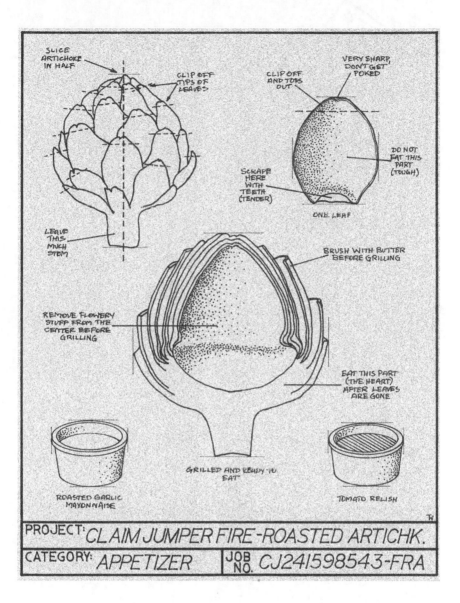

SLICE
ARTICHOKE
IN HALF

CLIP OFF
TIPS OF
LEAVES

VERY SHARP,
DON'T GET
POKED

CLIP OFF
AND TOSS
OUT

DO NOT
EAT THIS
PART
(TOUGH)

SCRAPE
HERE
WITH
TEETH
(TENDER)

ONE LEAF

LEAVE
THIS
MUCH
STEM

BRUSH WITH BUTTER
BEFORE GRILLING

REMOVE FLOWERY
STUFF FROM THE
CENTER BEFORE
GRILLING

EAT THIS PART
(THE HEART)
AFTER LEAVES
ARE GONE

ROASTED GARLIC
MAYONNAISE

GRILLED AND READY TO
EAT

TOMATO RELISH

PROJECT: *CLAIM JUMPER FIRE-ROASTED ARTICHK.*

CATEGORY: *APPETIZER*   **JOB NO.** *CJ241598543-FRA*

CLAIM JUMPER CHEESE POTATOCAKES

MENU DESCRIPTION: *"(Our most popular appetizer.) Parmesan, Cheddar & Monterey Jack cheeses, cilantro, onion, fresh dill & mashed potato lightly breaded and fried crispy topped with fresh cut chives. Served with herbed ranch salsa."*

This top-seller is a versatile side dish alternative to mashed potatoes, but also stands well on it's own as an appetizer. With cilantro, green onion, and three different cheeses in there, the flavor is the bomb. When you add a crispy breading and some herbed ranch salsa drizzled over the top, it's clear why this is the most popular appetizer on the huge Claim Jumper menu. Try dropping a pinch or two of cayenne pepper into the herbed ranch salsa for an extra spicy boost.

HERBED RANCH SALSA
½ cup sour cream
¼ cup seeded and diced tomato
   (about ½ tomato)
2 tablespoons minced onion
1 tablespoon white vinegar

1 teaspoon fresh minced cilantro
½ teaspoon salt
¼ teaspoon ground black pepper
pinch dried dill weed

POTATOCAKES

4 medium red potatoes, with skin
    (about 1 pound)
¼ cup shredded Cheddar cheese
¼ cup shredded Monterey Jack
    cheese
2 tablespoons shredded Parmesan
    cheese

1 green onion, chopped
½ teaspoon minced fresh cilantro
½ teaspoon salt
¼ teaspoon ground black pepper
¼ teaspoon garlic powder

BREADING

⅔ cup unseasoned breadcrumbs
    (Progresso is good)
⅓ cup all-purpose flour
½ teaspoon dried dill weed

1 egg, beaten
1 cup milk

2 to 3 cups vegetable shortening

GARNISH

fresh cut chives

1. Boil potatoes for 25 to 30 minutes or until mostly soft, but still slightly firm. Be careful not to overcook those boys. Your potatocakes will hold together best when the potatoes aren't too mushy.
2. As the potatoes boil make your herbed ranch salsa by combining all of the ingredients in a small bowl. Cover and chill this sauce until you need it.
3. Drain the potatoes and mash them with the skin on in a medium bowl. You don't need a completely smooth consistency for the potatoes. There should be some small chunks of potato in there. Add the remaining ingredients for the potatocakes and mix well.
4. Combine breadcrumbs with flour and ½ teaspoon dill in a large bowl. Combine beaten egg and milk in another large bowl. Measure about ⅓ cup of the potato mixture into your

hands and shape it into a patty about the size of a hamburger patty. Drop the potato mixture into the breading mixture, then into the egg and milk, then back into the breading, being sure to cover the entire surface of the potatocake with the breading. Arrange the potatocake on a plate and repeat the process with the remaining potato mixture. Cover and chill the potatocakes for about 1 hour, so that they'll be sure to stick together when fried.

5. Heat up the shortening in a skillet over medium/low heat. You should have about 1 inch of shortening in the pan. Fry the potatocakes for 2 to 4 minutes or until golden brown, then drain on a rack or paper towels.

6. Serve potatocakes with a bit of ranch salsa poured over the top and sprinkle with fresh cut chives.

• MAKES 6 POTATOCAKES.

•   •   •   •

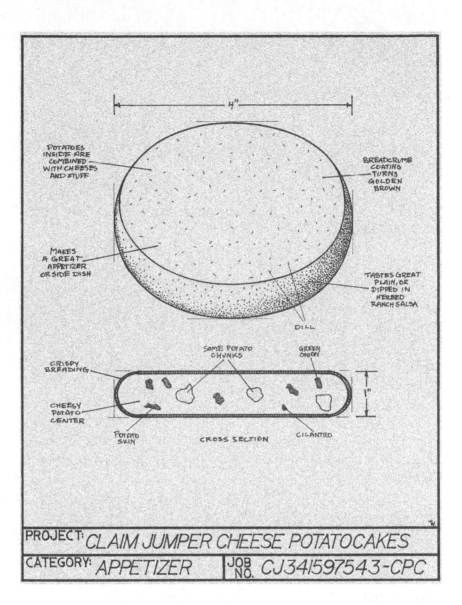

4"

POTATOES
INSIDE ARE
COMBINED
WITH CHEESES
AND STUFF

BREADCRUMB
COATING
TURNS
GOLDEN
BROWN

MAKES
A GREAT
APPETIZER
OR SIDE DISH

TASTES GREAT
PLAIN, OR
DIPPED IN
HERBED
RANCH SALSA

DILL

CRISPY
BREADING

SOME POTATO
CHUNKS

GREEN
ONION

1"

CHEESY
POTATO
CENTER

POTATO
SKIN

CROSS SECTION

CILANTRO

PROJECT: CLAIM JUMPER CHEESE POTATOCAKES

CATEGORY: APPETIZER | **JOB NO.** CJ341597543-CPC

CLAIM JUMPER SPICY THAI SLAW

MENU DESCRIPTION: *"Mixed greens, carrots, zucchini, green onions, peanuts and crunchy cappellini. Tossed in a sweet and spicy dressing."*

If you dig the sweet, sour, and spicy flavor combinations of Thai food, you'll love this tasty twist on coleslaw. Just find yourself a medium-size head of napa cabbage and a few other special ingredients and you're on your way to a perfect side dish for grilled grub, sandwiches, or as a quick solo snack. The menu mentions cappellini but we'll substitute with soba noodles that can be found in the supermarket aisle with other Asian foods (the rice vinegar and chili paste will be over there too). If you can't find soba noodles, the thicker chow mein noodles will also work. The mixed baby greens can often be found in ready-to-serve-plastic bags in the produce section. But the real secret ingredient for great tasting slaw is patience. The flavors of coleslaw improve after several hours in the cool box, and letting it sit overnight is even better.

DRESSING

⅓ cup rice vinegar
½ cup granulated sugar
1 tablespoon chili paste
    (sambal)

4 teaspoons fresh lime juice
2 teaspoons canola oil
½ teaspoon salt

2 ounces soba noodles, cooked (1 ½ cups)
10 cups thinly sliced napa cabbage (approx. 1 head)
2 cups mixed baby greens
1 ½ cups julienned carrot (approx. 1 carrot)

1 cup julienned zucchini, (approx. ½ zucchini)
1 cup chopped fresh cilantro
1 cup dry roasted unsalted peanuts
½ cup sliced almonds

1. Prepare the dressing first by combining the ingredients in a small bowl or glass measuring cup. Heat up this mixture in the microwave on high for 30 to 60 seconds or until dressing is hot, but not boiling. This will help to dissolve the sugar and salt. Stir the dressing well and set it aside to cool.

2. Cook 2 ounces of soba noodles following the directions on the package (the directions will say something like: "Cook noodles for 5 minutes in rapidly boiling water"). Drain the soba noodles, run cold water over them and let them sit to cool while you prepare the other ingredients.

3. Use a large sharp knife to thinly slice a medium head of napa cabbage. You can also use a mandoline to slice the cabbage into thin, uniform strips so that you have 10 cups of sliced cabbage. You can use a mandoline with a julienne attachment for slicing the carrots and zucchini as well. Make sure to chop the julienne slices into bite-size strips.

4. Chop the soba noodles into bite-size pieces, then combine them with the cabbage, baby greens, carrot, zucchini, cilantro, and nuts in a large bowl. Toss everything around real well while adding the dressing, then cover and chill the bowl for at least 4 hours. If you have the patience, wait overnight for it, because the cole slaw will taste even better. Your slaw should last for up to a week covered in the fridge.

• MAKES APPROXIMATELY 10 CUPS.

• • • •

CLAIM JUMPER
MEATLOAF

MENU DESCRIPTION: *"Our own special recipe made with fresh ground chuck, pork, mild onions, green peppers and more. Served with mashed potatoes, brown gravy and garlic toast."*

Here's a great meatloaf recipe to add to your mealtime repertoire. This luscious loaf combines ground chuck with ground pork along with breadcrumbs, green onion, garlic, carrot and green pepper for one of the best flavor experiences you'll get from a good old-fashioned American loaf of meat. Use a perforated nesting meatloaf pan if you've got one so that the fat drains out into the pan below. If you don't have one of those a regular loaf pan will still work fine. But use a large one. This recipe makes a pretty big beefy slab of goodness.

2 teaspoons vegetable oil
1 green onion, minced
2 cloves garlic, minced
2 tablespoons minced green bell
    pepper
2 tablespoons grated carrot
2 eggs, beaten
1 cup milk
2 teaspoons salt
½ teaspoon ground black pepper

½ teaspoon garlic powder
½ teaspoon onion powder
1½ pounds ground chuck
¾ pound ground pork
1 cup breadcrumbs (such as
    Progresso)
½ cup all-purpose flour
¼ cup ketchup plus an additional
    ¼ cup ketchup (for top)

1. Preheat oven to 350 degrees.
2. Sauté green onion, garlic, green pepper, and carrot in vegetable oil over medium heat for a couple minutes.
3. Combine beaten eggs with milk, salt, black pepper, garlic powder, and onion powder in a medium bowl.
4. In a large bowl, mix breadcrumbs and flour into ground chuck and ground pork with your hands. Add egg and milk mixture, sautéed veggies, ¼ cup ketchup and mix it up using your hands. Get in there and squish it all around for a while. Enjoy yourself.
5. Press the mixture into a meatloaf pan (the kind of pan with drainage holes in the bottom) or a large loaf pan. Bake for 30 minutes, then spread ¼ cup of ketchup over the top of the meatloaf and bake it for another hour. Let it sit for a bit after you remove it from the oven before you slice it to serve.

- SERVES 8.

• • • •

DENNY'S
FABULOUS
FRENCH TOAST

MENU DESCRIPTION: *"Three thick slices grilled golden brown and sprinkled with powdered sugar."*

This popular breakfast choice at America's number one diner chain takes center stage on the cover of the menu. Three slices of thick bread are dipped in a slightly sweet egg batter, browned to perfection and served up with a dusting of powdered sugar, some soft butter and thick maple syrup on the side. Find the thick-sliced Texas toast bread in your bakery, or use any white bread that's sliced around ¾-inch thick. This recipe will make enough for two servings of three slices each, and it's the perfect recipe for waking up a special someone with breakfast in bed. (Many points will be earned.)

4 eggs
⅔ cup whole milk
⅓ cup all-purpose flour
⅓ cup granulated sugar
½ teaspoon vanilla extract

¼ teaspoon salt
⅛ teaspoon ground cinnamon
6 slices thick bread (such as Texas toast)
3 tablespoons butter

GARNISH
powdered sugar
butter

ON THE SIDE

maple syrup

1. Whisk together eggs, milk, flour, sugar, vanilla, salt, and cinnamon in a large bowl.
2. Heat a large cast-iron or nonstick skillet over medium/low heat. When the pan is hot, add 1 tablespoon of butter. If butter smokes, your pan is too hot, turn down the heat.
3. Drop each bread slice into the batter for about 30 seconds per side. Let some of the batter drip off then drop the bread into the buttered pan. Cook each battered bread slice for 1½ to 2 minutes per side or until golden brown. Add more butter to the pan as needed to cook all the French toast.
4. Serve three slices of French toast per plate. Dust each serving with a little powdered sugar (tap it through a strainer), and include some maple syrup on the side.

- MAKES 2 SERVINGS.

•   •   •   •

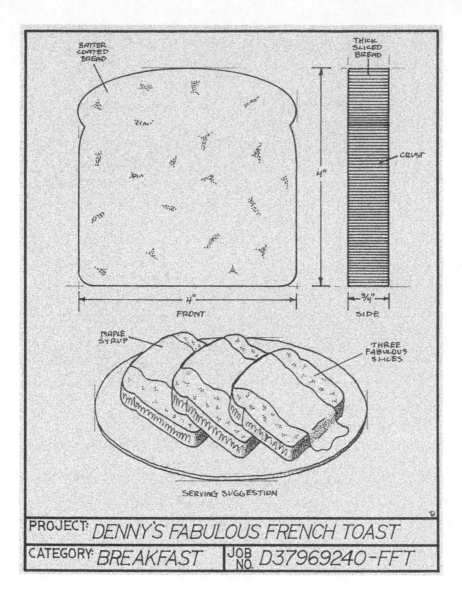

BATTER COATED BREAD

THICK SLICED BREAD

4"

CRUST

4"

FRONT

3/4"

SIDE

MAPLE SYRUP

THREE FABULOUS SLICES

SERVING SUGGESTION

PROJECT: *DENNY'S FABULOUS FRENCH TOAST*

CATEGORY: *BREAKFAST*

JOB NO. *D37969240-FFT*

DENNY'S
BBQ CHICKEN SANDWICH

MENU DESCRIPTION: *"A seasoned, grilled chicken breast topped with Cheddar cheese and a stack of thin crisp onion rings on a sesame seed bun with lettuce, tomato and a sweet hickory spread. Served with a side of BBQ sauce."*

With 1,527 restaurants across the country, Denny's is on top as America's largest full-service family restaurant chain. Sure, the chain's famous for its Grand Slam Breakfasts, but Denny's menu is filled with tasty choices for grub way past breakfast time. One such item is this chicken sandwich built with grilled chicken breast, lettuce, tomato, Cheddar cheese, crispy onion rings, and a secret sweet hickory spread. That hickory spread is one of the ingredients that makes this sandwich special. So the clone is here, and it requires an ingredient called hickory salt. You can find this blend of salt and hickory flavoring in the spice section from Spice Islands under the name "Old Hickory Smoked Salt." If you can't find that stuff, just substitute with ⅛ teaspoon salt and ⅛ teaspoon liquid hickory smoke. For even more flavor, Denny's serves the sandwich with a small dish of barbecue sauce that tastes remarkably similar to Bull's-Eye Original, so that's what we'll use. While homemade crunchy onion rings are the way to go for a true clone, you can certainly shortcut this step by using the canned French's French Fried Onions found in practically every supermarket.

SWEET HICKORY SPREAD

3 tablespoons butter
1 cup minced onion
2 teaspoons all-purpose flour
¼ cup molasses

¼ cup water
2 tablespoon white vinegar
⅛ teaspoon hickory salt

CRUNCHY ONION RINGS (SEE TIDBITS)

1 cup thinly sliced onion,
   separated into rings
1 cup milk
1 cup all-purpose flour

1 teaspoon salt
½ teaspoon ground black pepper
2 cups canola oil

2 skinless chicken breast fillets
vegetable oil
salt
ground black pepper
2 sesame seed hamburger buns

2 tablespoons melted butter
2 leaves green leaf lettuce
4 tomato slices
2 slices Cheddar cheese

ON THE SIDE
Bull's-Eye Original Barbecue Sauce

1. Prepare sweet hickory spread by melting 3 tablespoons butter over medium/low heat. Add 1 cup minced onion and sauté for 7 to 10 minutes or until the onions start to brown. Add 2 teaspoons flour and stir until the flour is mixed in. Let this cook for a minute or two, then add molasses, water, vinegar, and hickory salt. Simmer sauce for 3 to 4 minutes or until thick. Remove from heat and cover.

2. Make the crunchy onion rings by pouring milk into a large bowl. Combine flour, salt, and black pepper in another bowl. Dip onions in flour mixture first, then into milk and back into flour. Arrange all of the coated rings to a plate to rest while you heat up 2 cups canola oil in a large saucepan over

medium/low heat (you can also use a deep fryer for this step, just use the amount of oil required by the fryer manufacturer and set the temperature to 375 degrees). Test the oil by dropping in a pinch of flour. It should bubble. When the oil is hot, fry a handful of onion rings at a time in the oil until golden brown (3 to 5 minutes). Drain them on paper towels. (See Tidbits.)

3. To cook the chicken, preheat a skillet or griddle pan over medium heat. Pound your chicken with a kitchen mallet so that it has a uniform thickness of about ½ inch (it will plump a bit as you cook it), then trim any excess meat away that would hang off the sandwich. Rub each chicken breast with some canola oil, then sprinkle each breast with salt and a pinch of pepper. Grill chicken breast fillets for 4 to 6 minutes per side until done.

4. As your chicken cooks, spread a little melted butter on the faces of your two hamburger buns and toast the faces of the buns on another skillet or griddle set to medium heat until light brown.

5. Build each sandwich by first spreading some of the sweet hickory spread on the face of the bottom bun.

6. Tear a leaf of green leaf lettuce to fit on the bottom bun.

7. Arrange two tomato slices on the lettuce on each sandwich.

8. Stack the grilled chicken breast on the tomato slices.

9. Place a slice of Cheddar on the chicken breast on each sandwich.

10. Stack a handful of crunchy onion rings on the sandwich, then top the sandwich off with the crown bun. Serve with a small bowl of barbecue sauce on the side.

•   MAKES 2 SANDWICHES.

TIDBITS

You can skip step #2 by using the canned French's French Fried Onions. A small can will be plenty.

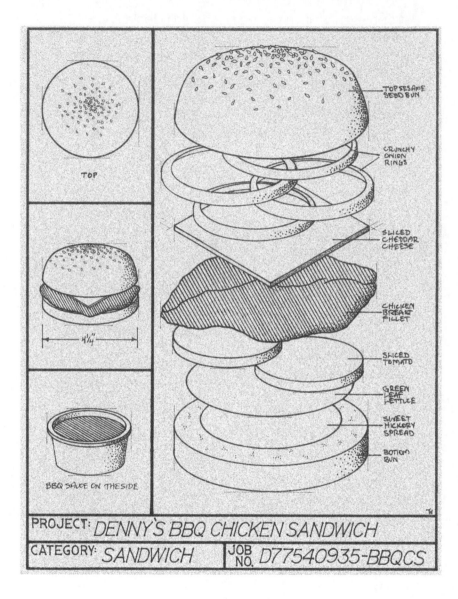

TOP

4¼"

BBQ SAUCE ON THE SIDE

TOP SESAME SEED BUN

CRUNCHY ONION RINGS

SLICED CHEDDAR CHEESE

CHICKEN BREAST FILLET

SLICED TOMATO

GREEN LEAF LETTUCE

SWEET HICKORY SPREAD

BOTTOM BUN

PROJECT: *DENNY'S BBQ CHICKEN SANDWICH*

CATEGORY: *SANDWICH* **JOB NO.** *D77540935-BBQCS*

DENNY'S
CLUB SANDWICH

MENU DESCRIPTION: *"Thinly sliced turkey, crisp bacon, lettuce and tomato on toasted white bread."*

Get out your toothpicks, because you'll have a hard time keeping the slices of this triple-decker sandwich from falling apart when slicing the only way you slice a true club sandwich: from corner to corner. This trusty, old-fashioned club sandwich recipe seems like it's been around forever, and yet this sandwich is still one of the top choices from Denny's for lunch. One day you'll find yourself with some white bread, sliced turkey, bacon, lettuce, tomato and mayo, and you'll realize you're just a *Top Secret Recipe* away from the secret stacking order to making the perfect club sandwich.

3 slices toasted white bread
4 ½ teaspoons mayonnaise
3 ounces sliced turkey breast
    (deli-sliced)

2 iceberg lettuce leaves
2 to 3 slices cooked bacon
2 tomato slices

1. Spread about 1 ½ teaspoons mayonnaise on one side of each toasted white bread slice.
2. Arrange the turkey breast on one slice of toast.
3. Tear or fold one iceberg lettuce leaf to fit on the sliced turkey.
4. Stack on another slice of toast with the mayo side facing up.

5. Break 2 or 3 slices of cooked bacon to fit on top of the second slice of toast.
6. Tear or fold the second lettuce leaf to fit on top of bacon.
7. Arrange the two tomato slices to fit on the lettuce.
8. Top off the sandwich with the last piece of toast turned with the mayo-coated side facing down.
9. Pierce the sandwich with four toothpicks between the corners, so that when the sandwich is sliced twice from corner to corner with a serrated knife, the toothpicks wind up in the center of each of the four slices.

• Makes 1 sandwich.

•   •   •   •

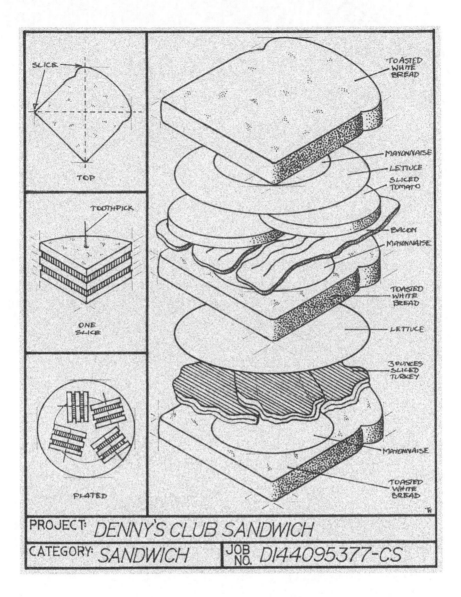

SLICE

TOP

TOOTHPICK

ONE
SLICE

PLATED

TOASTED
WHITE
BREAD

MAYONNAISE

LETTUCE

SLICED
TOMATO

BACON

MAYONNAISE

TOASTED
WHITE
BREAD

LETTUCE

3 OUNCES
SLICED
TURKEY

MAYONNAISE

TOASTED
WHITE
BREAD

PROJECT: *DENNY'S CLUB SANDWICH*

CATEGORY: *SANDWICH* **JOB NO.** *DI44095377-CS*

HARD ROCK CAFE HOMEMADE CHICKEN NOODLE SOUP

Give this simple soup clone a shot and I guarantee you'll never again want to eat chicken soup from a can. The recipe is a breeze since you use pre-cut chicken fillets—rather than cutting up a whole chicken—and you don't have to create a stock from scratch. Swanson sells a 32-ounce carton of chicken broth that's the perfect amount (4 cups) for this recipe.

1 pound skinless chicken breast fillets	½ cup diced celery (about 1 stalk)
1 pound skinless chicken thigh fillets	4 cups chicken broth
2 tablespoons vegetable oil	4 cups water
1 tablespoon butter	1 teaspoon salt
1 cup diced onion (about ½ of a medium onion)	1 teaspoon freshly ground black pepper
1 cup diced carrot (about 2 medium carrots, peeled)	1 teaspoon minced fresh parsley
	3 cups wide egg noodles (dry)

GARNISH
minced fresh parsley

1. Heat 2 tablespoons vegetable oil in a large skillet over medium heat. Sauté chicken breasts and thighs for 10 to 15 minutes or until lightly browned on both sides and cooked through. Remove chicken from the skillet to a cutting board to cool a bit.
2. Reduce heat to medium/low, add butter to skillet then toss in onion, carrot and celery. Slowly cook the veggies (sweat them) for 10 minutes, stirring often, or until carrots are beginning to soften.
3. Chop the chicken, then dump all of it, plus the veggies, chicken broth, water, salt, pepper and 1 teaspoon parsley into a large soup pot. Bring soup to a boil then reduce heat and simmer for 10 minutes. Add noodles and simmer for an additional 15 minutes or until noodles are soft. Serve with a pinch of minced fresh parsley sprinkled on top.

- MAKES 8 SERVINGS.

• • • •

HARD ROCK CAFE
BAR-B-QUE BEANS

If you like baked beans you'll go nuts over this clone recipe from the world's first theme restaurant chain. It's really easy to make too, since you just stir the ingredients into a covered casserole dish, and bake for an hour and a half. This makes the dish handy if transporting to another location for a party or potluck, since you can fill the dish, cover it, then pop it into the oven once you arrive. The only element that may give you pause is the pulled pork from the recipe that follows (on page 164) for Hard Rock Cafe Pig Sandwich. It's an effortless addition if you've got some of that pork on hand. If not, just leave that ingredient out. Or you could add a couple tablespoons crumbled cooked bacon. Either way the beans will still come out great as a nosh-worthy side dish or solo snack.

2 15-ounce cans pinto beans
   (with liquid)
2 tablespoons water
2 teaspoons cornstarch
½ cup ketchup
⅓ cup white vinegar
¼ cup brown sugar
2 tablespoons diced onion

1 teaspoon prepared mustard
½ teaspoon chili powder
¼ teaspoon salt
¼ teaspoon coarse ground black
   pepper
½ cup shredded pork (from recipe
   on page 164)

1. Preheat oven to 350 degrees.
2. Pour entire contents of the can of pinto beans into a casserole dish (with a lid).
3. Dissolve the cornstarch in a small bowl with the 2 tablespoons of water. Add this solution to the beans and stir.
4. Add the remaining ingredients to the dish, stir well and cover.
5. Bake for 90 minutes or until the sauce thickens. Stir every 30 minutes. After removing the beans from the oven, let the beans cool for 5 to 10 minutes before serving.

• SERVES 6 TO 8 AS A SIDE DISH.

•   •   •   •

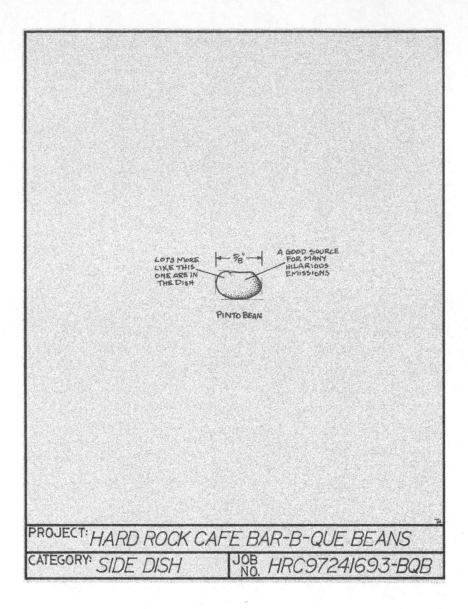

LOTS MORE
LIKE THIS
ONE ARE IN
THE DISH

5/8"

A GOOD SOURCE
FOR MANY
HILARIOUS
EMISSIONS

PINTO BEAN

PROJECT: *HARD ROCK CAFE BAR-B-QUE BEANS*

CATEGORY: *SIDE DISH*

JOB NO. *HRC97241693-BQB*

HARD ROCK CAFE COLESLAW

Smashing a guitar and hanging it on the wall will not give you the true Hard Rock Cafe experience unless you then eat a sandwich with this coleslaw served on the side. You have to be patient, though, since it's not something you can enjoy right away. Good coleslaw needs a little time to chill in the cool box—24 hours at least. The cabbage needs a chance to get it together with the other ingredients before rocking out at the gig inside your mouth.

1 ⅓ cups mayonnaise
3 tablespoons white vinegar
2 tablespoons plus 2 teaspoons
    granulated sugar
2 tablespoons milk

dash salt
8 cups chopped cabbage
    (1 head)
½ cup shredded carrot

1. Combine all ingredients except the cabbage and carrots in a large bowl and blend until smooth with an electric mixer.
2. Add cabbage and carrots and toss well.
3. Cover and chill overnight in the refrigerator. The flavors fully develop after 24 to 48 hours.

• SERVES 6 TO 8 AS A SIDE DISH.

• • • •

HARD ROCK CAFE
PIG SANDWICH

MENU DESCRIPTION: *"Select pork, hickory-smoked then hand-pulled, so it's tender and juicy. 'An old Southern delicacy' with our famous vinegar-based bar-b-que sauce. Served with fries, ranch beans and homemade coleslaw."*

Take a big honkin' bite out of one of these and you'll soon know why it's the Hard Rock Cafe's most popular sandwich. The pork is hickory smoked for 10 hours, but since we're impatient hungry people here, we'll cut that cooking time down to under 4 hours using a covered grill and carefully arranged charcoal. Just sprinkle wet hickory chips over the hot charcoal arranged around the inside edge of a grill (such as a round Weber), and let the smoking begin. You can certainly use an actual smoker if you've got one, and go the full 10 hours with this puppy. But while you're still waiting for your sandwiches, the rest of us will have already dragged our full, round bellies over to the couch for a nap. By the way, you should try to make your marinated cabbage a day ahead of time so it has time to soak up the flavors.

MARINATED CABBAGE

2 tablespoons white vinegar

1 tablespoon granulated sugar

4 cups thinly sliced cabbage

4 cups hickory smoking chips

RUB

2 tablespoons kosher salt

2 teaspoons cracked black pepper

1 teaspoon paprika

½ teaspoon onion powder

½ teaspoon ground sage

½ teaspoon dried thyme

¼ teaspoon ground cayenne
   pepper

1 boneless pork loin roast (3 to 4
   pounds)

vegetable oil

SAUCE

2 15-ounce cans tomato puree

1 cup apple cider vinegar

¾ cup brown sugar

2 tablespoons vegetable oil

½ teaspoon onion powder

½ teaspoon liquid hickory smoke

1 clove garlic, minced

¼ teaspoon salt

¼ teaspoon coarse ground black
   pepper

8 kaiser rolls

1. Make the marinated cabbage at least one day prior to building your sandwiches. Like coleslaw, this garnish needs some time to develop in the fridge. Combine the vinegar and sugar in a medium bowl. Add the cabbage, stir, cover the bowl and store it in the refrigerator until you are ready to make the sandwiches.

2. Put the wood chips in a bowl and cover with water. Let the wood soak for at least 1 hour. Light the charcoal after it has been arranged around the inside edge of your grill. You don't want coals directly under your pork. When the coals are hot, drain the water from the wood chips and sprinkle the chips over the top of the coals. You should now have smoke.

3. Combine the ingredients for the rub in a small bowl and mix well.

4. Rub some vegetable oil over the surface of the pork roast. Sprinkle the rub over the entire surface of the roast.

5. Place the roast in the center of your grill and put the lid on. Let the pork cook for 3 to 4 hours or until the internal temperature of the roast reaches 170 degrees.

6. As the pork cooks, make the sauce by combining the ingredi-

ents in a medium saucepan over medium/low heat. Let the sauce simmer for 15 to 20 minutes, then cover and remove from heat. Set this aside until your pork is ready.

7. When the pork is done, remove it from the grill and let it sit to cool for 15 to 20 minutes or until you can handle it. Now you want to tear the meat along the grain, making bite-size strips of shredded pork.

8. Put the shredded pork into a large saucepan over medium heat. Add 2 cups of the sauce to the pan and stir. Keep the rest of the sauce for later to serve on the side. Cook the pork for 15 minutes or until it is heated through.

9. Grill the faces of the rolls and stack about 1 cup of pork onto the bottom half of each roll. Add a rounded tablespoon of marinated cabbage on top of the pork, add a tablespoon or so of extra sauce on top of that, then cap off each sandwich with the top half of the roll. Serve with clones for the Hard Rock's coleslaw (page 163) and baked beans (page 160) on the side, if desired.

• MAKES 8 SANDWICHES.

• • • •

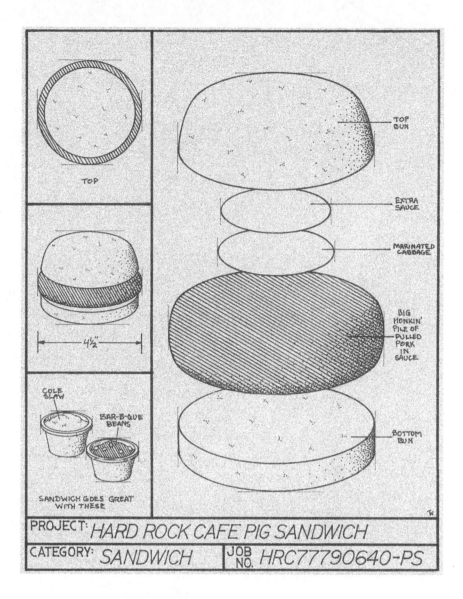

TOP

4½"

COLE SLAW

BAR-B-QUE BEANS

SANDWICH GOES GREAT WITH THESE

TOP BUN

EXTRA SAUCE

MARINATED CABBAGE

BIG HONKIN' PILE OF PULLED PORK IN SAUCE

BOTTOM BUN

PROJECT: *HARD ROCK CAFE PIG SANDWICH*

CATEGORY: *SANDWICH*   JOB NO. *HRC77790640-PS*

HOUSTON'S CHICAGO-STYLE SPINACH DIP

These days just about every casual dining chain has its version of this appetizer: spinach and artichoke hearts mixed with cheese and spices, served up hot with chips or crackers for dipping. Making the rounds over the years, I've tried many of them, and most formulas are nearly identical. That is, except for this one. Houston's makes their spinach dip special by using a blend of sour cream, Monterey Jack cheese and Parmigiano-Reggiano—the ultimate Parmesan cheese. Parmigiano-Reggiano is born in Italy and is usually aged nearly twice as long as other, more common Parmesan cheeses. That ingredient makes the big difference in this dip. So hunt down some of this special Parm at your well-stocked market or gourmet store, and you'll find out why Houston's spinach dip has been one of the most requested recipe clones at *TSR* Central.

One 12-ounce box frozen
    chopped spinach, thawed
½ cup chopped canned artichoke
    hearts (not marinated)
1 tablespoon chopped white onion
¼ cup heavy cream

¼ cup sour cream
1 ¼ cups shredded Monterey Jack
    cheese
⅓ cup grated Parmigiano-
    Reggiano cheese
¼ teaspoon garlic salt

ON THE SIDE
Corn tortilla chips

1. Mix together the spinach, chopped artichoke hearts, and onion in a microwave-safe glass or ceramic bowl. Cover bowl with plastic wrap, then cut a small slit in the center of the wrap so that the steam can sneak out. Microwave on high for 4 minutes. Keep spinach covered while you prepare the cream sauce.
2. Combine cream, sour cream, Jack cheese, grated Parmigiano-Reggiano cheese, and garlic salt in a medium saucepan over medium/low heat. Heat this up slowly for about 10 minutes or until the sauce reaches a simmer and thickens. Just don't let the mixture boil.
3. Add the spinach mixture to the sauce and continue to heat over medium/low. Cook for about 10 more minutes or until mixture reaches a thick dip-like consistency. Pour into a bowl and serve with tortilla chips for dipping (or crackers, bread, whatever you want).

• MAKES 2 CUPS.

• • • •

HOUSTON'S
HONEY-LIME VINAIGRETTE

This 38-unit casual dining chain may be small compared to many of the other chains whose food I've cloned, but Houston's has a huge following of loyal customers throughout the country. I know this because for many years the restaurant sat at the top of my "most requested clones" list. I was finally ready to take on the challenge, but since there are no Houston's where I live in Las Vegas, it required a road trip—this time to Orange County, California. A couple plane rides, a bit of driving, some walking and a stumble or two later, I had a cooler full of Houston's goodies secured safely back at the underground lab. After a few hours of chopping and mixing this simple sweet-and-sour salad slather from Houston's was cracked.

⅓ cup vegetable oil
¼ cup rice vinegar
¼ cup honey
2 tablespoons Grey Poupon Dijon
    mustard
1 tablespoon chopped fresh
    cilantro
2½ teaspoons fresh lime juice

1 teaspoon sesame oil
1½ teaspoons minced red bell
    pepper
1 teaspoon minced onion
¼ teaspoon freshly ground black
    pepper
pinch salt

1. Combine all ingredients in a small glass or ceramic bowl. Stir well.
2. Heat dressing in the microwave on high for 1 to 1½ minutes or until mixture begins to bubble. Remove dressing from microwave and whisk for 1 minute. This will emulsify the dressing and it should begin to thicken as it cools.
3. Cover and chill for 2 hours before serving.

- MAKES 1 CUP.

•   •   •   •

HOUSTON'S COLESLAW

It's not your typical coleslaw. The sweet pickle relish and green onion is a nice touch, and all that parsley really sets this dish apart from any other coleslaw I've tried. If you like coleslaw and you've never had this version at the restaurant, I encourage you to give this one a go.

¾ cup mayonnaise
3 tablespoons white vinegar
2 tablespoons granulated sugar
⅛ teaspoon salt
8 cups chopped green cabbage
   (1 head)

½ cup chopped fresh parsley
½ cup chopped green onion
   (green part only)
2 tablespoons sweet pickle relish
½ teaspoon celery seed

1. Whisk together mayonnaise, vinegar, sugar, and salt in a medium bowl.
2. Combine cabbage, parsley, green onion, and relish in a large bowl.
3. Pour the dressing over the cabbage and mix well. Add celery seed and mix, then cover the bowl and chill for at least 4 hours before munching out. Chilling the slaw overnight is even better.

• MAKES 8 SERVINGS.

• • • •

IHOP CINN-A-STACKS

Put away the maple syrup. Next time you whip up pancakes or French toast, try something new with this clone that makes your stacks taste like freshly baked cinnamon rolls. Spread the cinnamon sauce on each pancake or on each slice of cinnamon toast as you stack 'em up. Then drizzle the delicious cream cheese icing over the top. As for the pancakes, we've got some great clone recipes on pages 175 (IHOP Country Griddle Cakes) and 180 (IHOP Harvest Grain 'N Nut Pancakes). And there's a simple clone for Denny's Fabulous French Toast on page 148. This mouthwatering new product from America's favorite pancake chain is a "limited time only" offering, but a fabulous home clone is yours whenever you crave it.

CINNAMON SAUCE

¼ cup butter (salted)
¾ cup dark brown sugar
3 tablespoons half-and-half
1 tablespoon ground cinnamon

⅛ teaspoon salt
⅛ teaspoon ground cloves
1 tablespoon all-purpose flour

CREAM CHEESE ICING

4 ounces cream cheese, softened
1¼ cups powdered sugar

1 teaspoon lemon juice
¼ teaspoon vanilla extract

GARNISH
whipped cream

1. Melt butter in a small saucepan over medium heat. Add brown sugar, 2 tablespoons half-and-half, cinnamon, salt and cloves and cook while stirring constantly until mixture comes to a simmer. Immediately remove sauce from the heat, add remaining tablespoon of half-and-half and stir in the flour.
2. Combine ingredients for cream cheese icing in a medium bowl. Beat on low speed with an electric mixer until smooth. Spoon icing into a squirt bottle.
3. To assemble your dish, spread about a tablespoon of cinnamon sauce on top of each pancake, or on each slice of French toast as you stack them. A typical serving at the restaurant is two pancakes or two slices of French toast. Drizzle cream cheese icing over the top, and finish off your stack with a dollop of whipped cream.

- MAKES ENOUGH FOR AT LEAST 4 SERVINGS.

• • • •

IHOP
COUNTRY
GRIDDLE CAKES

MENU DESCRIPTION: *"Delicious blend of buttermilk and real Cream of Wheat."*

This nationwide chain, which is known for its big bargain breakfasts, serves an impressive number of non-breakfast items as well. In 1997, IHOP dished out over 6 million pounds of french fries and over half a million gallons of soft drinks. But it's the Country Griddle Cakes on the breakfast menu that inspired this *Top Secret Recipe*. The unique flavor and texture of this clone comes from the Cream of Wheat in the batter. Now you can have your pancakes, and eat your cereal too.

nonstick spray
1 ¼ cups all-purpose flour
1 ½ cups buttermilk
⅓ cup instant
    Cream of Wheat (dry)
1 egg

⅓ cup granulated sugar
1 teaspoon baking powder
1 teaspoon baking soda
¼ cup vegetable oil
½ teaspoon salt

1. Preheat a skillet over medium heat. Apply nonstick spray.
2. Combine all ingredients in a large bowl with a mixer set on medium speed. Mix until smooth, but don't over mix.
3. Pour the batter by ⅓-cup portions into the hot pan and

cook pancakes for 1 to 3 minutes per side or until brown. Repeat with remaining batter.

- MAKES 8 TO 10 PANCAKES.

• • • •

IHOP
COUNTRY OMELETTE

Sure, IHOP is famous for pancakes, but the joint makes a pretty killer omelette when put to the task. What makes this three-egg creation so cool is the top secret folding method. For all of IHOP's omelettes, the beaten eggs are mixed with the appropriate chunky ingredients, and the whole thing is poured out thin on a giant griddle. When the eggs have firmed up, two sides are folded over, the filling is positioned, and the omelette is rolled over once, twice, three times so it ends up looking like a burrito, sort of. Now we can execute the same egg origami at home with a 12-inch electric skillet, or a 12-inch stovetop griddle pan. You can find easy-to-cook hash brown potatoes in bags in the freezer section.

3 eggs
1/8 teaspoon salt
2 tablespoons diced cooked ham
2 tablespoons diced white onion

1/2 tablespoon butter
3 tablespoons cooked shredded
   hash brown potatoes
1/4 cup shredded Cheddar cheese

GARNISH
2 tablespoons sour cream

1. Heat a 12-inch electric skillet to 275 degrees (or heat a 12-inch griddle pan over medium low heat). Preheat oven to 300 degrees.

2. Add salt to eggs and beat for about 30 seconds. Stir in diced cooked ham and white onion.
3. Melt ½ tablespoon of butter in hot griddle or pan. When butter melts pour eggs into the pan and swirl the pan around to coat the bottom evenly. Use a spatula to evenly distribute ham and onion.
4. Cook eggs for 4 to 6 minutes or until top of omelette is mostly firm. Fold over 1-inch of top and bottom of the omelette. Sprinkle 2 tablespoons shredded cheddar cheese down omelette at about one-third of the way from the left side of the omelette. Arrange about 3 tablespoons of cooked hash brown potatoes on top of the cheese. Starting at the left end, use a spatula to roll the eggs over the filling ingredients. Continue rolling the omelette two more times. Use a spatula to lift the omelette onto an oven safe plate. Sprinkle 2 tablespoons of shredded Cheddar over the top of the omelette and place the plate in the 300 degree oven for 1 to 2 minutes or until the cheese has melted. If you're making more than one omelette, set your oven to 200 degrees to keep ready-to-eat omelettes on hold.
5. Just before serving, spoon 2 tablespoons of sour cream onto the middle of the omelette.

• MAKES 1 SERVING.

•   •   •   •

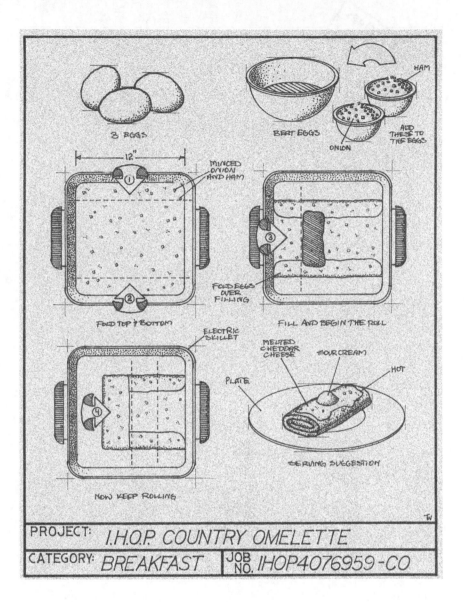

3 EGGS

BEAT EGGS

HAM

ONION

ADD THESE TO THE EGGS

12"

MINCED ONION AND HAM

①

②

FOLD TOP & BOTTOM

③

FOLD EGGS OVER FILLING

FILL AND BEGIN THE ROLL

ELECTRIC SKILLET

④

NOW KEEP ROLLING

MELTED CHEDDAR CHEESE

SOUR CREAM

HOT

PLATE

SERVING SUGGESTION

PROJECT:	*I.H.O.P. COUNTRY OMELETTE*	
CATEGORY: *BREAKFAST*	JOB NO.	*IHOP4076959-CO*

IHOP
HARVEST GRAIN 'N NUT
PANCAKES

MENU DESCRIPTION: *"Hearty grains, wholesome oats, almonds and English walnuts."*

Wholesome grains and nuts get it on in this clone for the signature pancakes from the country's largest pancake chain. The whole wheat flour and oats add more flavor, while the nuts pitch in for a crunch in every bite. Take a break from gummy, bland traditional pancakes. Make a breakfast that pacifies your pancake urge and leaves you feeling peppy.

¾ cup Quaker oats
¾ cup whole wheat flour
⅓ cup all-purpose flour

2 teaspoons baking soda	2 eggs
1 teaspoon baking powder	¼ cup granulated sugar
½ teaspoon salt	3 tablespoons finely chopped
1¼ cups buttermilk	blanched almonds
⅓ cup whole milk	3 tablespoons finely chopped
¼ cup vegetable oil	walnuts

1. Lightly oil a skillet or griddle and preheat it to medium heat.
2. Grind the oats in a blender or food processor until fine, like flour.

3. Combine oat flour, whole wheat flour, all-purpose flour, baking soda, baking powder and salt in a medium bowl.
4. In another bowl combine buttermilk, milk, oil, eggs and granulated sugar with an electric mixer until smooth. Combine dry ingredients with wet ingredients, add nuts and mix well by hand.
5. Ladle ⅓ cup of the batter onto the hot skillet and cook the pancakes for 1 to 3 minutes per side or until brown.

• MAKES 12 PANCAKES.

TIDBITS

You can cover and freeze these after they cool. To reheat, just put a stack in the microwave on high for 1 to 2 minutes.

•   •   •   •

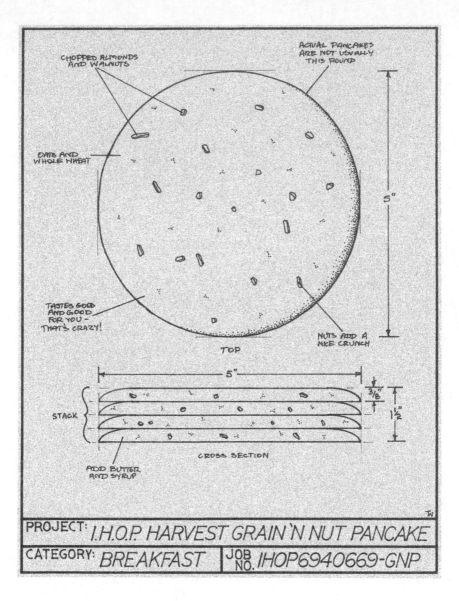

CHOPPED ALMONDS
AND WALNUTS

ACTUAL PANCAKES
ARE NOT USUALLY
THIS ROUND

OATS AND
WHOLE WHEAT

5"

TASTES GOOD
AND GOOD
FOR YOU —
THAT'S CRAZY!

NUTS ADD A
NICE CRUNCH

TOP

5"

STACK

3/8"

1½"

CROSS SECTION

ADD BUTTER
AND SYRUP

PROJECT: *I.H.O.P. HARVEST GRAIN 'N NUT PANCAKE*

CATEGORY: *BREAKFAST*   JOB NO. *IHOP6940669-GNP*

IHOP
PUMPKIN PANCAKES

During the holiday season this particular pancake flavor sells like ... well, you know. It's one of 16 varieties of pancakes served at this national casual diner chain. You can make your own version of these delicious flapjacks with a little canned pumpkin, some spices and traditional buttermilk pancake ingredients. Get out the mixer, fire up the stove, track down the syrup.

nonstick spray
2 eggs
1 ¼ cups buttermilk
4 tablespoons butter, melted
3 tablespoons canned pumpkin
¼ cup granulated sugar

¼ teaspoon salt
1 ¼ cups all-purpose flour
½ teaspoon baking powder
½ teaspoon baking soda
¼ teaspoon ground cinnamon
¼ teaspoon ground allspice

1. Preheat a skillet over medium heat. Coat pan with oil cooking spray.
2. Combine eggs, buttermilk, butter, pumpkin, sugar, and salt in a large bowl. Use an electric mixer to blend ingredients.
3. Combine remaining ingredients in a small bowl. Add dry ingredients to wet ingredients and blend with mixer on medium speed until smooth.
4. Pour the batter in ⅓-cup portions into the hot pan.
5. When the batter stops bubbling and edges begin to harden,

flip the pancakes. They should be dark brown. This will take from 1 to 3 minutes.

6. Flip the pancakes and cook other side for the same amount of time, until brown.

- MAKES 8 TO 10 PANCAKES.

• • • •

ISLANDS CHINA COAST SALAD DRESSING

This 30-store Hawaiian-themed chain of restaurants is known for its handmade burger buns, specialty sandwiches and taco platters with names like Shorebird, Pelican, Sandpiper, Baja, and Northshore. Some people, though, go to the Islands just for the China Coast salad. It's a huge bowl filled with sliced chicken breast, lettuce, red cabbage, julienned carrots, fried noodles, sesame seeds, mandarin orange wedges and chives, and then tossed with this top secret dressing. Many diners think the dressing's so good they ask for extra and discreetly smuggle it home. No more smuggling required. Now, with this simple formula, you can make your own clone at home and use it on any of your favorite bowls of green.

½ cup mayonnaise
5 tablespoons rice vinegar
2 tablespoons granulated sugar

2 tablespoons sesame oil
1 tablespoon soy sauce
¼ teaspoon garlic powder

Combine all ingredients in a medium bowl and mix with an electric mixer until blended and sugar is dissolved. Chill.

- MAKES 1 CUP.

• • • •

ISLANDS
ISLAND FRIES

MENU DESCRIPTION: *"Our famous fries are fresh cut daily from whole potatoes with the skins left on."*

Not only can I show you the best way to make french fries at home in this clone of Islands' top-selling version, but I'm also supplying you with a super simple way to make the same type of salt blend that Islands uses to make those fries so dang addicting. As with any good french fry recipe, you'll need to slice your potatoes into strips that are all equal thickness. That means you need a mandoline, or similar slicing device, that makes ¼-inch slices. Once you've got your potatoes cut, you must rinse and soak them in water to expel the excess starch. The frying comes in two stages: A quick blanching stage, and the final frying to put a crispy coating on the suckers. Islands uses a combination of peanut and vegetable oils in their fryers, so you simply combine the two in your home fryer. The whole process is not that tough once you get going, and certainly worth the effort if hungry mouths are waiting for the perfect homemade french fries. However, if you want to simplify the process because your hungry mouths aren't of the patient sort, you could certainly buy frozen french fries, cook 'em up following the instructions on the bag, and then sprinkle on this garlic/onion salt blend for a quick-and-easy kitchen clone.

GARLIC/ONION SALT

1 tablespoon garlic salt   ¼ teaspoon ground black pepper
1 teaspoon onion salt

FRIES

2 medium russet potatoes   3 to 5 cups peanut oil (fryer filled
3 to 5 cups vegetable oil (fryer   rest of the way)
    filled halfway)

1. Combine garlic salt, onion salt, and pepper in a small bowl.
2. Slice potatoes with a slicer or mandoline set to ¼-inch thick slices. Hold potato at a slight angle when slicing to produce fries that are about 2 to 3 inches in length.
3. Drop sliced potatoes into a bowl of water to rinse away starch. Pour out water, then fill bowl again. Pour out that water, then fill bowl again with water and add some ice. Let potatoes sit for 1 hour in the ice water.
4. Heat oils in fryer to 350 degrees.
5. When the potatoes are done soaking, drain them, then pour them out onto a clean dish towel. Blot fries dry.
6. When fries are dry drop about half into the hot oil and blanch for 2 to 3 minutes (fries should be soft in the center). Remove the fries onto a towel to cool. When all the fries are blanched, let them sit to cool for about 30 minutes. When fries are cool, fry them for the second time for 5 to 7 minutes or until fries are golden and crispy.
7. Pour fries onto a rack or towels to drain. Toss fries with several pinches of the garlic/onion salt and serve hot.

- SERVES 4.

•   •   •   •

ISLANDS
TORTILLA SOUP

☆　✌　💣　✏　☯　✂　☞

The entire process for making this soup, which Islands serves in "bottomless bowls," takes as long as 3 hours, but don't let that discourage you. Most of that time is spent waiting for the chicken to roast (up to 90 minutes—although you can save time by using a precooked chicken, see Tidbits) and letting the soup simmer (1 hour). The actual work involved is minimal—most of your time is spent chopping the vegetable ingredients. This recipe produces soup with an awesome flavor and texture since you'll be making fresh chicken stock from the carcass of the roasted chicken. As for the fried tortilla strip garnish that tops the soup, you can go the hard way or the easy way on that step. The hard way makes the very best clone and it's really not that hard: Simply slice corn tortillas into strips, fry the strips real quick, then toss the fried strips with a custom seasoning blend. The easy way is to grab a bag of the new habanero-flavored Doritos, which happen to be similar in spiciness to the strips used at the restaurant. Simply crumble a few of these chips over the top of your bowl of soup, and dig in.

4 to 5 pound whole roasting
　　chicken
2 tablespoons butter, melted
16 cups (1 gallon) water
1 medium Spanish onion, diced
　　(2 cups)
1 medium red bell pepper, diced
　　(1 cup)

2 medium carrots, diced
　　(1 cup)
2 Anaheim peppers, diced
　　(¾ cup)
2 cloves garlic, minced
　　(1 tablespoon)
4 6-inch yellow corn tortillas, diced
　　(1½ cups)

juice of 2 large limes
(3 tablespoons)
1 tablespoon salt
1 teaspoon chili powder

1 teaspoon ground cayenne
pepper
2 tablespoons minced fresh
cilantro

TORTILLA STRIPS

2 cups vegetable oil
6 6-inch yellow corn tortillas
1 teaspoon chili powder
1 teaspoon paprika

¾ teaspoon ground cayenne
pepper
½ teaspoon salt

GARNISH

1 cup shredded Monterey Jack
cheese

2 avocados, diced

1. Preheat oven to 375 degrees.
2. Rub the chicken with melted butter and sprinkle with salt and pepper. Place your clucker breast-side-up on a rack in a roasting pan. Roast chicken for 70 to 90 minutes or until the temperature in the center of the breast is 160 degrees. Remove chicken from the oven to cool, but don't get rid of the drippings in the roasting pan.
3. When chicken has cooled enough to handle, tear the meat off the bone. Throw away the skin, but keep all the bones. Add the bones to 16 cups of water in a soup pot. Bring to a boil, then reduce heat to a rapid simmer and find something to keep you busy for 30 minutes. This is a good time to finish chopping the veggies.
4. Spoon a tablespoon of fat from the roasting pan into a large skillet over medium heat. When the pan is hot, sauté onion, peppers, carrot and garlic for 10 minutes over medium/low heat.
5. After 30 to 45 minutes of simmering, remove chicken bones from the water, and add the sautéed vegetables,

plus the chicken meat, lime juice, salt, chili powder and cayenne pepper. Simmer soup for 1 hour, adding the cilantro to the pot about 30 minutes in.

6. As your soup simmers, heat up 2 cups of vegetable oil in a medium saucepan. Make your spicy tortilla strips by cutting a pile of 6 small corn tortillas in half. Slice the stacks into ¼-inch strips. Test the oil by dropping in one strip. If it bubbles rapidly, it's hot enough. Wait 4 minutes, then take out the sample and make sure it's crunchy. If your oil is ready, fry half of the strips at a time for 4 to 5 minutes or until they all come out crispy. Drain on paper towels. Combine the seasonings for the strips (chili powder, paprika, cayenne and salt) in a small bowl. Toss the tortilla strips with the seasoning in a large bowl until the strips are coated.

7. Serve each bowl of soup topped with a couple tablespoons of shredded Jack cheese, a couple tablespoons of diced avocado (one-quarter of an avocado), and handful of tortilla strips on top.

• MAKES 8 SERVINGS (1½ CUPS EACH).

TIDBITS

Home-roasting a chicken is easy, but if you want to save a little time you can just as well use one of the precooked whole chickens usually found in the deli section of your market. If you go that route, just pick up the recipe from step #3.

•   •   •   •

ISLANDS
YAKI SOFT TACOS

MENU DESCRIPTION: *"Three flour tortillas stuffed w/marinated chicken, teriyaki sauce, Jack cheese, pineapple, lettuce, tomatoes & scallions."*

If you love the sweet taste of teriyaki-marinated chicken, you'll dig the Yaki Soft Tacos at this Hawaiian-themed burger chain. Sure, Islands is famous for its burgers, but many also go for the several choices of soft tacos—and the one I've cloned here is the top-seller. After testing all popular brands of teriyaki sauce on the market, I found that none have the heavy ginger notes of the chain's version, so you'll want to make the sauce from scratch. Which is really no big deal, since it's an easy process and you'll end up with a teriyaki sauce/marinade that's better than any store version, and you can use it in all sorts of recipes. When you buy the canned pineapple, go for the 20-ounce can or get two 8-ounces cans. You'll need that much since you'll use the pineapple chunks in both the sauce and on the tacos (and you'll even use some of the juice from the can in your teriyaki sauce). When chopping the chunks, take the time to slice each chunk into quarters (length-wise, with the grain) so you get thin pineapple pieces that are the exact size of the stuff they use in the restaurant. Or you can find smaller pineapple chunks in some stores (see Tidbits).

TERIYAKI SAUCE

1¾ cups water
1 tablespoon cornstarch
¾ cup light brown sugar
½ cup soy sauce
½ cup canned pineapple chunks
(chunks sliced into quarters)

¼ cup juice from can of pineapple
chunks
½ teaspoon garlic powder
¼ teaspoon onion powder
2 teaspoons minced fresh ginger

12 chicken tenderloins
12 7-inch flour tortillas
2 cups shredded Monterey Jack
cheese
4 cups iceberg lettuce, chopped
very thin or shredded
1½ cups canned pineapple
chunks, (chunks sliced into
quarters)

1½ cups diced tomatoes (about
2 medium tomatoes)
½ cup chopped green onion
(green part only)

1. Make the teriyaki sauce by whisking cornstarch into the water in a medium saucepan. Add remaining ingredients, then bring mixture to a boil. Reduce heat and simmer for 7 to 10 minutes or until thicker. Let sauce cool before you use it for marinating.

2. When the sauce is cool, measure out 1 cup of sauce and set it aside. Use the remaining sauce to pour over chicken tenders in a medium bowl. Cover chicken and let it marinate for at least 6 hours. Overnight is even better.

3. When chicken has marinated, preheat a large skillet over medium/low heat. Wipe the pan with a little oil. Remove the chicken from the marinade (and toss out the marinade) and sauté chicken in the pan for 8 to 10 or until chicken is cooked through and browned on both sides. Slice each chicken filet into 3 or 4 pieces and spoon all the chicken into a medium bowl. Microwave the leftover 1 cup of teriyaki

sauce in the oven for 30 to 60 seconds or until it's hot. Pour the sauce over the sliced chicken in the bowl.

4. When you're ready to build the tacos, preheat another skillet over medium heat. Toss a tortilla into the pan for a minute, then flip it over and add 2 to 3 tablespoons of shredded cheese across the center of the tortilla. Let the tortilla sit in the pan for about a minute or so (until the cheese starts melting) then remove the tortilla and immediately spoon the equivalent of one chicken tender into the tortilla (3 or 4 chunks of chicken). Spoon about 1½ tablespoons teriyaki sauce from the cooked chicken bowl over the chicken in each taco.

5. Arrange about ⅓ cup shredded lettuce over the chicken in each taco. Follow that up with 1 to 2 tablespoons of pineapple chunks, 1 to 2 tablespoons diced tomato, and a couple pinches of chopped green onion. Repeat process for remaining tacos. The restaurant serves 3 tacos with each order.

• MAKES 12 TACOS (4 SERVINGS).

TIDBITS

If you can find them, Del Monte offers canned pineapple that's pre-cut into the perfect size for this recipe. And I love the name: They're called "Tidbits."

• • • •

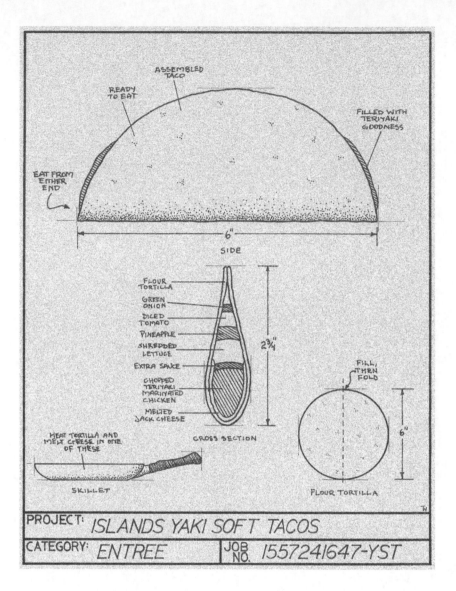

READY
TO EAT

ASSEMBLED
TACO

FILLED WITH
TERIYAKI
GOODNESS

EAT FROM
EITHER
END

6"

SIDE

FLOUR
TORTILLA

GREEN
ONION

DICED
TOMATO

PINEAPPLE

SHREDDED
LETTUCE

EXTRA SAUCE

CHOPPED
TERIYAKI
MARINATED
CHICKEN

MELTED
JACK CHEESE

2¾"

CROSS SECTION

HEAT TORTILLA AND
MELT CHEESE IN ONE
OF THESE

SKILLET

FILL,
THEN
FOLD

6"

FLOUR TORTILLA

PROJECT: ISLANDS YAKI SOFT TACOS

CATEGORY: ENTREE

JOB NO. 1557241647-YST

194

JOE'S CRAB SHACK
BLUE CRAB DIP

The number one appetizer on Joe's menu is called Blue Crab Dip, but you don't need blue crab to clone it. You don't even need to use fresh crab. I used some delicious lump crabmeat from Phillips Seafood that comes in 16-ounce cans (you'll find it at Costco, Sam's Club, Wal-Mart, and Von's) and the dip came out amazing. You could also use crabmeat that comes in 6-ounce cans found at practically every supermarket—you'll need two of them. Just be sure to get the kind that includes leg meat, and don't forget to drain off the liquid before you toss it in.

one 8-ounce pkg. cream cheese, softened
2 cups crabmeat (canned is fine)
¼ cup diced green onion
1 tablespoon minced mild red chili pepper

1 tablespoon mild green chili pepper (Anaheim)
¼ teaspoon salt
¼ teaspoon ground white pepper
2 tablespoons shredded Parmesan cheese

GARNISH

paprika

1 teaspoon minced fresh parsley

1. Preheat oven to broil.
2. Combine cream cheese with crab, green onion, chili peppers, salt and white pepper in a medium bowl. Stir well to combine.

3. Spread mixture into the bottom of an oven-safe dish. Use a wide dish for this so that the dip is only about an inch deep in the bottom.
4. Sprinkle Parmesan cheese over the surface of the dip.
5. Broil for 3 to 4 minutes or until cheese on top begins to brown.
6. Sprinkle paprika over the dip, followed by fresh minced parsley. Serve with tortilla chips or crackers for dipping.

- MAKES APPROX. 2 CUPS (SERVES 4 TO 6 AS AN APPETIZER).

JOE'S CRAB SHACK
GARLIC KING CRAB LEGS

These legs from the king of crabs come already cooked at your supermarket (usually previously frozen), so we won't have to boil them long to finish them off. But we do want to give them a long enough bath to get the flavor of garlic into the meat. To aid in this process we need to poke several holes in the shell along each leg so that the garlic water can seep in. Use the handle end of a nut-cracker (the kind that is often served with crab to help crack the shells), or the back end of a wooden spoon to make those holes. This step also makes removing the shells easier when eating the crab. And you don't have to worry about peeling the garlic cloves. Just pound 'em flat with a mallet or foil-wrapped brick and toss 'em into the water.

1 cup vegetable oil	1 tablespoon dried parsley flakes
2 large heads garlic	2 pounds king crab legs

ON THE SIDE
melted butter

1. Fill a large pot halfway with water. Add oil and bring to a boil. Crush all of the unpeeled garlic cloves with a mallet. When the water and oil comes to a boil add the garlic and parsley flakes and boil for 15 minutes.

2. Cut the crab legs in half so that they will fit into the pot. Use the handle end of a thin wooden spoon or nutcracker to poke several holes in the shell of each crab leg. This will allow the flavor of the garlic to seep into the crab. Lower the crab into the pot and boil for 5 to 6 minutes.
3. Remove crab legs and drain. Arrange one pound of crab on each plate. Serve with melted butter on the side.

• SERVES 2.

• • • •

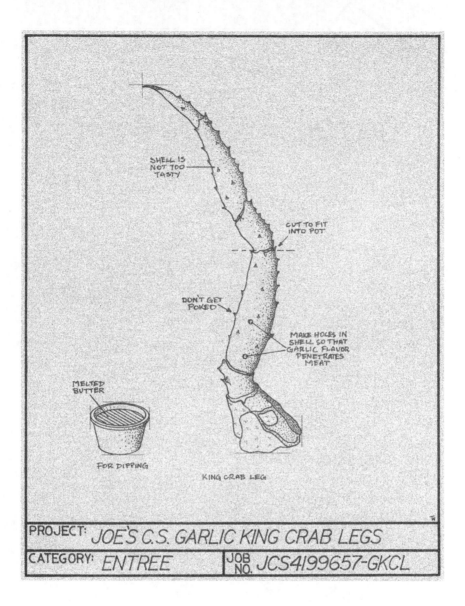

SHELL IS NOT TOO TASTY

CUT TO FIT INTO POT

DON'T GET POKED

MAKE HOLES IN SHELL SO THAT GARLIC FLAVOR PENETRATES MEAT

MELTED BUTTER

FOR DIPPING

KING CRAB LEG

PROJECT: *JOE'S C.S. GARLIC KING CRAB LEGS*

CATEGORY: *ENTREE*

JOB NO. *JCS4I99657-GKCL*

LONE STAR STEAKHOUSE LETTUCE WEDGE SALAD

Why waste time chopping up the lettuce when you can just hack a head into four chunks, dress it up and serve? This unique presentation is not only easy to make, but is also a deliciously different way to serve your next salad. The creamy bleu cheese dressing is a breeze to craft from scratch and tastes much better than anything you'll buy in a store. Add a bit of extra crumbled bleu over the top, some freshly diced tomatoes, and you're well on your way to a fancy-pants side salad that'll surely impress.

BLEU CHEESE DRESSING

¾ cup mayonnaise
½ cup buttermilk
¼ cup crumbled bleu cheese
½ teaspoon granulated sugar

¼ teaspoon ground black pepper
¼ teaspoon garlic powder
⅛ teaspoon onion powder
⅛ teaspoon salt

1 head iceberg lettuce
1 cup crumbled bleu cheese

1 cup diced tomato (1 large tomato)

1. Use an electric mixer to combine all ingredients for bleu cheese dressing in a medium bowl.
2. Slice a head of iceberg lettuce into quarters through the

stem end. Cut the stem off of the wedges and arrange each one on a plate.

3. Spoon about ¼ cup of bleu cheese dressing over each lettuce wedge.

4. Sprinkle ¼ cup of crumbled bleu cheese over the dressing.

5. Sprinkle ¼ cup of diced tomato over the top and serve.

• MAKES 4 SERVINGS.

•   •   •   •

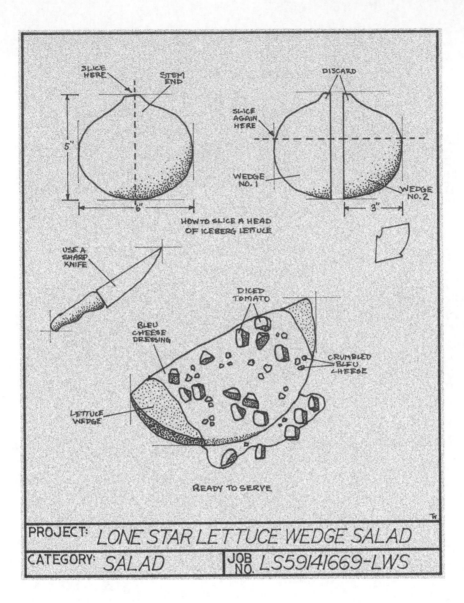

SLICE HERE
STEM END
DISCARD
5"
SLICE AGAIN HERE
6"
WEDGE NO. 1
WEDGE NO. 2
3"

HOW TO SLICE A HEAD
OF ICEBERG LETTUCE

USE A SHARP KNIFE

DICED TOMATO
BLEU CHEESE DRESSING
CRUMBLED BLEU CHEESE
LETTUCE WEDGE

READY TO SERVE

PROJECT:	LONE STAR LETTUCE WEDGE SALAD	
CATEGORY: SALAD	JOB NO.	LS59141669-LWS

LONE STAR
STEAKHOUSE
BAKED SWEET POTATO

Sweet potatoes are not related to the more common russet potatoes and are often confused with yams in the grocery store and on menus (the yam is actually starchier and less flavorful). Just be sure you're buying sweet potatoes when you get to the produce section—even the produce stockers get mixed up! Although these puppies are not really potatoes, the baking times are the same. And when you spoon on some butter and sprinkle cinnamon/sugar over the top, you've got a treat that tastes more like dessert than a versatile side dish.

4 sweet potatoes
vegetable oil
3 tablespoons granulated sugar

1 ½ teaspoons ground cinnamon
½ cup whipped butter

1. Preheat oven to 350 degrees. Rub a little oil on the skin of the sweet potato and bake it for 45 to 75 minutes (bigger sweet potatoes take longer to cook). When they are done, the outside will have darkened and the inside will be soft. You may see liquid from the sweet potato oozing out when it's close to done.

2. As potatoes bake, combine sugar and cinnamon in a small bowl.
3. To serve, slice a sweet potato down the center. Add two tablespoons of whipped butter, and sprinkle some cinnamon/sugar over the top.

• MAKES 4 SERVINGS.

•   •   •   •

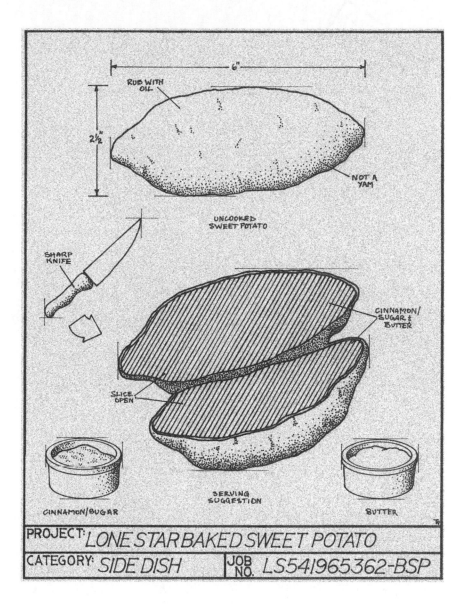

6"

RUB WITH OIL

2½"

NOT A YAM

UNCOOKED SWEET POTATO

SHARP KNIFE

CINNAMON/ SUGAR & BUTTER

SLICE OPEN

SERVING SUGGESTION

CINNAMON/SUGAR

BUTTER

PROJECT: *LONE STAR BAKED SWEET POTATO*

CATEGORY: *SIDE DISH*   JOB NO. *LS541965362-BSP*

LONE STAR STEAKHOUSE LONE STAR CHILI

MENU DESCRIPTION: *"Meaty and spicy, served piping-hot with chopped onions, shredded cheddar, and a whole jalapeno."*

This chain makes a tasty chili that warms the bones on a nippy day. This clone recipe is easy to make, low in fat, and delicious. And if it's super brisk outside, you might want to add an additional tablespoon of diced jalapeno to the pot to aggressively stoke those internal flames.

1 pound ground beef
1 diced onion
1 tablespoon diced fresh jalapeno pepper
1 15-ounce can kidney beans with liquid
1 14.5-ounce can peeled diced tomatoes

1 8-ounce can tomato sauce
1 cup water
1 tablespoon apple cider vinegar
1 teaspoon salt
1 teaspoon chili powder
¼ teaspoon garlic powder
1 bay leaf

GARNISH

grated Cheddar cheese
diced onion

canned whole jalapeno chili peppers

1. Brown ground beef in a large saucepan over medium heat. Drain fat.
2. Add onion and pepper and sauté for about two minutes.
3. Add remaining ingredients and simmer for 1 hour, stirring occasionally. Serve one cup in a bowl with the optional cheese, diced onion and whole jalapeno garnish on top.

• MAKES 4 SERVINGS.

•   •   •   •

MARGARITAVILLE CRAB, SHRIMP AND MUSHROOM DIP

MENU DESCRIPTION: *"Our signature appetizer . . . jumbo lump blue crab meat, gulf shrimp and mushrooms, simmered in a Cajun cream sauce and served with toasted garlic bread. We make it here so you know it's good!"*

This dips rocks, and I'm not the only one who thinks so. According to the Margaritaville menu, it's the theme chain's signature appetizer. And what's not to like: Delicious blue crab, little bay shrimp and sliced mushrooms are all swimming in a Cajun-style cream sauce, topped with melted Cheddar and Jack cheeses, and broiled until the cheese melts . . . oh, hold me back. Serve up your clone with slices of freshly toasted buttery garlic bread and you've got a great party snack. The restaurant version is a tiny little serving that's barely enough for two, so I've supersized this clone recipe to make enough dip to satisfy the Brady Bunch—if Alice sits out.

DIP

2 tablespoons butter
¼ cup minced celery
¼ cup minced white onion
1 teaspoon crushed red pepper
    flakes

2 cups heavy cream
1 ½ cups sliced white mushrooms
1 cup blue crab
1 cup bay shrimp, cooked
    (smallest shrimp)

¼ teaspoon salt
1 cup shredded Cheddar
    cheese

1 cup shredded Monterey Jack
    cheese
2 green onions, sliced

BREAD

2 loaves Italian bread
½ cup butter, melted (1 stick)

½ teaspoon dried parsley flakes
¼ teaspoon garlic powder

1. Melt 2 tablespoons of butter over low heat in a large saucepan. Add celery, white onion and red pepper flakes and simmer slowly (sweat) the ingredients over low heat for 20 minutes. You don't want the ingredients to turn brown; rather, you want them to cook slowly until the celery softens and the onion begins to turn translucent.

2. Add cream, mushrooms, crab, shrimp and salt to the pan. Turn the heat up a bit until the liquid begins to bubble, then bring the heat back down and let the mixture simmer for 20 minutes or until it reduces to about ½ the volume and becomes thick. Watch the saucepan carefully to make sure the mixture doesn't bubble over. In the meantime, crank your oven up to broil.

3. Prepare the bread by cutting the loaves into ½-inch thick slices. Combine the dried parsley flakes and garlic powder with a stick of melted butter in a small bowl. Brush some of this garlic butter on each side of each bread slice and toast the bread under the hot broiler for 1 to 2 minutes per side or until the bread is toasted to a light brown.

4. When the dip has thickened pour it into an 8x8-inch casserole dish. Combine the shredded Cheddar and Jack cheese and sprinkle the cheese mixture over the dip. Broil the dip for 3 to 4 minutes or until the cheese is melted. Sprinkle sliced green onions over the top and serve hot with the

garlic toast on the side, and some spoons or forks for spreading the dip onto the toast.

- MAKES 6 TO 8 SERVINGS.

• • • •

MARGARITAVILLE
JAMAICA MISTAICA WINGS

MENU DESCRIPTION: *"Come back to Jamaica! Our wings tossed in habanero-honey wing sauce with cucumber sticks and house-made mango ranch dipping sauce."*

Oh, wings. You gotta love those flavorful little non-functioning chicken parts. When they're good, they're real good. And these little guys from Jimmy Buffett's chain of island-themed restaurants rock my tiny inflatable boat. The preparation is no big secret: fry the wings, add the sauce. But it's that habanero honey sauce recipe that makes these suckers so addicting. Add to that an easy-to-make mango ranch dipping sauce and you're off on a nonstop cruise to chicken wing paradise. The restaurant serving size is for 10 wings, but these *Top Secret* sauces will be enough for 30 wings, and you'll need it! If I have one word of caution it's to be very careful mincing that habanero. You may even want to use rubber gloves to handle it. This is the hottest pepper in the world, folks, so if you touch the minced pieces with your bare fingers, and then proceed to touch a crucial and sensitive body part, you'll discover one big "mistaica" real fast.

HABANERO HONEY SAUCE

1 cup water
1 6-ounce can tomato paste
½ cup Worcestershire sauce
¼ cup honey
¼ cup molasses

1 teaspoon minced habanero pepper (1 pepper)
1 teaspoon crushed red pepper flakes
1 teaspoon ground black pepper

½ teaspoon onion powder
½ teaspoon chili powder
½ teaspoon dried minced onion
½ teaspoon dried parsley

¼ teaspoon garlic powder
⅛ teaspoon liquid hickory smoke
⅓ cup white vinegar

MANGO RANCH DIPPING SAUCE

1 8-ounce bottle Hidden Valley
    Ranch dressing
¼ cup mango juice (Kern's is
    good)

½ jalapeno, minced

6 to 10 cups vegetable oil (as
    required by fryer)
10 chicken wings

salt
pepper

ON THE SIDE

cucumber sticks

1. Prepare habanero honey sauce by combining all ingredients except the vinegar in a large saucepan. Bring mixture to a boil, then reduce heat and simmer sauce for 1 hour uncovered, or until sauce reduces to about half of its original volume and thickens. Remove sauce from heat, mix in ⅓ cup white vinegar and cover.
2. Make the mango ranch dipping sauce by combining the ingredients in a small bowl. Cover and chill sauce until needed.
3. In your deep fryer, bring 6 to 10 cups of vegetable oil (or whatever is required by your fryer) to 375 degrees.
4. Drop in the wings and fry for 8 to 12 minutes or until the wings become golden brown. Drain wings for a few minutes on paper towels. Sprinkle with salt and pepper.
5. Put wings in a large metal or glass bowl, add ½ cup of the habanero honey sauce and toss the wings until they are all

coated. Serve with dipping sauce on the side and cucumber sticks, if desired.

- MAKES 10 WINGS (PLUS SAUCE FOR 20 MORE).

• • • •

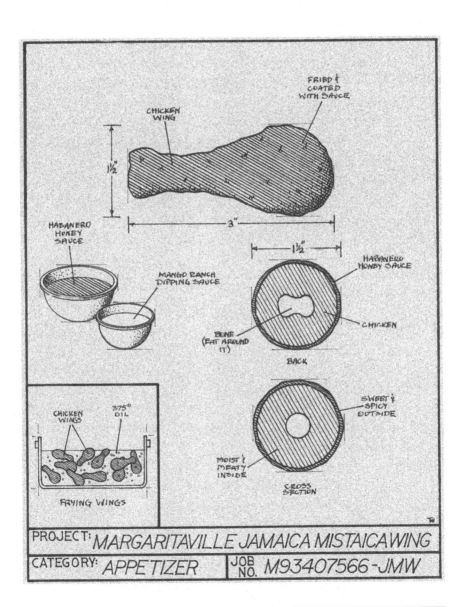

CHICKEN WING

FRIED & COATED WITH SAUCE

1½"

3"

HABANERO HONEY SAUCE

MANGO RANCH DIPPING SAUCE

1½"

HABANERO HONEY SAUCE

BONE (EAT AROUND IT)

CHICKEN

BACK

CHICKEN WINGS

375° OIL

SWEET & SPICY OUTSIDE

MOIST & MEATY INSIDE

CROSS SECTION

FRYING WINGS

PROJECT: MARGARITAVILLE JAMAICA MISTAICAWING

CATEGORY: APPETIZER   JOB NO. M93407566-JMW

MARGARITAVILLE
KEY LIME PIE

MENU DESCRIPTION: *"A true taste of the tropics. National award-winning recipe."*

Many of the key lime pie recipes circulating, including the recipe found on bottles of key lime juice, have a glaring error: They don't make enough filling to fit properly into a standard 9-inch graham crust pie shell. That's probably because those recipes are designed around one 14-ounce can of sweetened condensed milk. But come on, if we're going to make a beautifully thick key lime pie like the one served at Jimmy Buffett's Margaritaville restaurants we need to use something like 1½ cans of sweetened condensed milk, or, more accurately, two cups of the stuff. The clone recipe for the pie is a simple one that's for sure, with only four ingredients including the pie shell. But don't stop there. I'm also including a special way to make mango sauce by simply reducing a couple cans of Kern's mango juice. And there's a raspberry sauce recipe here that's made easily with frozen raspberries. These two sauces are used to jazz up the plate at the restaurant and are certainly optional for your clone version, even though I've made them as easy as, um, you know.

2 cups sweetened condensed milk   ⅔ cup key lime juice
6 egg yolks   1 graham cracker pie shell

MANGO SAUCE

2 11.5-ounce cans Kern's
   mango juice

RASPBERRY SAUCE

1 ½ cups water   ½ cup granulated sugar
2 cups frozen raspberries

GARNISH

canned whipped cream
4 thin lime slices, halved

1. Preheat oven to 325 degrees.
2. Use an electric mixer on medium speed to combine sweetened condensed milk, egg yolks, and lime juice. Mix just until ingredients are combined.
3. Pour filling into graham pie shell and bake on middle rack for 20 minutes or until filling jiggles only slightly when shaken. Cool. Cover pie and chill in refrigerator for a couple hours before serving.
4. Make mango sauce by bringing two cans of Kern's mango juice to a boil in a medium saucepan over medium heat. Reduce heat and simmer for 30 minutes or until sauce thickens. Cover and chill.
5. Make raspberry sauce by combining water and raspberries in a medium saucepan over medium heat. Bring to a boil then reduce heat and simmer raspberries for 10 minutes. Use a potato masher or a large spoon to crush the raspberries as they boil. Strain raspberry seeds from water, then put the liquid back into the saucepan and add the sugar. Bring mixture back to a boil, reduce heat and simmer for 15 to 20 minutes or until the sauce thickens. Cover and cool sauce until you are ready to serve the pie.

6. Prepare dessert by dribbling some mango sauce and some raspberry sauce onto a small plate (you can use spoons or squirt bottles for this). Place a slice of pie onto the sauce, add a dollop of whipped cream to the top of the pie slice with one half of a thin lime slice on top of the whipped cream.

• MAKES 8 SERVINGS.

•   •   •   •

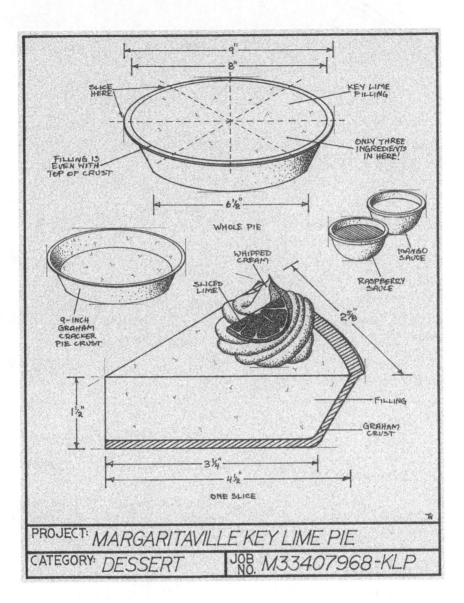

9"
8"
SLICE HERE
KEY LIME FILLING
FILLING IS EVEN WITH TOP OF CRUST
ONLY THREE INGREDIENTS IN HERE!
6½"
WHOLE PIE

MANGO SAUCE
RASPBERRY SAUCE

9-INCH GRAHAM CRACKER PIE CRUST

WHIPPED CREAM
SLICED LIME
2⅝"
FILLING
GRAHAM CRUST
1½"
3¼"
4½"
ONE SLICE

PROJECT: *MARGARITAVILLE KEY LIME PIE*

CATEGORY: *DESSERT*

JOB NO. *M33407968-KLP*

MARIE CALLENDER'S LEMON CREAM CHEESE PIE

MENU DESCRIPTION: *"Our melt-in-your-mouth cream cheese pie with a tangy lemon topping."*

Here's a great double-layered pie with lemon topping covering a creamy cheesecake filling. It's two great pies in one dessert. This creation has been huge seller for Marie Callender's, and I've had nothing but raves from anyone who's tried it—including a couple high fives and one affectionate rabbit punch. Make the crust from scratch like the pros using the recipe here, or take the easy route with a premade graham cracker crust found in the baking aisle. Either way it's pie heaven.

CRUST

1 cup graham cracker crumbs
¼ cup butter, melted (½ stick)

2 tablespoons granulated sugar

CREAM CHEESE FILLING

one 8-ounce pkg. cream cheese, softened
¼ cup granulated sugar

½ teaspoon vanilla extract
1 egg

LEMON FILLING

½ cup granulated sugar
2 tablespoons cornstarch
dash salt
1 cup water

2 egg yolks
2 tablespoons fresh lemon juice
1 tablespoon butter

1. Preheat oven to 350 degrees.
2. Make the crust by combining the graham cracker crumbs with melted butter and sugar in a small bowl. Press the crust mixture into an 8-inch pie pan.
3. Prepare the cream cheese filling by mixing cream cheese with ¼ cup sugar, vanilla and an egg using an electric mixer. Mix well until smooth. Pour cream cheese filling into graham cracker crust and bake for 30 to 35 minutes or until center is cooked. A knife stuck in the middle of the filling should come out mostly clean.
4. As the pie cools, make the lemon filling by combining ½ cup sugar with cornstarch, salt and water in a small saucepan. Set mixture over low heat and bring to a simmer, stirring often.
5. Whisk in egg yolks, then add lemon juice and butter. When mixture simmers again immediately remove it from the heat.
6. Pour the lemon filling over the cream cheese filling, and let the pie cool. When cool, chill pie in the refrigerator for several hours before serving. Slice into 6 pieces to serve restaurant-size portions.

• MAKES 6 SERVINGS.

• • • •

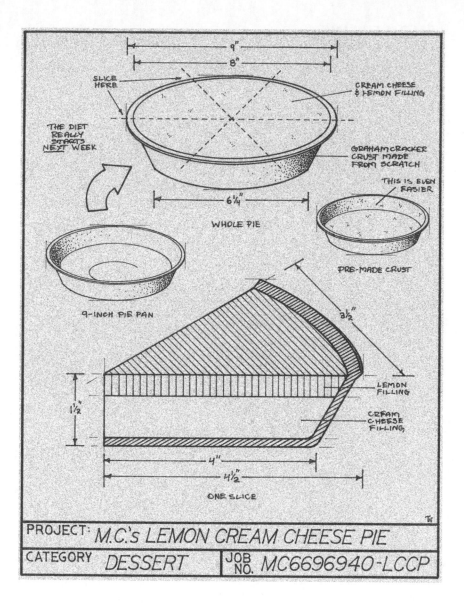

9"

8"

SLICE
HERE

CREAM CHEESE
& LEMON FILLING

THE DIET
REALLY
STARTS
NEXT WEEK

GRAHAM CRACKER
CRUST MADE
FROM SCRATCH

6¼"

THIS IS EVEN
EASIER

WHOLE PIE

9-INCH PIE PAN

PRE-MADE CRUST

3½"

LEMON
FILLING

CREAM
CHEESE
FILLING

1½"

4"

4½"

ONE SLICE

TW

PROJECT: *M.C.'s LEMON CREAM CHEESE PIE*

CATEGORY *DESSERT*   JOB NO. *MC6696940-LCCP*

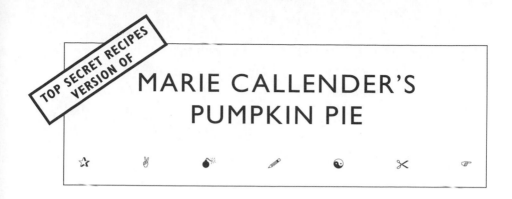

MARIE CALLENDER'S PUMPKIN PIE

MENU DESCRIPTION: *"Our famous pumpkin pie has just the right amount of spice."*

The vittles from Marie Callender's have made an impression beyond the chain's West Coast roots with home-style packaged entrees and side dishes available in frozen food sections of supermarkets across the country. But pie making is where the chain excels. A fresh slice of a Marie Callender's pie is as close as you'll get to homemade heaven this side of grandma's porch window. This clone is an obvious selection, since the restaurant sells more pumpkin pies than any other, even in non-holiday months. This clone is a perfect opportunity to improve on icky pumpkin pie recipes (like those found on cans of canned pumpkin, for example) in many ways. For one thing, there's no need to use canned evaporated milk when fresh whole milk and cream is so much better. Also, I've added a little brown sugar in there to contribute hints of molasses that go so well with the pumpkin and spices. And three eggs, versus two found in many recipes, will add to the richness and firmness of the cooked filling. After mixing the filling we'll let it sit for a bit while waiting for the oven to preheat. This way it can come closer to room temperature, and the pie filling will bake more evenly. And then, of course, you've got the crust. Marie Callender's pie crust is a treat, and the clone recipe included here—which uses a chilled combination of butter and shortening—results in the perfect mix of flavor and flakiness.

¼ cup butter, softened (½ stick)
¼ cup vegetable shortening
1 ¼ cups all-purpose flour
1 tablespoon granulated sugar

¼ teaspoon salt
1 egg yolk
2 tablespoons ice water

FILLING

3 eggs
1 15-ounce can pumpkin
½ cup granulated sugar
¼ cup packed dark brown sugar
1 teaspoon ground cinnamon
½ teaspoon salt

½ teaspoon ground ginger
¼ teaspoon ground cloves
¼ teaspoon ground nutmeg
¾ cup whole milk
¼ cup heavy cream

1. Prepare the crust by beating together the butter and short-ening until smooth and creamy. Chill until firm.
2. Sift together the flour, sugar and salt in a medium bowl.
3. Using a pastry knife or fork, cut the chilled butter and short-ening into the dry ingredients until the flour is mixed in and it has a crumbly texture. Mix egg yolk and ice water into the dough with a spoon then form it into a ball with your hands. Don't work the dough too much or your crust will lose its flakiness. Flakey crust is good crust. Cover dough ball with plastic wrap to sit until the filling is ready.
4. Prepare filling by beating eggs. Add pumpkin and stir well to combine.
5. Combine sugars, cinnamon, salt, ginger, cloves, and nutmeg in a small bowl. Stir spice mixture into the pumpkin. Mix in milk and cream.
6. Preheat oven to 425 degrees. While oven preheats let filling sit so that it can come closer to room temperature.
7. Unwrap pie dough, then roll it flat on a floured surface and line a 9-inch pie dish.
8. When oven is hot pour filling into pie shell, and bake for 15 minutes. Reduce heat to 350 degrees and bake for another

50 to 60 minutes or until a knife stuck in the middle comes out clean.

9. Cool pie, then chill. Slice chilled pie into 6 pieces to serve restaurant-size portions. Whipped cream on top is optional, but highly recommended.

* MAKES 6 SERVINGS.

• • • •

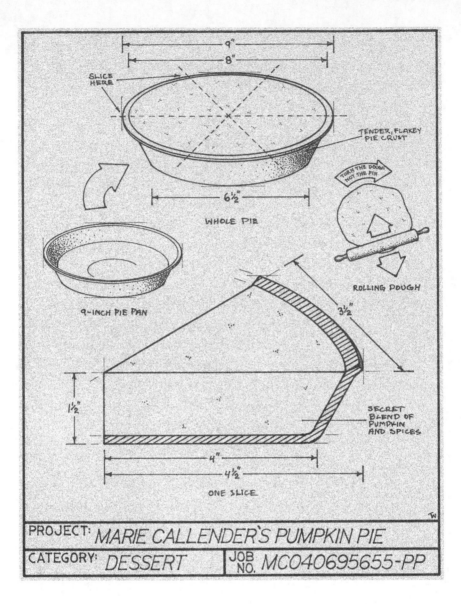

9"

8"

SLICE HERE

TENDER, FLAKEY PIE CRUST

6½"

WHOLE PIE

9-INCH PIE PAN

TURN THE DOUGH NOT THE PIN

ROLLING DOUGH

3½"

SECRET BLEND OF PUMPKIN AND SPICES

1½"

4"

4½"

ONE SLICE

PROJECT: *MARIE CALLENDER'S PUMPKIN PIE*

CATEGORY: *DESSERT*

JOB NO. *MC040695655-PP*

MIMI'S CAFE CARROT RAISIN BREAD

It's dark, moist and delicious, and it comes in a breadbasket to your table at this French-themed West Coast casual restaurant chain. Now the tastiest carrot bread ever can be yours to create at home with a couple of grated carrots, molasses, raisins and chopped walnuts. You'll be baking this one in the oven for at least an hour. That should be enough time to warm up the house and send amazing smells wafting through every room. Line the carpet with newspaper to catch the family drool.

1 ½ cups all-purpose flour
1 teaspoon cinnamon
1 teaspoon baking powder
1 teaspoon baking soda
1 teaspoon salt
1 cup vegetable oil
1 cup plus 2 tablespoons
    granulated sugar

3 eggs
¼ cup molasses
½ teaspoon vanilla extract
1 cup shredded carrot
1 cup raisins
¾ cup chopped walnuts

1. Preheat oven to 350 degrees.
2. Combine flour, cinnamon, baking powder, baking soda, and salt in a large mixing bowl.
3. In another bowl, combine oil, sugar, eggs, molasses, and vanilla with an electric mixer. Add shredded carrot and mix. Add raisins and walnuts and mix well by hand.

4. Pour flour mixture into the other ingredients and stir until combined.
5. Pour batter into two ungreased 8-inch loaf pans. Bake for 60 minutes, or until done.

• MAKES 2 LOAVES.

• • • •

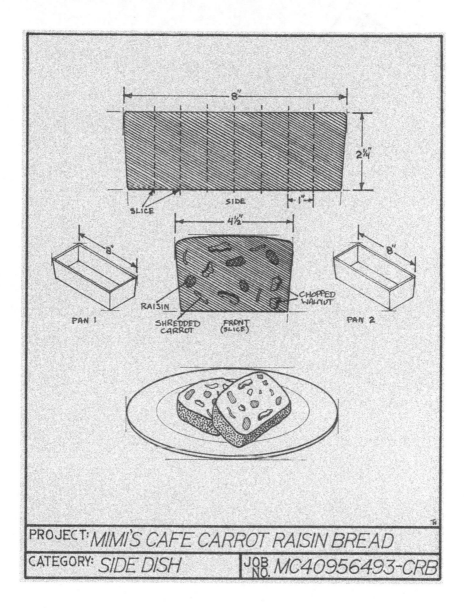

8"

2¼"

SLICE

SIDE

1"

4½"

PAN 1

8"

RAISIN

SHREDDED CARROT

FRONT (SLICE)

CHOPPED WALNUT

PAN 2

8"

TM

PROJECT: *MIMI'S CAFE CARROT RAISIN BREAD*

CATEGORY: *SIDE DISH*

JOB NO. *MC40956493-CRB*

MIMI'S CAFE
CORN CHOWDER

Arthur Simms was in the restaurant business for many years before he opened the first Mimi's Cafe with his son, Tom, in Anaheim, California in 1978. Back in the Golden Age of Hollywood Arthur was the guy running things in the MGM Studios commissary where, on any given day, Jean Harlow, Clark Gable and Judy Garland might stop in for a grazing. Arthur named his New Orleans–influenced, bistro-style restaurant after a woman he met and fell in love with in Paris during the war. Today it's Tom who runs the show at this growing 93-unit chain where regulars return for the staple favorites including the French Market Onion Soup (on page 230), Carrot Raisin Bread (on page 225) and the delicious Corn Chowder, cloned here.

2 tablespoons butter
2 large celery stalks, chopped
    (about 1 ½ cups)
½ cup diced white onion
4 cups water
1 russet potato, peeled and cut
    into ½-inch cubes (about
    2 cups)
1 bay leaf

1 15-ounce can cream-style corn
    (with liquid)
1 15-ounce can whole kernel corn
    (with liquid)
2 teaspoons granulated sugar
½ teaspoon salt
⅛ teaspoon ground white pepper
½ cup all-purpose flour
1 ½ cups half-and-half

GARNISH

minced fresh parsley

1. Sauté celery and onion in the butter for 5 minutes in a large saucepan or stock pot. Don't brown.
2. Add 4 cups of water, chopped potato, and bay leaf. Bring to a boil, then reduce heat and simmer for 15 minutes, stirring occasionally.
3. Add creamed corn (with liquid), canned whole corn (with liquid), sugar, salt, and white pepper and simmer for 20 minutes, stirring occasionally.
4. Combine flour with half-and-half and stir until smooth. Add this mixture to the soup and simmer for an additional 10 to 15 minutes, until thick.
5. Serve by spooning a 1-cup portion into a small bowl and sprinkle a little minced fresh parsley on top.

• MAKES 2 QUARTS (EIGHT 1-CUP SERVINGS).

•   •   •   •

MIMI'S CAFE FRENCH MARKET ONION SOUP

☆   ✌   💣   ✎   ☯   ✂   ☞

You might not think that a tough World War II flying ace would open a restaurant called "Mimi's," but that's exactly what happened in the 1970s. Arthur J. Simms flew spy missions over France during the war and helped liberate a small French town near Versailles. After the war, Arthur ran the commissary at MGM studios in Hollywood, stuffing the bellies of big-time celebs like Judy Garland, Clark Gable and Mickey Rooney. He later joined his son, Tom, in several restaurant ventures including one called "French Quarter" in West Hollywood. This was the prototype for the French-themed Mimi's Cafe. In 1978, the first Mimi's opened in Anaheim, California. Today there are over 90 Mimi's in the chain with a new one opening every other week; all of them serving this amazing French onion soup that's topped with not one, not two . . . *three* different cheeses. Oui!

¼ cup butter
3 medium white onions, sliced
3 14-ounce cans beef broth
   (Swanson is best)
1 teaspoon salt
¼ teaspoon garlic powder
3 tablespoons Kraft grated
   Parmesan cheese

6 to 12 slices French bread
   (baguette)
6 slices Swiss cheese
6 slices mozzarella cheese
6 tablespoons shredded Parmesan
   cheese

1. Sauté onions in melted butter in a large soup pot or saucepan for 15 to 20 minutes or until onions begin to brown and turn transparent.
2. Add beef broth, salt and garlic powder to onions. Bring mixture to a boil, then reduce heat and simmer uncovered for 1 hour. Add the grated Parmesan cheese in the last 10 minutes of cooking the soup.
3. When soup is done, preheat oven to 350 degrees and toast the French bread slices for about 10 to 12 minutes or until they begin to brown. When bread is done, set oven to broil.
4. Build each serving of soup by spooning about 1 cup of soup into an oven-safe bowl. Float a toasted slice or two of bread on top of the soup, then add a slice of Swiss cheese on top of that. Place a slice of mozzarella on next and sprinkle 1 tablespoon of shredded Parmesan cheese over the top of the other cheeses.
5. Place the soup bowl on a baking sheet and broil for 5 to 6 minutes or until the cheese begins to brown.

- MAKES 6 SERVINGS.

•   •   •   •

OLIVE GARDEN LIMONCELLO LEMONADE

Need a simple cocktail for a hot day when the thought of lemonade makes your mouth water? Try this one. You start crafting this new signature blender drink by making lemon syrup from scratch from lemon juice, sugar and water. Track down some limoncello—an Italian lemon liqueur—and Smirnoff citrus vodka (or your favorite citrus vodka). Now you're just a press of the blender button away from being refreshed.

¼ cup hot water
¼ cup granulated sugar
4 teaspoons lemon juice
1 ounce Smirnoff citrus vodka

1 ounce limoncello liqueur
4 ounces lemonade (Minute Maid
   or Country Time)
1 to 2 cups ice

GARNISH
slice of lemon

1. Make lemon syrup by combining hot water, sugar and lemon juice.
2. When syrup is cool, make drink by combining ¾ ounce of lemon syrup with citrus vodka, limoncello, lemonade and ice in a blender. Blend on high speed until ice is crushed. Start

with one cup of ice and add additional ice, if needed, to make drink slushy. Serve in a 16-ounce glass with a straw and a thin slice of lemon on the rim of the glass.

• MAKES 1 DRINK.

•   •   •   •

OLIVE GARDEN BRUSCHETTA

MENU DESCRIPTION: *"A traditional topping of roma tomatoes, fresh basil and extra-virgin olive oil. Served with freshly toasted ciabatta bread."*

Olive Garden's recently redesigned bruschetta recipe improves on the Italian chain's previous version. The tomato salad includes a little sun-dried tomato and balsamic vinegar, and it is now served in a separate dish rather than on the bread. Now the bread doesn't get soggy. The tomatoes are finely diced before mixing with the other ingredients, and the ciabatta bread is sprinkled with a little grated Parmesan cheese before it's toasted. Try to find a nice, chewy loaf of Italian bread for this dish—get the best bread in the store. The better your bread, the better your bruschetta.

3 firm roma tomatoes, finely
    diced (about 1 ½ cups)
1 tablespoon minced fresh basil
2 teaspoons minced garlic
2 teaspoons diced marinated
    sun-dried tomatoes
2 teaspoons extra virgin olive oil
1 teaspoon balsamic vinegar

¼ teaspoon salt

9 to 10 slices ciabatta bread (or
    Italian bread)
1 tablespoon grated Parmesan
    cheese
pinch dried parsley flakes

1. Toss diced tomatoes with basil, garlic, sun-dried tomatoes, olive oil, vinegar, and salt in a medium bowl. Cover and chill 1 hour.
2. When you are ready to serve the dish, preheat oven to 450 degrees.
3. Combine Parmesan cheese with dried parsley in a small bowl. Arrange the bread slices on a baking sheet. Sprinkle a couple pinches of the Parmesan cheese mixture over each bread slice. Bake for 5 minutes or until the bread starts to crisp.
4. Pour tomato mixture into a serving dish (strain off the liquid), and serve it up alongside the toasted bread slices.

- SERVES 4.

• • • •

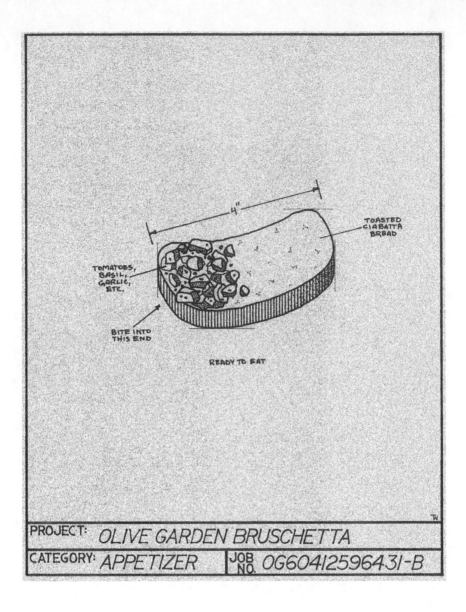

4"

TOASTED
CIABATTA
BREAD

TOMATOES,
BASIL,
GARLIC,
ETC.

BITE INTO
THIS END

READY TO EAT

TW

PROJECT:	OLIVE GARDEN BRUSCHETTA	
CATEGORY: APPETIZER	JOB NO.	OG60412596431-B

OLIVE GARDEN
SICILIAN SCAMPI

MENU DESCRIPTION: *"Large shrimp sautéed in extra-virgin olive oil with white wine, garlic and lemon."*

Once you have the onion, garlic and parsley all chopped up, this clone of a top appetizer pick at the Garden takes only a few minutes to assemble. Cooks at Olive Garden speed up the process by using what they call "scampi butter"—chilled blocks of butter with all the spices, garlic, and onions already in it—so that each serving is prepared quickly and consistently without any tedious measuring. When the shrimp is done, each one is placed on the inside end of five toasted Italian bread slices which have been arranged on the plate in a spoke-like fashion (you can also use a French baguette with the slices cut at an extreme angle). One shrimp is also placed in the middle of the plate, and the delicious sauce is poured over the top. I've included diced roma tomato here as an optional garnish, since one Olive Garden used it, but another location on the other side of town did not. As for the shrimp, use medium-size (they're called 31/40) that are already peeled, but with the tails left on. Then all you have to do to butterfly them is make a deep cut (don't go all the way through) on the outside of the shrimp where the vein was. As the shrimp cooks, they will curl and spread open.

2 tablespoons butter
1 tablespoon olive oil
1 teaspoon minced white onion
1 teaspoon minced garlic
1 tablespoon Chablis wine
6 fresh medium shrimp, butterfly
    cut with tails on
1 teaspoon lemon juice
½ teaspoon minced fresh parsley

pinch salt
pinch ground black pepper
pinch crushed red pepper flakes
1 tablespoon heavy cream
1 tablespoon sliced canned black
    olives

5 slices Italian bread, toasted

OPTIONAL GARNISH
½ diced roma tomato
freshly grated Parmesan cheese

1. Toast the sliced Italian bread on a sheet pan in your oven set to broil, or in a toaster oven. The bread should toast for 1 to 2 minutes on each side, or until light brown. Arrange the bread slices in a spoke-like fashion on a serving plate then dance over to the stove to whip up the scampi.
2. Heat a small skillet over medium heat. Add 2 tablespoons butter and 1 tablespoon olive oil to the pan.
3. When the butter has melted add the minced onion and garlic. Make sure your heat isn't up too high or the garlic may burn, and turn brown and bitter. When the onion and garlic have sautéed for just a few seconds, add the wine to the pan.
4. Immediately add the shrimp to the pan.
5. After you add the shrimp, quickly add the lemon juice, parsley, salt, black pepper, and crushed red pepper and cook shrimp for 1 to 2 minutes, tossing occasionally.
6. After a minute or two, when the shrimp is done, add the cream and olives. Cook for 15 seconds or so, then use tongs to place one shrimp on the end of each bread slice (the ends that are in the center of the plate), and place one shrimp in the center of the plate (not on bread). Pour the sauce from the pan over the shrimp and serve the dish with a diced

roma tomato sprinkled over the top and freshly grated Parmesan cheese, if that's your thing.

• Makes an appetizer for two.

• • • •

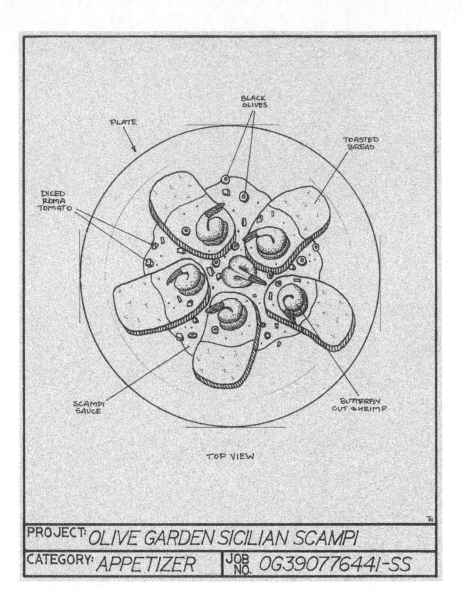

BLACK
OLIVES

PLATE

TOASTED
BREAD

DICED
ROMA
TOMATO

SCAMPI
SAUCE

BUTTERFLY
CUT SHRIMP

TOP VIEW

PROJECT:	*OLIVE GARDEN SICILIAN SCAMPI*	
CATEGORY:	*APPETIZER*	JOB NO. *OG39077644I-SS*

OLIVE GARDEN STUFFED MUSHROOMS

MENU DESCRIPTION: *"Parmesan, Romano and mozzarella cheese, clams and herb breadcrumbs baked in mushroom caps."*

Breadcrumbs, clams and three types of cheese are baked into white mushroom caps in this clone of a top pick from Olive Garden's appetizer menu. Simply mix all the stuffing ingredients together in a bowl, fill the mushroom caps, sprinkle on some minced red bell pepper, cover the mushrooms with a blanket of mozzarella cheese slices, and bake. After 15 minutes you'll have a great appetizer or hors d'oeuvre for 4 to 6 people— that's twice the serving size of the dish from the restaurant.

⅓ cup Progresso breadcrumbs
    (herb flavor)
¼ cup canned minced clams
    (drain liquid)
1 tablespoon shredded Parmesan
    cheese
1 tablespoon shredded Romano
    cheese
½ teaspoon minced garlic

3 tablespoons chicken broth
12 medium white button
    mushrooms with stems
    removed
3 tablespoons butter, melted
2 tablespoons minced red bell
    pepper
2 to 3 slices mozzarella cheese
½ teaspoon minced fresh parsley

1. Preheat oven to 450 degrees.
2. Combine breadcrumbs, clams, Parmesan cheese, Romano cheese, and garlic in a medium bowl. Use your hands to mix everything together. Add the chicken broth 1 tablespoon at a time and stir after each addition with a spoon. Keep the stuffing fluffy by not over stirring.
3. Fill each of the mushroom caps with 1 to 2 teaspoons of the stuffing (depending on the size of the mushroom). Keep the filling pretty loose but make the top surface flat to support the sliced cheese. Arrange the stuffed mushrooms in a shallow baking dish with the stuffing facing up.
4. Use a brush to dab melted butter over each mushroom. Add enough so that the butter trickles down the sides of each mushroom and rests in the baking dish. Pour any leftover butter into the dish, then scoot the mushrooms next to each other.
5. Sprinkle the minced red bell pepper over the tops of the stuffed mushrooms.
6. Arrange the slices of cheese over the mushrooms. Tear the slices to cover all of the mushrooms leaving no stuffing un-covered.
7. Bake the mushrooms for 12 to 15 minutes or until the cheese is golden brown.
8. When the mushrooms come out of the oven immediately sprinkle them with ½ teaspoon of minced parsley and serve.

*   SERVES 4 TO 6 AS AN APPETIZER.

•   •   •   •

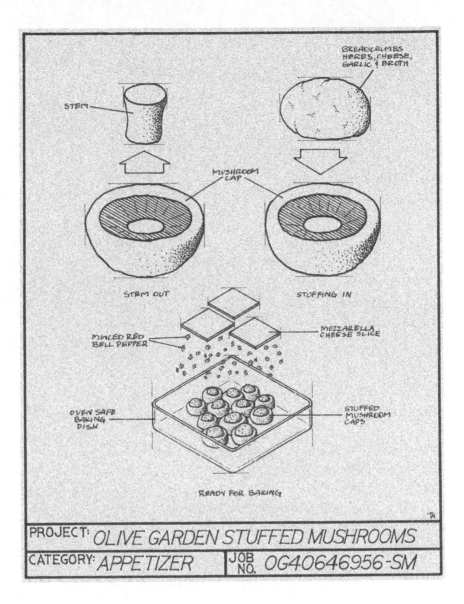

STEM

BREADCRUMBS, HERBS, CHEESE, GARLIC & BROTH

MUSHROOM CAP

STEM OUT

STUFFING IN

MINCED RED BELL PEPPER

MOZZARELLA CHEESE SLICE

OVEN SAFE BAKING DISH

STUFFED MUSHROOM CAPS

READY FOR BAKING

PROJECT: *OLIVE GARDEN STUFFED MUSHROOMS*

CATEGORY: *APPETIZER*   JOB NO. *OG40646956-SM*

OLIVE GARDEN
TOASTED RAVIOLI

Sold as a finger-food appetizer along with marinara dipping sauce, Olive Garden's delicious breaded ravioli can be cloned with ease using one of several varieties of premade raviolis carried in just about any supermarket. It's best to use the fresher raviolis found in the refrigerated section, but you can also use frozen raviolis; you just have to let them thaw first before breading them. The Toasted Ravioli at O.G. has a beefy inside, but you can use any ravioli that tickles your fancy including chicken, sausage, vegetarian, or cheese. As for the breading, find Progresso brand Italian style breadcrumbs. Contadina is another popular brand, but their version is much too salty for a good clone.

6 to 10 cups canola oil (as
    required by fryer)
1 egg, beaten
1 cup milk
1 cup Progresso Italian style
    breadcrumbs

12 premade beef raviolis (fresh, or
    if frozen, thawed)
1 tablespoon grated Parmesan
    cheese

ON THE SIDE
½ cup marinara sauce, warmed

1. Preheat the oil in your deep fryer to 325 degrees.
2. Combine the beaten egg with the milk in shallow bowl. Pour the breadcrumbs into another shallow bowl.
3. Bread the ravioli by dipping each one in the milk and egg, then into the breadcrumbs. Arrange the breaded ravioli on a plate and let them sit for 5 minutes so that the breading sticks like a champ.
4. When the raviolis have rested, drop a handful into the oil. Depending on the size of your fryer, you may want to fry the raviolis in batches so they aren't too crowded. Fry the breaded raviolis for 1 to 2 minutes or until they're golden brown. Remove them to a draining rack or a paper-towel lined plate.
5. When all the raviolis are cooked, arrange them on a serving plate and sprinkle 1 tablespoon of grated Parmesan cheese over the top. Serve the dish with a small bowl of warmed marinara sauce on the side for dipping.

- SERVES 3 TO 4 AS AN APPETIZER.

• • • •

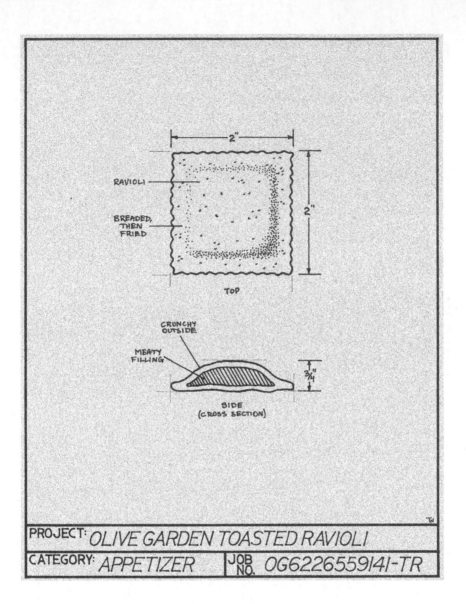

RAVIOLI

BREADED,
THEN
FRIED

2"

2"

TOP

CRUNCHY
OUTSIDE

MEATY
FILLING

3/4"

SIDE
(CROSS SECTION)

PROJECT: OLIVE GARDEN TOASTED RAVIOLI

CATEGORY: APPETIZER   JOB NO. OG6226559141-TR

OLIVE GARDEN PASTA E FAGIOLI

MENU DESCRIPTION: *"White and red beans, ground beef, tomatoes and pasta in a savory broth."*

It's amazing how many lousy clone recipes for this delicious chili-like soup are floating around the Internet. Cooking message boards, and questionable sites that claim to have "actual restaurant recipes" have for years passed off numerous versions only to have disappointed home chefs waste ingredients. What's puzzling is they leave out major ingredients that you can clearly see in the real thing, like the carrots, or ground beef, or two kinds of beans. Others don't even get the pasta right—it's obviously ditali pasta, which are short little tubes. So, if you want the taste of Olive Garden's famous Pasta e Fagioli at home, this may be the only recipe out there that will live up to a side-by-side taste test. Beware of imitation imitations!

1 pound ground beef
1 small onion, diced (1 cup)
1 large carrot, julienned (1 cup)
3 stalks celery, chopped (1 cup)
2 cloves garlic, minced
2 14.5-ounce cans diced tomatoes
1 15-ounce can red kidney beans
   (with liquid)
1 15-ounce can Great Northern
   beans (with liquid)

1 15-ounce can tomato sauce
1 12-ounce can V-8 juice
1 tablespoon white vinegar
1½ teaspoons salt
1 teaspoon dried oregano
1 teaspoon dried basil
½ teaspoon ground black pepper
½ teaspoon dried thyme

½ pound (½ pkg.) ditali pasta

1. Brown the ground beef in a large saucepan or pot over medium heat. Drain off most of the fat.
2. Add onion, carrot, celery and garlic and sauté for 10 minutes.
3. Add remaining ingredients, except pasta, and simmer for 1 hour.
4. About 50 minutes into the simmering, cook the pasta in 1½ to 2 quarts of boiling water over high heat. Cook for 10 minutes or just until pasta is *al dente,* or slightly tough. Drain.
5. Add the pasta to the large pot of soup. Simmer for 5 to 10 minutes more and serve.

- SERVES 8.

•   •   •   •

OLIVE GARDEN MINESTRONE SOUP

MENU DESCRIPTION: *"Fresh vegetables, beans and pasta in a light tomato broth—a vegetarian classic."*

This classic Italian soup is jam-packed with beans, zucchini, onion, tomatoes, carrots, pasta, and spices; but O.G.'s secret formula doesn't include chicken broth. Canned vegetable broth found in the soup aisle of most markets works as a base here in this secret formula that bursts with flavor as a purely vegetarian dish.

3 tablespoons olive oil
1 cup minced white onion (about 1 small onion)
½ cup chopped zucchini
½ cup frozen cut Italian green beans
¼ cup minced celery (about ½ stalk)
4 teaspoons minced garlic (about 4 cloves)
4 cups vegetable broth (Swanson is good)
2 15-ounces cans red kidney beans, drained
2 15-ounce cans small white beans or Great

Northern beans, drained
1 14-ounce can diced tomatoes
½ cup julienned or shredded carrot
2 tablespoons minced fresh parsley
1½ teaspoons dried oregano
1½ teaspoons salt
½ teaspoon ground black pepper
½ teaspoon dried basil
¼ teaspoon dried thyme
2 bay leaves
3 cups hot water
4 cups fresh baby spinach
½ cup small seashell pasta

1. Heat olive oil over medium heat in a large saucepan or stock-pot. Sauté onion, zucchini, green beans, celery and garlic in the oil for 5 minutes or until onion begins to turn translucent.
2. Add broth to pot, plus drained beans, tomatoes, carrot, spices, bay leaves, and hot water. Bring soup to a boil, then reduce heat and simmer for 20 minutes.
3. Add spinach leaves and pasta and cook for an additional 20 minutes or until desired soupy thickness.

• MAKES ABOUT EIGHT 1 ½-CUP SERVINGS.

• • • •

OLIVE GARDEN CHICKEN SCAMPI

MENU DESCRIPTION: *"Chicken breast tenderloins sautéed with bell peppers, roasted garlic and onions in a garlic cream sauce over angel hair."*

This dish is a big favorite of Olive Garden regulars. Chicken tenderloins are lightly breaded and sautéed along with colorful bell peppers and chopped red onion. Angel hair pasta is tossed into the pan along with a healthy dose of fresh scampi sauce. Then it's time to ring the dinner bell. If you're cooking for two, you can prepare this dish for the table in one large skillet, saving the remaining ingredients for another meal. If you're making all four servings at once, you need two skillets. By the way, if you can't find fresh chicken tenderloins (the tender part of the chicken breast), you can usually find big bags of them in the freezer section. If that's how you buy them, you'll have plenty left over after this recipe, but they're really good to have around.

SCAMPI SAUCE

3 tablespoons butter
2 tablespoons minced white onion
¼ cup minced garlic (8 to 12 cloves)
1½ cups Chablis wine
½ teaspoon salt
½ teaspoon Italian seasoning

½ teaspoon crushed red pepper flakes
¼ teaspoon ground black pepper
2 teaspoons minced fresh parsley
1 cup heavy cream

5 to 6 quarts water

16 ounces angel hair pasta

4 tablespoons olive oil

12 chicken tenderloins

½ cup all-purpose flour

1 green bell pepper, cut into bite-size strips

1 red bell pepper, cut into bite-size strips

1 yellow bell pepper, cut into bite-size strips

1 chopped red onion

2 teaspoons minced fresh parsley

OPTIONAL GARNISH
freshly grated Parmesan cheese

1. Make scampi sauce by melting butter in a preheated pan over medium/low heat. Add 2 tablespoons minced white onion and sauté for 2 to 4 minutes or until the onion begins to brown. If the butter begins to burn, turn down the heat. When the onion is beginning to brown, add the minced garlic and sauté for another 30 seconds. Don't let the garlic burn. After about 30 seconds add the wine, salt, Italian seasoning, red pepper flakes, and black pepper, and bring mixture to a simmer. Simmer for approximately 15 to 18 minutes or until the sauce has reduced by half. Add parsley and heavy cream and simmer uncovered for about 10 minutes. Do not let mixture reach a boil.

2. Bring 4 quarts of water to a boil in a large pot. Add the angel hair pasta and cook for about 4 minutes or until pasta is al dente, or mostly tender with just a slight toughness. Drain the pasta in a colander or sieve when done, then hit it with some cold water to prevent sticking and to keep it from cooking further.

3. If preparing all four servings, preheat the oil in 2 large skillets over medium heat (if making just 2 servings, you'll need only one skillet and half of the total ingredients—save the rest for another meal). Lightly salt and pepper the chicken tenderloins, then coat each one in the flour that has been measured into a large bowl. Arrange all of the coated tenderloins

on a plate before sautéing 6 tenderloins in each pan. Cook the tenderloins for 3 to 5 minutes on one side or until golden brown.

4. When the chicken is brown on one side, flip each of the pieces, and move them to the side of the pans, then add an even amount of the sliced peppers and chopped red onion to the center of each skillet. Continue cooking the chicken and vegetables for 4 to 6 minutes or until the chicken is browned and the veggies are beginning to brown on the edges.

5. Divide the scampi sauce in half and pour it over the chicken and other ingredients in each pan. Add 2 portions of pasta to each pan, then toss everything a bit and continue to cook for a couple minutes or until the pasta is heated through. Prepare each dish by serving equal amounts of pasta onto each of four plates. Use a spoon or tongs to add the peppers and onion on top of each pile of pasta. Arrange three chicken tenderloins onto the center of the pasta.

6. Sprinkle each plate with about ½ teaspoon of fresh parsley and serve it up with freshly grated Parmesan cheese if desired.

• MAKES 4 SERVINGS (BUT CAN BE EASILY DIVIDED INTO 2 SEPARATE SERVINGS FOR 2).

•   •   •   •

OLIVE GARDEN CHOCOLATE LASAGNA

☆   ✌   💣   ✏   ☯   ✂   ☞

MENU DESCRIPTION: *"Layers of rich chocolate cake and sweet buttercream icing."*

To simplify this clone recipe, we'll start with a box of cake mix and tweak it a bit to add a little cherry flavor. The buttercream frosting spread between the three layers of the "lasagna" is a breeze to make from scratch. The real secret to this *Top Secret Recipe* is how we put it all together. You've got to make two slices through the edge of the baked cake to create the three thin layers, so grab a long serrated knife. Lay down some wax paper under the cake to help you turn the cake while you slice. Slide the whole thing over near the edge of the counter so that you can keep the knife parallel to the countertop, and you should have no trouble at all. Another technique is to drag a long piece of dental floss through the cake twice. The floss will glide right through the cake with ease, giving you two clean slices. You can use your favorite chocolate cake mix for the recipe, but be sure not to use one with pudding in it or one that is "extra moist." (Duncan Hines Moist Deluxe is one such brand.) These mixes make slicing and layering difficult because the baked cake falls apart so easily.

1 18.25-ounce box dark chocolate or chocolate fudge cake mix (not too moist)
1 ¼ cups water
⅓ cup vegetable oil
3 eggs
2 teaspoons cherry extract
vegetable shortening

BUTTERCREAM FROSTING

1 ½ cups butter, softened
  (3 sticks)
4 cups powdered sugar ·
¼ cup milk

½ teaspoon vanilla extract

4 ounces semi-sweet chocolate,
  chilled

1. Make the cake in a 13x9-inch baking pan following instructions on the box of cake mix, but add cherry extract to the
mix. (Preheat oven to 350 degrees; mix cake mix, water, oil,
and eggs together in a large bowl; pour batter into pan
greased generously with shortening.) Allow the cake to cool
completely.
2. When cake is cool, make buttercream frosting by first whipping the soft butter in a large bowl with an electric mixer on
high speed. Add two cups of the powdered sugar, mix well,
then add remaining powdered sugar. Add ¼ cup of whole
milk and vanilla, then mix on high speed for 2 minutes or
until frosting is smooth and creamy.
3. Turn cake out of the pan onto wax paper. Using both hands,
carefully flip the cake over, so that it's right-side up, onto another strip of wax paper. Now you're going to cut through
the cake twice, creating three layers. We'll start at the
bottom slice. First slide the cake over to the edge of your
kitchen counter. This way you can drop your hand with the
knife down below the counter at the edge to get a nice,
straight cut through the cake. Using a long bread knife or
other long serrated knife, cut through the bottom third of
the cake. Spin the cake and wax paper so that you can cut
through all sides (your knife probably won't get all the way
through to the other side). When the cake is sliced, carefully
flip the top section over onto the other sheet of wax paper.
Frost the bottom layer of cake with approximately ⅓ of the
buttercream frosting. Break the chilled semi-sweet chocolate
into little bits that are a tad smaller than chocolate chips. A
good way to do this is to put the chilled chocolate into a
large zip-top bag, then use the handle of a butter knife to

smash the unsuspecting chocolate into pieces. Sprinkle about ⅓ of the chocolate bits over the frosting on the bottom layer.

4. Turn the top section back over onto the bottom layer. Again, slice through the top section creating the final two layers. Carefully flip the top over onto the wax paper, and frost the new layer as you did with the first layer, adding chocolate bits as well. You may, at this point, wish to slice the top into thirds across the width of the cake. This makes flipping over the top layer much easier. It's also how you're going to slice the cake later, so you'll never see the cuts. Any cracks or breaks are no big deal since you'll just cover up the goofs with frosting.

5. Carefully reassemble the top section on the rest of the cake. If you have a large bulge in the center of the cake, you may wish to slice that off so that the cake is flatter on top. Throw that slice away. Frost the top of the cake with the remaining frosting, then sprinkle on the remaining chocolate bits.

6. The cake is served as triangular slices. So, slice it up by first cutting through the middle of the cake, lengthwise. Next cut across the cake through the middle (widthwise) twice. Now you have six slices that just need to be cut from corner to corner one time each, creating 12 triangular slices. Chill any cake you don't eat that day.

• MAKES 12 SERVINGS.

• • • •

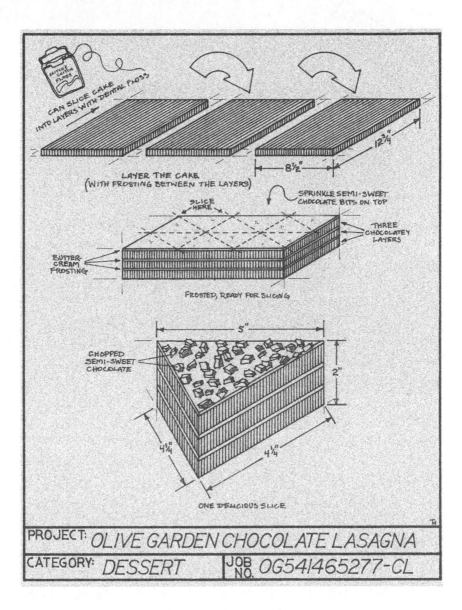

CAN SLICE CAKE INTO LAYERS WITH DENTAL FLOSS

LAYER THE CAKE
(WITH FROSTING BETWEEN THE LAYERS)

8½"

12¾"

SLICE HERE

SPRINKLE SEMI-SWEET CHOCOLATE BITS ON TOP

THREE CHOCOLATEY LAYERS

BUTTER-CREAM FROSTING

FROSTED, READY FOR SLICING

5"

CHOPPED SEMI-SWEET CHOCOLATE

2"

4¼"

4¼"

ONE DELICIOUS SLICE

PROJECT: OLIVE GARDEN CHOCOLATE LASAGNA

CATEGORY: DESSERT

JOB NO. OG541465277-CL

OLIVE GARDEN
FROZEN TIRAMISU

The amazing Frozen Tiramisu—a dessert in a glass—requires espresso syrup that you can clone with sugar and either espresso or strong coffee. Each serving requires just a little of the syrup, so you'll have plenty left over for additional servings of the cocktail for your happy toasting partners.

¼ cup hot espresso
¼ cup granulated sugar
¾ ounce Tuaca liqueur

¾ ounce Kahlua liqueur
1 cup vanilla ice cream
1 cup ice

GARNISH
whipped cream   cocoa

1. Make espresso syrup by combining hot espresso with granulated sugar.
2. When espresso syrup is cool, make drink by combining ½ ounce of the espresso syrup with Tuaca, Kahlua, vanilla ice cream and ice in a blender on high speed and blend until smooth. Serve in a tall 16-ounce glass, with whipped cream on top. Sprinkle a little cocoa on top of the whipped cream (tap it through a mesh strainer), and serve drink with a straw.

• MAKES 1 DRINK.

• • • •

OLIVE GARDEN
LEMON CREAM CAKE

☆   ✌   💣   ✏   ☯   ✄   ☞

MENU DESCRIPTION: *"Delicate white cake and lemon cream filling with a vanilla crumb topping."*

I like simple. So, to keep this clone as uncomplicated as possible, I've designed the recipe using a common white cake mix. I picked Betty Crocker brand, but any white cake mix you can get your hands on will do. Just note that each brand (Duncan Hines, Pillsbury, etc.) requires slightly different measurements of additional ingredients (oil, eggs). Follow the directions on the box for mixing the batter, then pour it into a greased 10-inch springform pan and bake until done. The filling recipe is a no-brainer and the crumb topping is a cinch. When your cake is assembled, stick it in the fridge for a few hours, and soon you'll be serving up 12 cloned slices of the addictive Olive Garden dessert.

CAKE
1 18.25-ounce box Betty Crocker
   white cake mix
1 ¼ cups water

⅓ cup vegetable oil
3 egg whites

LEMON CREAM FILLING
8 ounces cream cheese, softened
2 cups powdered sugar

3 tablespoons lemon juice
1 cup heavy whipping cream

VANILLA CRUMB TOPPING
½ cup all-purpose flour
½ cup powdered sugar

¼ cup cold butter
½ teaspoon vanilla extract

GARNISH
powdered sugar

1. Make white cake following the directions on the box. Pour batter into a greased 10-inch cake pan or springform pan, and bake at 350 degrees for 40 to 45 minutes. Allow cake to cool completely when it comes out of the oven.

2. Make lemon cream filling by mixing cream cheese and powdered sugar in a medium bowl with an electric mixer until smooth. Mix in lemon juice.

3. Whip cream in a large bowl with an electric mixer on high speed until it forms stiff peaks. Fold cream cheese mixture with whipped cream. Stir gently by hand until blended.

4. Make crumb topping by combining flour and powdered sugar in a medium bowl. Add butter and dribble in the vanilla extract. Use your hands to mix cold butter into flour and sugar. Break butter into smaller and smaller pieces as you incorporate it into the dry ingredients. Be sure not to press the mixture together. You want to end up with a very crumbly consistency with pieces no bigger than a pea. (If you have trouble making small crumbs, pop the bowl into your fridge for a few minutes.) Chill this crumb topping until you are ready to use it.

5. When the cake is cool, slice it in half through the middle and remove the top. Spread all but ½ cup of the lemon cream mixture onto the bottom half of the cake, then carefully replace the top half of the cake.

6. Spread the remaining ½ cup of cream filling over the top and sides of the cake. Sprinkle the crumb topping on top of the cake and press it onto the sides all the way around the cake.

7. Now chill the cake for at least 3 hours before you serve it. When you are ready to dig in, slice cake into 12 slices. Serve each slice topped with powdered sugar tapped through a strainer.

• SERVES 12.

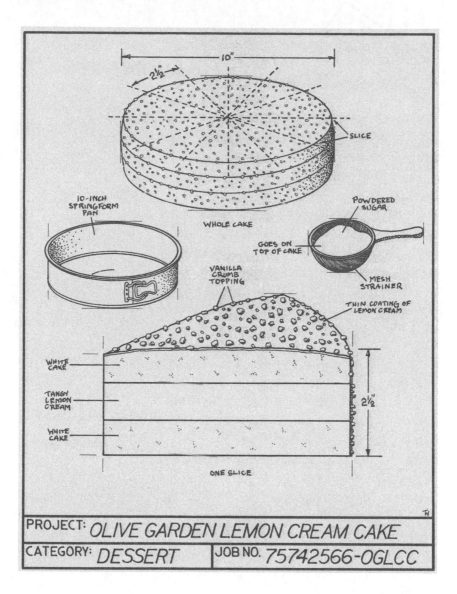

10"

2½

SLICE

10-INCH
SPRINGFORM
PAN

WHOLE CAKE

POWDERED
SUGAR

GOES ON
TOP OF CAKE

MESH
STRAINER

VANILLA
CRUMB
TOPPING

THIN COATING OF
LEMON CREAM

WHITE
CAKE

TANGY
LEMON
CREAM

2½

WHITE
CAKE

ONE SLICE

PROJECT: *OLIVE GARDEN LEMON CREAM CAKE*

CATEGORY: *DESSERT*   **JOB NO.** *75742566-OGLCC*

OLIVE GARDEN
TIRAMISU

MENU DESCRIPTION: *"The classic Italian dessert. A layer of creamy custard set atop espresso-soaked ladyfingers."*

In Italian, *tiramisu* means "pick me up" or "cheer me up." And when you taste the delicious combination of mascarpone cheese (sometimes referred to as Italian cream cheese), cream cheese, ladyfingers, espresso and Kahlua it will be hard not to smile. Olive Garden's tiramisu is very dense, which sets it apart from most tiramisu recipes that require the cheese mixture to be folded into whipped cream. This technique, however, makes a tiramisu that is too fluffy and light to be a decent clone. Besides, the whipped cream hides the cheese flavors, and that's just not a good way to make this tiramisu. So get out your double boiler for the egg yolks (a metal bowl over a saucepan of simmering water will also do) and snag some ladyfingers (ladyfingers are miniature cakes about the size of two fingers side-by-side). You can either make your own espresso, use extra strong coffee as a substitute, or, next time you're at Starbucks, order up a quadruple shot of espresso to go.

4 egg yolks
2 tablespoons milk
⅔ cup granulated sugar
2 cups mascarpone cheese
¼ teaspoon vanilla extract

1 cup heavy cream
20 to 24 ladyfingers
½ cup cold espresso
¼ cup Kahlua coffee liqueur
2 teaspoons cocoa powder

1. Fill a medium saucepan halfway with water and bring it to a boil over medium/high heat, then reduce the heat so that the water is simmering. Whisk egg yolks, milk and sugar together in a medium metal bowl, then place the bowl on top of the saucepan (you can also use a double boiler for this step). Stir the mixture often for 8 to 10 minutes or until the mixtures thickens. Remove the bowl from the heat, and to it add the 2 cups of mascarpone cheese and the vanilla. Get in there and whisk the cheese like the dickens until it smoothes out.
2. In a separate bowl, whip the cream with an electric mixer until thick.
3. Slowly fold the whipped cream into the mascarpone mixture until it's completely incorporated, but don't over mix or that goodness could lose its fluff and flatten out on you.
4. Combine the espresso and Kahlua in a large, shallow bowl. One-by-one, quickly dip each ladyfinger in the espresso. The ladyfinger will soak up the espresso/Kahlua mixture like a sponge, so dip quickly. Arrange half of the dipped ladyfingers side-by-side on the bottom of an 8x8-inch serving dish or baking pan.
5. Spoon about half of the cheese mixture over the ladyfingers, then add another layer of soaked ladyfingers on top of the cheese mixture.
6. Spoon the remaining cheese mixture over the second layer of ladyfingers and spread it evenly.
7. Put two teaspoons of cocoa powder in a tight-mesh strainer and gently tap the side of the strainer to add an even dusting of cocoa powder over the top of the dessert.
8. Cover and chill for several hours. To serve, slice the dessert twice across and down creating 9 even portions. And don't worry about how that first serving looks—it's always the hardest to get out.

• MAKES 9 SERVINGS.

•   •   •   •

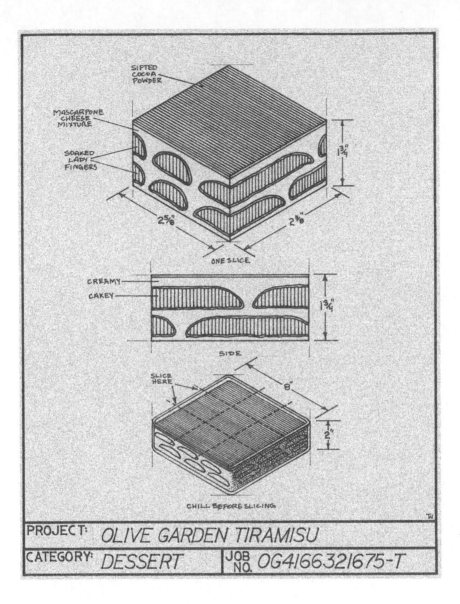

SIFTED COCOA POWDER

MASCARPONE CHEESE MIXTURE

SOAKED LADY FINGERS

2⅝"

2⅛"

1¾"

ONE SLICE

CREAMY

CAKEY

1¾"

SIDE

SLICE HERE

8"

2"

CHILL BEFORE SLICING

PROJECT:	*OLIVE GARDEN TIRAMISU*	
CATEGORY: *DESSERT*	JOB NO.	*OG4166321675-T*

ORIGINAL PANCAKE HOUSE APPLE PANCAKE

MENU DESCRIPTION: *"Oven baked with fresh apples and pure Sikiyan cinnamon glaze."*

Fresh, high-quality ingredients and traditional recipes are what make this growing chain a frequent favorite for anyone who stops in. The star of the show is the incredible apple pancake, the chain's signature dish. To make a dead-on clone, Granny Smith apples are sautéed in butter, brown sugar and cinnamon, then allowed to cool for a bit. That way, when the batter is poured into the pan the apples and glaze stay anchored to the bottom. This technique also prevents the glaze from penetrating into the batter as the pancake bakes since there is now an apple barrier preventing any mixing of the ingredients. When the pancake comes out of the oven it's flipped over onto a plate and the apples are smiling away at you right there on top, dripping with a delicious cinnamon-sugar glaze. You won't need any syrup for this one, that's for sure. Just a light dusting of powdered sugar, if you like, then get ready for an apple pancake unlike any other.

2 medium Granny Smith apples, peeled and sliced (about 16 to 20 slices each)

3 tablespoons butter (salted)
½ cup light brown sugar
¾ teaspoon ground cinnamon

3 eggs
⅓ cup whole milk
⅓ cup heavy cream
2 tablespoons granulated sugar

¼ teaspoon salt
¼ teaspoon vanilla
½ cup all-purpose flour

OPTIONAL GARNISH

powdered sugar

1. Peel and quarter two Granny Smith apples. Slice the core from each of the quarters, then slice the quarters into 4 to 5 slices each. Melt 3 tablespoons butter in a 9- or 10-inch skillet. If you've got a skillet that isn't nonstick, such as cast-iron, that's the best kind for this recipe, although any oven-safe skillet this size will still work. Add brown sugar, cinnamon and the sliced apples and sauté for 10 minutes, stirring occasionally. Turn off the heat and let the pan sit for one hour so that the apples and glaze will stick to the bottom when the batter is poured on top.
2. Preheat oven to 475 degrees.
3. In a medium bowl, beat eggs with an electric mixer. Mix in milk, cream, sugar, salt and vanilla. Mix until sugar is dissolved. Sift in flour and mix until smooth. Let batter rest for about 10 minutes.
4. After the apples have cooled for an hour, pour the batter over the apples and pop the whole thing into the oven for 16 to 18 minutes or until the top begins to brown. Remove it from the oven, cool for one minute, and then use a spatula to loosen the pancake around the edges. Put a plate on top of the pan and invert the pan and plate together so that the pancake comes out upside down on the plate. Serve with an optional dusting of powdered sugar over the top.

• MAKES 1 LARGE PANCAKE.

TIDBITS

You can substitute ⅔ cup half-and-half for the ⅓ cup heavy cream and ⅓ cup whole milk, but I found that using the cream and milk separately makes for a fluffier texture and better clone.

• • • •

ORIGINAL PANCAKE HOUSE GERMAN PANCAKE

MENU DESCRIPTION: *"Oven baked. Dusted with powdered sugar, served with lemon and butter."*

It was in 1953 when Les Highet and Erma Huenke opened their first Original Pancake House in Portland, Oregon, using traditional pancake recipes handed down through the generations. Now, with over 100 restaurants in 25 states, this breakfast chain is generating a huge cult following. That's probably because many of the authentic ethnic pancake recipes can't be found at IHOP, and this is a clone recipe for one of them. The German pancake is baked at a high temperature in a skillet, where it puffs up radically in the oven, then settles down as it comes out. It's dusted with powdered sugar, and served with whipped butter and lemon wedges on the side. Delicious. You can also apply maple syrup, if that's your thing. A cast-iron skillet seems to work best for this recipe (just as they used back in the day), but you can get away with nonstick, if that's all you've got. If that's the case, you should know that the pancake will morph more radically in a nonstick pan and practically overflow the skillet—especially if it isn't a deep one. Even so, once you get it out of the oven it will shrink back down and taste just as amazing.

3 large eggs	2 tablespoons granulated sugar
⅓ cup whole milk	¼ teaspoon salt
⅓ cup heavy cream	¼ teaspoon vanilla

½ cup all-purpose flour   1 tablespoon melted butter
                                       (salted)

GARNISH
powdered sugar

SERVE WITH
lemon wedges   maple syrup
butter

1. Preheat oven to 475 degrees.
2. In a medium bowl, beat eggs with an electric mixer. Mix in milk, cream, sugar, salt and vanilla. Mix until sugar is dissolved. Sift in flour and mix until smooth. Let batter rest for about 10 minutes.
3. Coat the bottom of a 9- or 10-inch oven-safe skillet (cast-iron is best) with melted butter. Pour batter into the pan, and bake for 14 to 16 minutes or until golden brown on top and dark brown around the edges. Pancake will rise substantially while cooking. Remove the pancake from the oven and let it sit for about a minute. Loosen the pancake around the edge with a spatula, then slide it out of the pan onto a plate. Dust with powdered sugar, and serve with lemon wedges, butter and syrup on the side.

- MAKES 1 LARGE PANCAKE.

TIDBITS

You can substitute ⅔ cup half-and-half for the ⅓ cup heavy cream and ⅓ cup whole milk, but I found that using the cream and milk separately makes for a fluffier texture and better clone.

•   •   •   •

TOP SECRET RECIPES VERSION OF

OUTBACK STEAKHOUSE HONEY WHEAT BUSHMAN BREAD

Along with your meal at this huge national steakhouse chain, comes a freshly baked loaf of dark, sweet bread, served on its own cutting board with soft whipped butter. One distinctive feature of the bread is its color. How does the bread get so dark? Even though this recipe includes molasses and cocoa, these ingredients alone will not give the bread its dark chocolate brown color. Usually commercially produced breads that are this dark—such as pumpernickel or dark bran muffins—contain caramel color, an ingredient often used in the industry to darken foods. Since your local supermarket will not likely have this mostly commercial ingredient, we'll create the brown coloring from a mixture of three food colorings—red, yellow and blue. If you decide to leave the color out, just add an additional 1 tablespoon of warm water to the recipe. If you have a bread machine, you can use it for kneading the bread (you'll find the order in which to add the ingredients to your machine in Tidbits). Then, to finish the bread, divide and roll the dough in cornmeal, and bake on a sheet pan in your home oven.

DOUGH

1¼ cups warm water	1 tablespoon cocoa
2 teaspoons granulated sugar	1 teaspoon salt
2¼ teaspoons (1 pkg.) yeast	2 tablespoons butter, softened
2 cups bread flour	¼ cup honey
1¾ cups whole wheat flour	2 tablespoons molasses

COLORING

1¼ teaspoons red food coloring	1 teaspoon blue food coloring
1 teaspoon yellow food coloring	cornmeal for dusting

1. Mix sugar with warm water, then dissolve the yeast in the solution. In five minutes the solution will begin to foam as the yeast begins its gassy dance party.
2. While the yeast is waking up, mix the flours, cocoa, and salt in a large bowl. Mix butter into the dry mixture with your hands. Make an impression in the middle of the dry mixture. Add the honey and molasses into the well. Mix the food coloring with the yeast solution, then pour the solution into the well. Stir from the middle bringing the dry mixture into the wet stuff, slowly at first, then quickly as you incorporate all the ingredients. You will eventually have to use your hands to combine everything. Knead the dough for 10 minutes on a lightly floured surface, then roll the dough into a ball and place it into a covered bowl in a warm place for 1 to 1½ hours or until it has doubled in size.
3. When the dough has doubled, separate it into 6 even portions. Roll each dough portion into logs that are 6 inches long and 2 inches wide. Pour cornmeal onto your rolling surface. Moisten your hands then rub water onto each dough log and roll it in the cornmeal. Arrange the rolled dough on a baking sheet and cover it with plastic wrap. Set the dough in a warm spot to rise for another hour or so until the loaves have doubled in size.

4. Preheat the oven to 350 degrees. Uncover the dough and bake it for 35 to 40 minutes in the hot oven. When the bread is done, take it out of the oven and let it cool for 10 to 15 minutes. Serve the bread with a sharp bread knife and butter on the side. If you want whipped butter, like you get at the restaurant, just use an electric mixer on high speed to whip some butter until it's fluffy.

• MAKES 6 SMALL LOAVES.

TIDBITS

If you'd like to use a bread machine to knead the dough, just add the ingredients in the following order: Mix the food coloring with the water, then add the colored water to the bread pan followed by the flours, sugar, salt, butter, cocoa, honey, molasses, and yeast. Set the machine to knead and walk away. When the dough's done kneading and rising, go to step #3 of this recipe and take it from there.

•   •   •   •

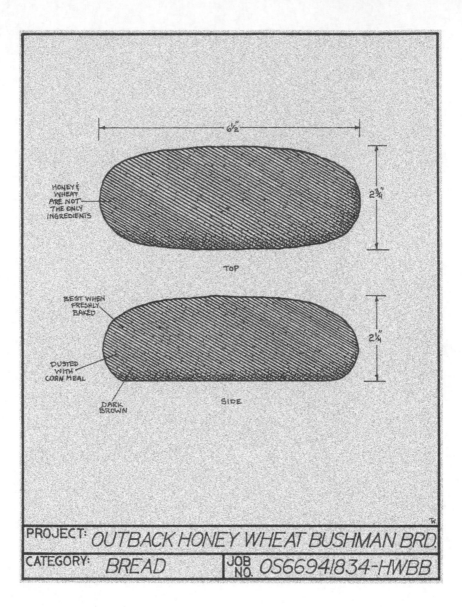

6½"

HONEY &
WHEAT
ARE NOT
THE ONLY
INGREDIENTS

2¾"

TOP

BEST WHEN
FRESHLY
BAKED

2¼"

DUSTED
WITH
CORN MEAL

DARK
BROWN

SIDE

PROJECT: *OUTBACK HONEY WHEAT BUSHMAN BRD.*

CATEGORY: *BREAD*   **JOB NO.** *OS66941834-HWBB*

OUTBACK STEAKHOUSE GRILLED SHRIMP ON THE BARBIE

MENU DESCRIPTION: *"Seasoned and served with Outback's own Remoulade sauce."*

This recipe makes the same size appetizer serving that you get in the restaurant. That's only 6 shrimp—enough for me, but what are you guys having? Thank goodness the remoulade sauce and the shrimp seasoning formulas yield enough for more, so you can grill up to a pound of shrimp with this cool clone. You can often find bags of frozen shrimp that have been peeled, but with the tails left on. Those are perfect for this recipe.

REMOULADE SAUCE
½ cup mayonnaise
1 tablespoon stone ground mustard
2 teaspoons milk
1¼ teaspoons prepared horseradish
1 teaspoon minced celery
1 teaspoon minced white onion
1 teaspoon minced green bell pepper
¼ teaspoon minced fresh parsley
¼ teaspoon white vinegar
¼ teaspoon paprika
⅛ teaspoon ground black pepper
⅛ teaspoon ground cayenne pepper
pinch salt

SHRIMP SEASONING

½ teaspoon salt
¼ teaspoon garlic powder
¼ teaspoon onion powder
¼ teaspoon ground black
    pepper

¼ teaspoon chili powder
¼ teaspoon granulated
    sugar
⅛ teaspoon cayenne pepper
dash ground allspice

6 large shrimp (21 to 25 per
    pound), thawed if frozen
fresh lemon juice

1 tablespoon butter, melted
minced fresh parsley

1. Preheat your grill to high heat.
2. Make the remoulade sauce by mixing the ingredients to-gether in a small bowl. Cover and chill this sauce until you are ready to use it.
3. Prepare the shrimp seasoning by mixing the spices together in a small bowl.
4. Remove the shell from the shrimp. Keep the last segment of the shell and the tail. Remove the black vein that runs down the back of the shrimp. Stick a skewer through the middle of each shrimp. Push them together on the skewer so that they are "spooning" each other.
5. Squeeze some fresh lemon juice over the cuddling shrimp.
6. Brush melted butter generously over the top of the shrimp.
7. Sprinkle a bit of the seasoning on next. Don't use a heavy coating of seasoning
8. Place the shrimp onto your hot grill with the seasoning side down. Brush some more butter over the other side of the shrimp followed by another light sprinkle of seasoning.
9. After 3 minutes or so the face-down side of the shrimp should be browned and showing some light charring. Flip the shrimp over and grill for an additional 2 to 3 minutes or until browned on the other side.
10. Remove the shrimp from the grill and slide them off the

skewer onto a slice of garlic butter coated bread (see Tidbits). Sprinkle with a pinch of fresh parsley.

- MAKES 1 TO 2 SERVINGS.

TIDBITS

It is best to use a clone for the Bushman Bread (on page 269) as a bed for your shrimp. Just slice an inch-thick piece off through the middle of the bread. This will give you a slice that is about 8 inches long and 2 to 3 inches wide. Crush a clove of garlic and mix it with your leftover melted butter. Brush this garlic butter on both sides of the bread and toast it until lightly brown. If you don't feel up to making the bread, you can use any bread you might have around that is in the shape of a hoagie roll. Or you may just wish to serve the shrimp on its own without the bread bed.

•　•　•　•

LEAVE ON TAIL SECTION

SKEWER

TASTY SPICE BLEND

SIX PEELED RAW SHRIMP

REMOVE SKEWER BEFORE SERVING

THIS GOES ON THE "BARBIE"

DIP SHRIMP IN HERE

BREAD IS BRUSHED WITH GARLIC BUTTER

REMOULADE SAUCE

SERVE ON A SLICE OF BREAD

PROJECT: *OUTBACK GRILLED SHRIMP ON BARBIE*

CATEGORY: *APPETIZER* JOB NO. *OS58941554-GSOTB*

OUTBACK STEAKHOUSE KOOKABURRA WINGS

MENU DESCRIPTION: *"Known as Buffalo chicken wings here in the States."*

No, Outback Steakhouse is not the country's largest importer of Australian woodland kingfisher wings. Despite the name, these tasty wings don't come from the wild birds also known as kookaburras. Instead, this appetizer is made the old fashioned way—with good ol' American chickens. And as with the traditional recipe, these wings are coated with Louisiana hot sauce; but it's the breading that makes them unique. This clone recipe uses a secret blend of powdered cheese sprinkles and spices. Kraft powdered cheese can be found near the Kraft Parmesan cheese or near the macaroni and cheese kits in your supermarket. If you can't track it down, use Molly McButter cheese sprinkles. If you can't find that, get a box of macaroni and cheese (it's cheap) and use the cheese from inside there. Keep the leftover macaroni noodles for a pasta recipe later.

10 chicken wing drumettes (see Tidbits)

6 to 10 cups vegetable shortening or oil (amount required by your fryer)

WING COATING

2 tablespoons all-purpose flour
1 tablespoon Kraft Macaroni &
    Cheese cheddar cheese
    topping (or Molly McButter
    cheese sprinkles)
1 ¼ teaspoons salt
1 teaspoon chili powder

¾ teaspoon ground black pepper
½ teaspoon cayenne pepper
¼ teaspoon paprika
¼ teaspoon onion powder
¼ teaspoon garlic powder
⅛ teaspoon ground cumin
dash ground cloves

2 tablespoons Crystal brand
    Louisiana hot sauce

1 teaspoon water

ON THE SIDE

bleu cheese dressing

celery sticks

1. Preheat shortening (you may also use vegetable or canola oil) to 375 degrees.
2. Make the spiced breading for your wings by combining the wing coating ingredients (flour through cloves) in a medium bowl. Stir well.
3. Dip each wing, one at a time into the breading. Give each one a light coating of the stuff. Arrange the breaded wings on a plate and let them sit uncovered in the refrigerator for about 15 minutes.
4. When the shortening or oil is hot, lower the wings into it. Fry for 7 to 10 minutes, or until the wings are brown.
5. While the wings are frying, mix the hot sauce and water together in a small bowl.
6. When the wings are done, drain them for a moment on paper towels or a rack. Drop the hot wings into a large plastic container with a lid. Pour the sauce over the wings. Cover the container and gently shake it to coat the wings with sauce.

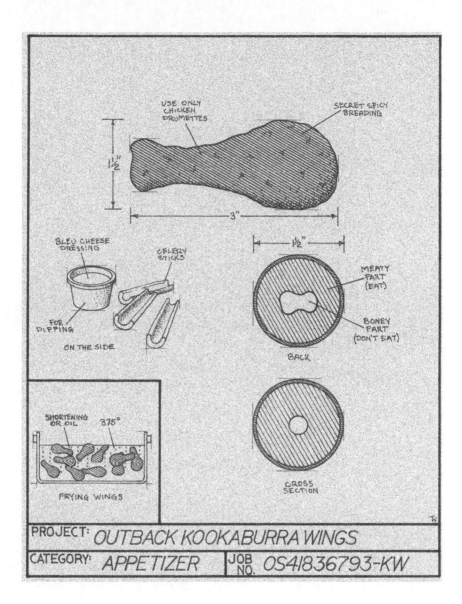

USE ONLY
CHICKEN
DRUMETTES

SECRET SPICY
BREADING

1½"

3"

1½"

BLEU CHEESE
DRESSING

CELERY
STICKS

FOR
DIPPING

ON THE SIDE

MEATY
PART
(EAT)

BONEY
PART
(DON'T EAT)

BACK

SHORTENING
OR OIL

375°

FRYING WINGS

CROSS
SECTION

PROJECT: *OUTBACK KOOKABURRA WINGS*

CATEGORY: *APPETIZER* JOB NO. *OS41836793-KW*

7. Use tongs to remove the wings from the container. Arrange them on a plate with bleu cheese dressing and celery sticks on the side.

- MAKES 2 TO 3 SERVINGS AS AN APPETIZER.

TIDBITS

There are two types of frozen chicken wings out there—the giant party wings that come with a couple dozen pieces per bag, and the smaller wings with nearly twice the number per bag. These smaller wings are what the restaurant uses and what you should use for this recipe. Because of the size of the bigger wings, they just don't fry up as well.

Also, you should know that most restaurants use shortening for frying. That's what I suggest you use if you want your wings closer to the real thing.

•   •   •   •

OUTBACK STEAKHOUSE BLEU CHEESE DRESSING

If you've had the Kookaburra Wings from Outback, then you've tasted the chain's thick and creamy bleu cheese dressing served up on the side. Use this stuff when you need an excellent dipping sauce for your next batch of wings, or just pour it over a salad and dive in.

1 cup mayonnaise
2 tablespoons buttermilk or whole milk
1 tablespoon crumbled bleu cheese

⅛ teaspoon coarse ground black pepper
⅛ teaspoon onion powder
⅛ teaspoon garlic powder

1. Mix all ingredients together by hand in a small bowl until smooth.
2. Cover and chill for 30 minutes before serving.

• MAKES 1 CUP.

• • • •

OUTBACK STEAKHOUSE CAESAR SALAD DRESSING

You can't buy it in the stores, but now you can make it from scratch in mere minutes. Best of all, this dressing keeps for a couple weeks in the fridge in a covered container . . . if it's even around that long.

1 cup mayonnaise	2 cloves garlic, pressed
¼ cup egg substitute	2 teaspoons granulated sugar
¼ cup grated Parmesan cheese	½ teaspoon coarse ground
2 tablespoons water	pepper
2 tablespoons olive oil	¼ teaspoon salt
1 ½ tablespoons lemon juice	¼ teaspoon dried parsley flakes,
1 tablespoon anchovy paste	crushed fine

1. Combine all ingredients in a medium bowl. Use an electric mixer to beat ingredients for about 30 seconds.
2. Cover bowl and chill for several hours so that flavors can develop.

• MAKES APPROXIMATELY 2 CUPS.

• • • •

OUTBACK STEAKHOUSE HONEY MUSTARD SALAD DRESSING

Outback makes their sauces and salad dressings from scratch every day following master formulas in a corporate cookbook. Now you've got a secret recipe of your own that will easily duplicate the taste of their hugely popular house honey mustard recipe. You'll need just three basic ingredients and about two minutes of free time to make it.

½ cup mayonnaise
¼ cup honey

2 tablespoons Grey Poupon Dijon mustard

Combine all ingredients in a medium bowl. Cover and chill to store.

• MAKES ¾ CUP.

• • • •

OUTBACK STEAKHOUSE RANCH SALAD DRESSING

This always-popular growing restaurant chain makes a tasty version of creamy ranch dressing for its house and Queensland salads. To get the same unique flavor and creaminess of the original at home, mates, you'll need one teaspoon of Hidden Valley Ranch instant salad dressing mix swimming in there with the mayo and buttermilk and other spices. Since there's three teaspoons of dressing mix per packet, you'll now be able to make three batches of dressing with one envelope of dressing mix.

1 teaspoon Hidden Valley Ranch salad dressing mix (Buttermilk Recipe)
1 cup mayonnaise
½ cup buttermilk

¼ teaspoon coarse grind black pepper
⅛ teaspoon paprika
⅛ teaspoon garlic powder

1. Combine all ingredients in a medium bowl. Mix well.
2. Cover bowl and chill dressing for at least 30 minutes before serving.

• MAKES 1½ CUPS.

TIDBITS

Make sure you are using the Hidden Valley Ranch dressing mix that says "Buttermilk Recipe." It's the one that comes in 0.4 ounce packets. Any other mix won't work as well for this clone.

• • • •

OUTBACK STEAKHOUSE TANGY TOMATO DRESSING

So many folks expressed interest in a knockoff of this dressing that I couldn't put it off any longer. Suited up in protective gear and tricked out with safety goggles, I set out to tackle the tangy beast. Now, fresh out of the underground laboratory, comes this simple formula for re-creating Outback's popular sour/sweet salad topper in your own cozy kitchen.   Mix it together, heat it up, cool it down, and store it in the fridge until salad time.

½ cup plus 1 tablespoon ketchup
⅓ cup water
¼ cup granulated sugar
¼ cup white vinegar
2 tablespoons olive oil
¼ teaspoon paprika

¼ teaspoon coarse grind black
   pepper
¼ teaspoon garlic powder
¼ teaspoon cayenne pepper
⅛ teaspoon onion powder
pinch dried thyme

Combine all ingredients in a small saucepan over medium heat. Bring to a boil, whisking often, then reduce heat and simmer, uncovered, for 5 minutes. Cover the dressing until cool, then pop it in the refrigerator to chill out.

• MAKES 1 CUP.

• • • •

OUTBACK STEAKHOUSE CINNAMON APPLE OBLIVION

MENU DESCRIPTION: *"Vanilla ice cream covered in cinnamon apples and pecans topped with caramel sauce."*

Roll a scoop of creamy vanilla ice cream in homemade candied pecans. Surround the ice cream with warm cinnamon apples and drizzle caramel over the top. Sprinkle fresh cinnamon-butter croutons on the dessert and you've got an irresistible clone that will make your diet cry "uncle!" For the croutons, the restaurant uses leftover Honey Wheat Bushman Bread (clone on page 269). But if you don't have plans to make that one you can use any sweet bread from the store, such as Hawaiian Sweet Bread or Pillsbury Honey White Bread.

CANDIED PECANS

½ cup granulated sugar

2 tablespoons water

½ teaspoon cinnamon

1 teaspoon butter

1¼ cups chopped pecans

CINNAMON CROUTONS

2 cups cubed Bushman Bread
    (or any sweet bread)

⅓ cup salted butter (⅔ stick)

2 tablespoons granulated sugar

½ teaspoon ground cinnamon

CINNAMON APPLES

1 20-ounce can apple pie filling
¼ teaspoon ground cinnamon
1 tablespoon brown sugar
1 quart vanilla ice cream

½ cup caramel topping
  (Smucker's is good)
1½ cups whipped cream
4 fresh strawberries

1. For candied pecans, combine ½ cup granulated sugar, 2 tablespoons water, 1 teaspoon butter, and ½ teaspoon cinnamon in a small saucepan over medium heat. Heat until mixture boils and all sugar granules are dissolved.
2. Add chopped pecans to mixture and stir for 1 to 2 minutes over heat. Be sure that all pecans are well-coated.
3. Pour mixture onto a large plate and continue to stir until mixture hardens and begins to break up. You should be able to separate all of the nuts.
4. For the croutons, preheat the oven to 300 degrees. Pour the slice bread cubes onto an ungreased cookie sheet and bake for 15 to 20 minutes or until the bread has turned light brown. Stir halfway through cooking time.
5. Melt the butter in a skillet over medium heat. Pour baked croutons into the pan and sauté until the bread is coated with butter. Combine the 2 tablespoons of sugar and ½ teaspoon of cinnamon in a small bowl. Sprinkle this mixture over the croutons while stirring so that the croutons are coated with cinnamon/sugar. Remove croutons from the heat and pour them onto a plate to cool.
6. Prepare apples by carefully mixing them with ¼ teaspoon cinnamon and 1 tablespoon of brown sugar in a large bowl. You want to be sure you don't stir hard enough to break up the apples. Microwave the apples for 1 to 2 minutes or until hot.
7. To assemble the dessert, first roll four cup-size scoops of ice cream in the pecan pieces. You can do this step ahead of time if you like, keeping the pecan-covered scoops in your freezer.
8. Place an ice cream scoop onto a small plate, then pour about

a tablespoon of caramel over the ice cream. Dribble another tablespoon around the base of the ice cream onto the plate.

9. Spread the hot apples around the base of the ice cream being sure to divide them evenly amongst the four servings.
10. Divide the croutons into four portions and sprinkle them on the apples around the base of the ice cream scoop on each plate.
11. Spread a generous portion of whipped cream onto the top of each scoop of ice cream.
12. Top off each dish with a fresh strawberry.

• MAKES 4 SERVINGS.

•   •   •   •

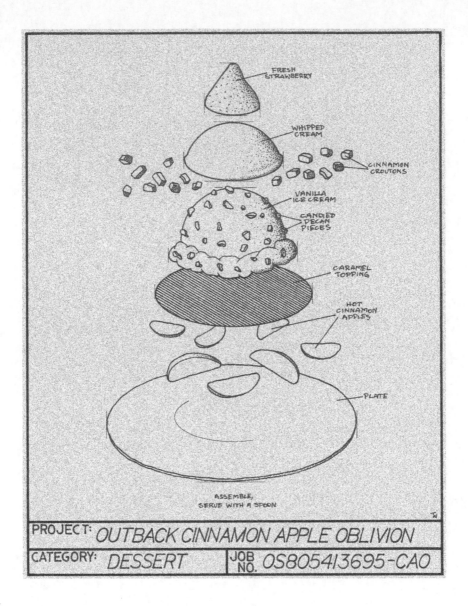

FRESH STRAWBERRY

WHIPPED CREAM

CINNAMON CROUTONS

VANILLA ICE CREAM

CANDIED PECAN PIECES

CARAMEL TOPPING

HOT CINNAMON APPLES

PLATE

ASSEMBLE, SERVE WITH A SPOON

PROJECT:	OUTBACK CINNAMON APPLE OBLIVION	
CATEGORY: DESSERT	JOB NO.	OS805413695-CAO

OUTBACK STEAKHOUSE SYDNEY'S SINFUL SUNDAE

MENU DESCRIPTION: *"Vanilla ice cream rolled in toasted coconut, covered in chocolate sauce and topped with whipped cream."*

Here's an easy-to-make dessert that will give you a cool way to use the vanilla ice cream that's calling to you from the freezer. The key to this recipe is to plan ahead just a bit by placing your serving plates into the freezer (give 'em at least 30 minutes). While the plates are chilling out, you toast some coconut flakes in the oven. After that, it's all about the presentation. You can top your master-piece with canned whipped cream or make your own from the simple recipe included here.

WHIPPED CREAM
1 cup heavy whipping cream
3 tablespoons granulated sugar

½ teaspoon vanilla extract
pinch salt

1 cup shredded coconut
4 large scoops vanilla ice cream

1 cup fudge topping
8 large, ripe strawberries

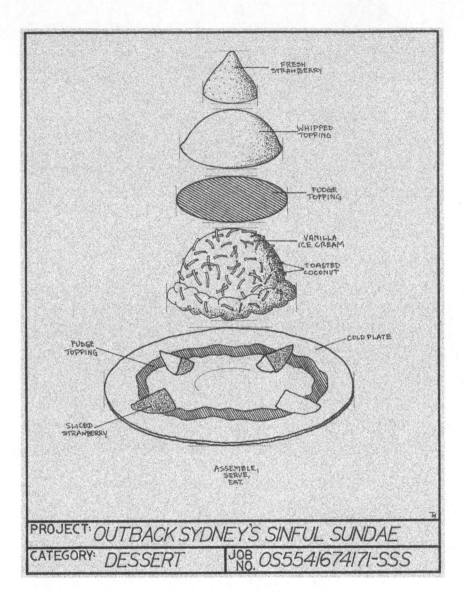

FRESH STRAWBERRY

WHIPPED TOPPING

FUDGE TOPPING

VANILLA ICE CREAM

TOASTED COCONUT

COLD PLATE

FUDGE TOPPING

SLICED STRAWBERRY

ASSEMBLE, SERVE, EAT.

PROJECT:	*OUTBACK SYDNEY'S SINFUL SUNDAE*	
CATEGORY: *DESSERT*	JOB NO.	*OS554I674I7I-SSS*

1. Put four dinner plates into the freezer.
2. Make whipped cream by combining cream with sugar, vanilla and salt with an electric mixer on high speed. It helps if the bowl has been chilled ahead of time. When cream makes stiff peaks, cover and chill until you need it.
3. Preheat the oven to 300 degrees.
4. Spread the coconut over the bottom of the inside of a large oven pan. Shake the pan a little to spread the coconut evenly.
5. Bake the coconut for 25 to 30 minutes or until the coconut is a light, golden brown. You may have to stir or shake the coconut in the last 10 minutes to help it brown evenly. Allow the coconut to cool on a plate or in a large bowl.
6. Heat up the fudge topping for 15 to 20 seconds in the microwave. Get the plates out of the freezer and make a circle of fudge on each of the plates.
7. Roll each scoop of ice cream in the coconut until it is well coated. Press down on the ice cream to help the coconut stick. Place a coconut-covered scoop of ice cream onto the center of the plate, then spoon about 2 tablespoons of fudge over the top of the ice cream.
8. Use an ice cream scoop to scoop a large portion of whipped cream and stack it on each of the scoops of ice cream.
9. Cut the stems from the strawberries. Cut four of the strawberries lengthwise into quarters. Position the sliced strawberries around the base of each scoop of ice cream on the ring of fudge. Place a whole strawberry onto the whipped cream on the top of each dessert. Serve with a spoon and a smile.

- MAKES 4 SERVINGS.

•　•　•　•

P. F. CHANG'S MAI TAI

MENU DESCRIPTION: *"It's our signature recipe."*

Bring the tropical spirit of this drink to your house with a clone of this potent cocktail from the growing Chinese bistro chain. Mai tai is Tahitian for "out of this world," and P. F. Chang's recipe is one of the best and most authentic. The secret to a true mai tai is found in the original recipe developed by Trader Vic in 1944: It's almond-flavored syrup called "orgeat." You can find the sweet stuff in stores that sell coffee flavorings (Torani is one very popular brand), or from bar supply outlets. Not only can you use the orgeat for making the best cocktails on the planet, but you can also use the syrup to wake up your next cup of java. If you can't find orgeat, there's a clone recipe included in Tidbits.

1 ½ ounces Bacardi light rum
¾ ounce triple sec
¾ ounce orgeat syrup
3 ounces orange juice

3 ounces pineapple juice
splash Bacardi 151 rum
splash dark rum

GARNISH
pineapple wedge
maraschino cherry

1. Fill a 16-ounce glass with ice.
2. Add the light rum, triple sec, orgeat, orange juice, and pineapple juice; then give the drink a quick stir.
3. Splash the 151 and dark rum on top. Do not stir.
4. Make a small cut in the pineapple wedge, then stick a toothpick into the pineapple wedge on the opposite edge. Pierce a maraschino cherry onto the toothpick. Slip the pineapple slice onto the rim of the glass (into the cut that you made). Add a straw, and serve.

• MAKES 1 DRINK.

TIDBITS

You can maker a pretty close version of orgeat syrup from scratch by dissolving ½ cup granulated sugar in ½ cup boiling water. Add ½ teaspoon of almond extract and ¼ teaspoon coconut extract. Cool before using, then measure as you would the real thing.

•　•　•　•

P. F. CHANG'S CHANG'S SPARE RIBS

☆   ✌   💣   ✏   ☯   ✂   ☞

MENU DESCRIPTION: *"Wok-seared with Chang's barbecue sauce."*

One of the most popular eats on P. F. Chang's kickin' appetizer menu are the spare ribs that arrive slathered with Asian-style barbecue sauce. The Asian flavor comes from the addition of sweet hoisin sauce to a fairly rudimentary barbecue sauce formula. Chang's menu says these ribs are spare ribs although they appear to be much smaller, more like baby backs. You can certainly use either for this recipe, just be sure to trim the ribs first, since the restaurant version is lean, clean ribs with no extra meat or fat hanging off. There are several ways to cook pork ribs—P. F. Chang's likes to boil theirs first then move on to a quick deep fry. After that, the ribs are tossed with the sauce in wok and served piping hot. A serving of these ribs at the restaurant is 6 individual ribs, but since a full rack is as many as 12 ribs, this recipe will make twice what you get in a serving at the bustling bistro.

SAUCE

1 cup ketchup	1 tablespoon rice vinegar
1 cup light corn syrup	
½ cup hoisin sauce	1 rack pork spare ribs
½ cup water	4 cups vegetable oil
⅓ cup light brown sugar, packed	1 teaspoon sesame seeds
2 tablespoons minced onion	1 tablespoon diced green onion

1. Make the sauce by combining ingredients in a medium saucepan over medium heat. Bring mixture to a boil, then reduce heat and simmer for 5 minutes, until thick. Cool.
2. To cook the ribs the P. F. Chang's way, you will need to first boil them in water. Heat up 12 to 16 cups of water in a large saucepan or Dutch oven. Add a couple teaspoons of salt to the water. As water boils, trim the excess fat and meat off the ribs. Slice between the bones of each rib to separate the ribs. When the water is boiling, toss the ribs in, bring the water back to a boil and boil the ribs for 12 to 14 minutes. No pink will show when they are done. Remove ribs to a plate to cool.
3. When the ribs have cooled you can either store them in an airtight bag in the refrigerator until you are ready for the final cooking step, or you can move on to that step now by heating up 4 cups of vegetable oil in a large saucepan over medium heat. The oil should be about 375 degrees. You can also use a deep fryer for this step, but your fryer will likely require more oil.
4. When the oil is hot, drop 4 to 6 ribs at a time into the oil. Fry for 2 to 4 minutes or until the meat browns. Drain off the ribs on a rack or paper towels. Fry all the ribs before moving on to the next step.
5. Heat a wok or large skillet over medium heat. When the pan is hot, toss in all the ribs and coat with the sauce. Simmer the ribs in the sauce for about a minute while stirring and dump the ribs onto a serving plate when they are all coated with sauce.
6. Sprinkle the ribs with sesame seeds and about a tablespoon of diced green onion, and serve with a pile of napkins.

- SERVES 2 TO 4 AS AN APPETIZER.

•　•　•　•

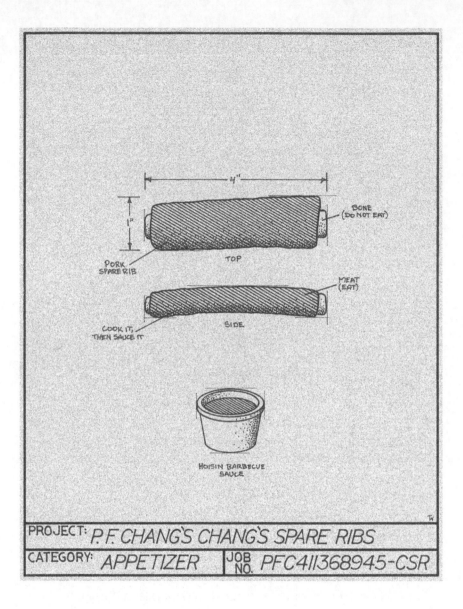

4"

1"

BONE
(DO NOT EAT)

PORK
SPARE RIB

TOP

MEAT
(EAT)

COOK IT,
THEN SAUCE IT

SIDE

HOISIN BARBECUE
SAUCE

PROJECT: *P.F. CHANG'S CHANG'S SPARE RIBS*

CATEGORY: *APPETIZER*   JOB NO. *PFC411368945-CSR*

P. F. CHANG'S
CHICKEN IN SOOTHING
LETTUCE WRAPS

MENU DESCRIPTION: *"Quickly cooked spiced chicken served with cool lettuce cups."*

Throw in a few initials with a little twist on the last part, and you have the name of Paul Fleming and Philip Chiang's Chinese bistro creation, P. F. Chang's. Since the first location opened in Scottsdale, Arizona, in 1993, over 124 new ones have sprouted up across the country—in more than 33 states. No matter the location, it's this dish that gets first raves. Like the very-dead McDonald's McD.L.T. hamburger, which disappeared around the time the first P. F. Chang's opened, the contrasting textures of the cool crispy lettuce and the hot meat filling come together in your mouth for a tasty oral dance party. According to waiters, those little dark bits in the chicken filling mix are "black mushrooms," and there's a good chance your local supermarket doesn't stock them. But a great alternative can be found in the Asian food section—canned straw mushrooms. Just remember to chop the chicken, water chestnuts and mushrooms up real good for the final sauté. Slip this filling into a lettuce cup, fold it up like a taco, add a little "special sauce," get down tonight.

SPECIAL SAUCE
¼ cup granulated sugar   2 tablespoons soy sauce
½ cup water   2 tablespoons rice vinegar

2 tablespoons ketchup

1 tablespoon lemon juice

⅛ teaspoon sesame oil

1 tablespoon Chinese hot mustard
powder (see Tidbits)

2 teaspoons water

1 to 3 teaspoons chili garlic sauce

STIR FRY SAUCE

2 tablespoons soy sauce

2 tablespoons dark brown sugar

½ teaspoon rice vinegar

3 tablespoons vegetable oil

2 skinless chicken breast fillets

1 cup diced water chestnuts

⅔ cup diced straw mushrooms

3 tablespoons chopped green onion

1 teaspoon minced garlic (1 clove)

1 cup fried maifun rice sticks (see
Tidbits)

4 to 5 iceberg lettuce cups

1. Make the special sauce (for spooning over your lettuce wraps) by dissolving the ¼ cup sugar in ½ cup water in a small bowl. Add 2 tablespoons soy sauce, 2 tablespoons rice vinegar, 2 tablespoons ketchup, 1 tablespoon lemon juice and ⅛ teaspoon sesame oil. Mix well and refrigerate this sauce until you're ready to serve the lettuce wraps. Combine the 2 teaspoons water with the Chinese hot mustard and set this aside as well. Eventually you will add your desired measurement of Chinese mustard and garlic chili sauce to the special sauce mixture to pour over your lettuce wraps. In the restaurant chain, waiters prepare the sauce at your table the same way, depending on your desired heat level. I'll talk more about that later.

2. Prepare the stir fry sauce by mixing the soy sauce, brown sugar, and rice vinegar together in a small bowl.

3. To prepare the filling for your lettuce wraps, bring 2 tablespoons of the vegetable oil to high heat in a wok or large frying pan. Sauté the chicken breasts for 4 to 5 minutes per side or until done. Remove chicken from the pan to cool. Keep the oil in the pan.

4. As the chicken cools be sure your water chestnuts and mush-rooms have been diced to about the size of small peas.
5. When you can handle the chicken, hack it up with a sharp knife so that no piece is bigger than a dime. With the wok or pan on high heat, add the remaining tablespoon of vegetable oil. Add the chicken, garlic, water chestnuts and mushrooms to the pan. Add the stir fry sauce to the pan and sauté the mixture for a couple minutes then spoon it into a dish lined with a bed of fried rice noodles (maifun).
6. Serve chicken with a side of lettuce cups. Make these lettuce cups by slicing the top off of a head of iceberg lettuce right through the middle of the head. Pull your lettuce cups off of the outside of this slice.
7. Make the special sauce at the table by adding your desired measurement of mustard and chili sauce to the special sauce blend: 1 teaspoon each of mustard and chili sauce for mild, 2 teaspoons each for medium and 3 teaspoons of each for hot. Stir well.
8. Assemble lettuce wraps by spooning filling into a lettuce cup, adding special sauce over the top, folding the sucker up like a taco, then munching down upon it with reckless abandon.

- SERVES 2 TO 3 AS AN APPETIZER.

TIDBITS

Follow the directions on the package for frying the maifun (rice sticks)—usually by pouring 2 inches of vegetable oil into a pan and heating to around 400 degrees. Add maifun, a little at a time, and when it floats to the top remove it to a paper towel. The rapid noodle expansion is actually quite exciting.

Rather than powdered Chinese hot mustard, you can instead use the kind that comes already prepared in the bottle so that you don't have to add water. Your choice.

• • • •

P. F. CHANG'S
SHRIMP DUMPLINGS

MENU DESCRIPTION: *"Served with a ginger chili pepper soy sauce. (Pan-fried or steamed.)"*

Shrimp Dumplings from P. F. Chang's are scrumptious mounds of shrimp and other yummy ingredients wrapped in wonton wrappers and steamed. You can also order them pan-fried, which makes the bottom of each little package a nice crispy brown. The dumplings are served with a soy-based dipping sauce that can be cloned by combining six ingredients in a saucepan. Recreating that part was easy. But those dumplings—oh, man! I must have gone through a couple boatloads of shrimp trying to figure out the best way to get my filling to hold together like the real thing. I tried adding egg and cornstarch and potato starch and flour to pureed cooked shrimp, but all I got was a shrimp mush that made the dumplings starchy and less flavorful than the real deal. It was only when I remembered hearing about how years ago shrimp molds were created into which pureed raw shrimp was poured and then cooked, creating uniform shrimp shapes that still had the taste and texture of unprocessed shrimp. No binders necessary. So get out your food processor and prepare yourself for the not-so-pretty sight of pulverized raw shrimp. At least you don't have to worry about the size of the shrimp you buy for this recipe, since you're going to mash up the little dudes anyway.

SAUCE

½ cup water
¼ cup soy sauce
2 tablespoons granulated sugar
1 tablespoon rice vinegar

1 tablespoon chopped green
    onion (green part only)
½ teaspoon chili oil

FILLING

½ pound raw shrimp (peeled and
    deveined)
1 tablespoon finely minced carrot
1 tablespoon finely minced green
    onion
½ teaspoon minced fresh ginger

½ teaspoon minced fresh garlic
¼ teaspoon salt
¼ teaspoon granulated sugar

8 wonton wrappers
1 egg, beaten

1. Make dipping sauce by simmering ingredients over medium heat for 1 minute. Remove the sauce from the heat and set it aside to cool.
2. Make shrimp filling for the dumplings by pureeing the shrimp in a food processor until it makes a smooth paste. Add carrot, green onion, ginger, garlic, salt, and sugar and pulse the food processor a couple times to mix.
3. Measure a heaping tablespoon of this filling into the center of a wonton wrapper. Brush beaten egg on each of the top four edges. Bring two opposite corners up to meet in the middle and press together over the filling. Bring the other two opposite corners up and pinch all the edges together making a square package with sealed edges. Repeat with the remaining ingredients and let the dumplings sit for about ten minutes in the refrigerator so that the "egg glue" sets up.
4. Prepare a steamer with hot water. When the water is simmering and steaming nicely drop in the dumplings (four at a time if your steamer is small) and steam them for 15 minutes. Serve these immediately if you want steamed dumplings. To clone the pan-fried version heat up some vegetable oil that's about ¼-inch deep in a skillet over medium heat. When the

oil is hot place the steamed dumpling with the flat side down in the oil and sauté for a couple of minutes or until the bottom is golden brown. Serve with the dipping sauce.

• SERVES 2 TO 4 (MAKES 8 DUMPLINGS).

• • • •

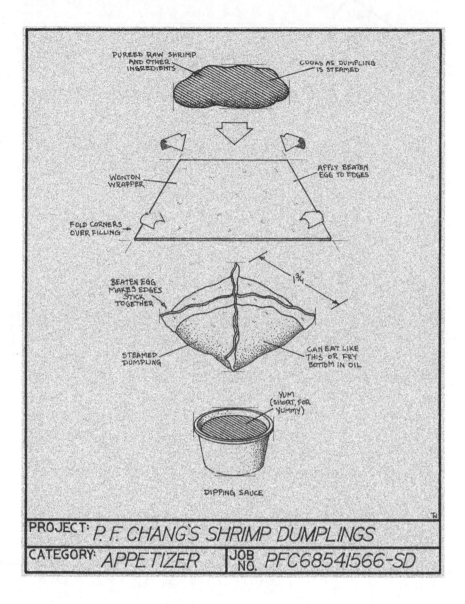

PUREED RAW SHRIMP AND OTHER INGREDIENTS

COOKS AS DUMPLING IS STEAMED

WONTON WRAPPER

APPLY BEATEN EGG TO EDGES

FOLD CORNERS OVER FILLING

BEATEN EGG MAKES EDGES STICK TOGETHER

1¾"

STEAMED DUMPLING

CAN EAT LIKE THIS OR FRY BOTTOM IN OIL

YUM (SHORT, FOR YUMMY)

DIPPING SAUCE

PROJECT: P. F. CHANG'S SHRIMP DUMPLINGS

CATEGORY: APPETIZER

JOB NO. PFC68541566-SD

P. F. CHANG'S GARLIC SNAP PEAS

MENU DESCRIPTION: *"Stir-fried with garlic."*

This is a standard side dish at the country's hottest Chinese dinner chain, and it'll take you just a couple minutes to duplicate at home as a good veggie side for any entrée, Chinese or otherwise. It's especially good when you're pressed to slam together a last-minute vegetable to go with tonight's dinner. You can certainly stay traditional and use a wok for this, but I always just use a medium-size nonstick skillet. The trick is to sauté the snap peas quickly over pretty high heat, tossing often, until they're hot, yet still crispy and bright green. You get the garlic in right at the end, and then quickly pop it off the heat so the garlic doesn't scorch. You don't want anyone getting "bitter garlic face."

2 cups fresh sugar snap peas
2 teaspoons vegetable oil
⅛ teaspoon salt

dash ground black pepper
2 cloves garlic, minced

1. Prepare snap peas by cutting off the tips on each end of the pods.
2. Preheat oil in a wok or medium skillet over medium/high heat.
3. Sauté snap peas in oil with salt and black pepper for 2½ to 3 minutes, tossing often, until peas are cooked, but still crispy.

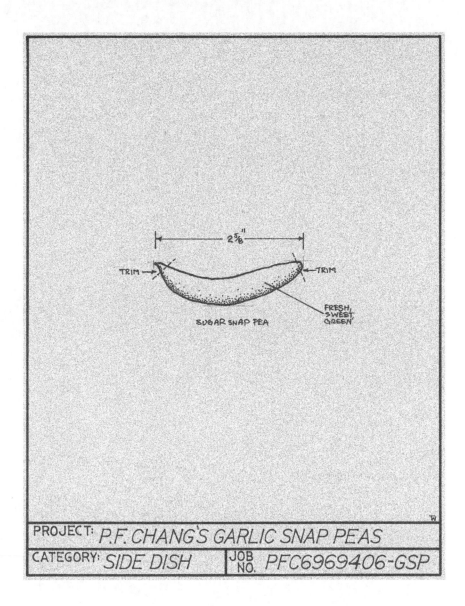

$2\frac{5}{8}''$

TRIM →

← TRIM

FRESH, SWEET, GREEN

SUGAR SNAP PEA

PROJECT: *P.F. CHANG'S GARLIC SNAP PEAS*

CATEGORY: *SIDE DISH*

JOB NO. *PFC6969406-GSP*

The pods should begin to get a few dark brown scorched spots developing on them when they're done. Add minced garlic, toss a bit more, then immediately pour the snap peas out onto a serving platter. If you keep the garlic in too long it could burn and get bitter on you, so don't leave it in the hot pan for any longer than about 10 seconds.

- SERVES 2 TO 4.

• • • •

P. F. CHANG'S
CHANG'S SPICY CHICKEN

MENU DESCRIPTION: *"Lightly dusted, stir-fried in a sweet Szechwan sauce. (Our version of General Chu's.)"*

The sweet and spicy zing in the secret sauce sets this recipe apart as one of P. F. Chang's top picks. If you're looking for something simple to make with those chicken breasts sitting in the fridge, this is a good choice. Once the sauce is finished all you have to do is sauté your chicken and combine. And you'll probably want to make up a little white or brown rice, like at the restaurant. If you can't find straight chili sauce for this recipe, the more common chili sauce with garlic in it will work just as well.

SAUCE

2 teaspoons vegetable oil
2 tablespoons chopped garlic
   (3 to 4 cloves)
3 tablespoons chopped green
   onions (about 3 onions)
1 cup pineapple juice
2 tablespoons chili sauce
2 tablespoons rice vinegar

4 teaspoons granulated sugar
1 teaspoon soy sauce
2 tablespoons water
½ teaspoon cornstarch

1 cup vegetable oil
2 skinless chicken breast fillets
⅓ cup cornstarch

1. Make the sauce by heating 2 teaspoons vegetable oil in medium saucepan. Sauté the garlic and onion in the oil for just a few seconds, not allowing the ingredients to burn, then quickly add the pineapple juice, followed by chili sauce, vinegar, sugar, and soy sauce.
2. Dissolve cornstarch in 2 tablespoons water and add it to the other ingredients in the saucepan. Bring mixture to a boil and continue to simmer on medium/high heat for 3 to 5 minutes or until thick and syrupy.
3. Heat 1 cup vegetable oil in a wok or a medium saucepan over medium heat.
4. While oil heats up, chop chicken breast fillets into bite-size pieces. In a medium bowl, toss chicken pieces with cornstarch until dusted.
5. Sauté coated chicken in the hot oil, stirring occasionally, until light brown. Remove chicken to a rack or paper towels to drain for a moment. Pour chicken into a medium bowl, add sauce and toss well to coat chicken. Serve immediately with rice on the side.

- SERVES 2.

• • • •

P. F. CHANG'S
DAN-DAN NOODLES

MENU DESCRIPTION: *"Scallions, garlic and chili peppers stir-fried with ground chicken nesting on hot egg noodles. Garnished with shredded cucumber and bean sprouts."*

To clone P. F. Chang's take on this traditional Chinese noodle dish you should use a wok, but I found that a large saucepan works well too. Sauté a couple chicken breasts ahead of time and give them a chance to cool so you can finely mince them up. The menu says the chicken is "ground" but it's actually more of a fine mince. Get out the cleaver, if you've got one, and chop away. Or just use a big chef's knife. You can prepare the chicken ahead of time and keep it covered in the fridge until you're ready to make the dish. Once you've got the chicken hacked up, you'll have tasty noodles on the table in less than 10 minutes.

2 chicken skinless breast fillets,
    cooked and minced
    (approx. 2 cups)
1 6-ounce pkg. chow mein
    noodles, cooked
2 tablespoons vegetable oil
1 tablespoon minced garlic
¼ cup chopped green onions
    (green part only)

6 tablespoons soy sauce
½ cup chicken broth
¼ cup dark brown sugar
1 teaspoon chili-garlic sauce
4 teaspoons cornstarch
½ cup water

GARNISH

½ cup julienned English cucumber   ½ cup bean sprouts

1. Cook chicken fillets first by simply sautéing them in a skillet in a little oil for 10 to 12 minutes. Let the chicken fillets cool, and then mince them into little bits with a sharp knife.
2. Prepare noodles following the directions on the package: boil noodles for 3 to 5 minutes in 8 to 10 cups water.
3. Make sauce by heating oil over medium heat in a saucepan or wok. Add garlic and green onion and sauté for just a few seconds, being careful not to burn the garlic. Add the soy sauce, chicken broth, brown sugar and chili-garlic sauce. Combine the cornstarch with ½ cup water and stir it into the sauce. Simmer sauce for about 2 minutes or until it thickens.
4. When the sauce is thick, add the chicken and simmer for an additional 5 minutes.
5. Pile cooked noodles onto a serving plate. Spoon chicken and sauce over the top of the noodles, then garnish with julienned cucumber on one side and bean sprouts on the other.

• SERVES 4.

P. F. CHANG'S
LEMON PEPPER SHRIMP

MENU DESCRIPTION: *"Stir-fried with chives and bean sprouts."*

Chefs at P. F. Chang's China Bistro cook most dishes in heavy woks over extremely high heat with sparks flying and flames nipping at their noses. The special stove is designed so that the tall fires work at the back end of the wok, away from the chef. The well-ventilated stove is built with a steady stream of running water nearby to thin sauces and rinse the woks after each dish is prepared. Since we don't have those phat, bad-boy stoves at home, the challenge is to tweak the recipe for standard kitchen equipment. Using a gas stove and a wok will get you the best duplicate, but this recipe can be knocked off nicely with a large skillet, if that's all you've got. Things are moving fast back in those P. F. Chang's kitchens. The chefs are well-trained, but they eyeball measurements for sauces with a ladle, so each wok-prepared dish is going to come out a little different. Considering this, I figured the best way to get a good clone would be to order the dish several times. I averaged the flavors by combining several batches of sauce (requesting extra on the side) into one large bowl, and then used that mixture to create the recipe. This technique works great for recipes like this one where the sauce is key, and measurements at the restaurant aren't exactly scientific. The shrimp is lightly breaded—they use potato starch, but cornstarch is a good substitute—and flash fried in oil. Strain the shrimp out of the oil, add it back to the pan with the sauce, and you've got yourself a clone.

SAUCE

1 tablespoon vegetable oil
2 tablespoons chopped
   garlic
½ teaspoon minced
   ginger
⅓ cup soy sauce
¾ cup water
2 teaspoons cornstarch
¼ cup dark brown sugar
2 teaspoons lemon juice

2 teaspoons coarse grind black
   pepper

1 pound medium raw shrimp
   (31/40 count), shelled and
   deveined
½ cup cornstarch
1 cup vegetable oil
4 thin lemon slices, each cut into
   quarters

GARNISH

1 teaspoon vegetable oil
2 large green onions

1 cup bean sprouts

1. Make sauce by heating 1 tablespoon oil in a wok or large saucepan over medium heat. Sauté garlic and ginger in the hot oil for about 15 seconds being careful not to burn the garlic. Add the soy sauce, then dissolve cornstarch in the water and add the mixture to the pan. Add brown sugar, lemon juice and black pepper and bring mixture to a boil. Simmer for two minutes then remove it from the heat.

2. Coat all the shrimp generously with cornstarch. Let the shrimp sit for about five minutes so that the cornstarch will adhere better.

3. Heat a cup of oil in a wok or large skillet over medium heat. Add the shrimp to the pan and sauté for 3 to 4 minutes or until the shrimp start to turn light brown. Strain the shrimp out of the oil with a slotted spoon or spider and dump oil. Replace shrimp back in the wok along with the lemon slices, sauté for a minute, then add the sauce to the pan. Toss everything around to coat the shrimp thoroughly. Cook for another minute or so until the sauce thickens on the shrimp.

4. As the shrimp cooks, heat up 1 teaspoon of oil in a separate

medium saucepan. Cut the green part of the green onions into 3-inch lengths. Add those green onion slices and bean sprouts to hot oil along with a dash of salt and pepper. Sauté for a couple minutes until green onions begin to soften.

5. Build the dish by pouring the green onions and sprouts onto a serving plate. Dump the shrimp over the veggies and serve.

* SERVES 2.

•   •   •   •

P. F. CHANG'S MONGOLIAN BEEF

MENU DESCRIPTION: *"Quickly cooked steak with scallions and garlic."*

Beef lovers go crazy over this one at the restaurant. Flank steak is cut into bite-size chunks against the grain, then it's lightly dusted with potato starch (in our case we'll use cornstarch), flash-fried in oil, and doused with an amazing sweet soy garlic sauce. The beef comes out tender as can be, and the simple sauce sings to your taste buds. I designed this recipe to use a wok, but if you don't have one a skillet will suffice (you may need to add more oil to the pan to cover the beef in the flash-frying step). P. F. Chang's secret sauce is what makes this dish so good, and it's versatile. If you don't dig beef, you can substitute with chicken. Or you can even brush it on grilled salmon.

SAUCE

2 teaspoons vegetable oil
½ teaspoon minced
    ginger
1 tablespoon chopped garlic
½ cup soy sauce
½ cup water

¾ cup dark brown sugar

1 cup vegetable oil
1 pound flank steak
¼ cup cornstarch
2 large green onions

1. Make the sauce by heating 2 teaspoons of vegetable in a medium saucepan over medium/low heat. Don't get the oil too hot or you'll get a major spatter when adding the other liquids. Add ginger and garlic to the pan and quickly add the soy sauce and water before the garlic scorches. Dissolve the brown sugar in the sauce, then raise the heat to about medium and boil the sauce for 2 to 3 minutes or until the sauce thickens. Remove it from the heat.

2. Slice the flank steak against the grain into ¼-inch thick bite-size slices. Tilt the blade of your knife at about a forty-five degree angle to the top of the steak so that you get wider cuts.

3. Dip the steak pieces into the cornstarch to apply a very thin dusting to both sides of each piece of beef. Let the beef sit for about 10 minutes so that the cornstarch sticks.

4. As the beef sits, heat up one cup of oil in a wok (you may also use a skillet for this step as long as the beef will be mostly covered with oil). Heat the oil over medium heat until it's nice and hot, but not smoking. Add the beef to the oil and sauté for just two minutes, or until the beef just begins to darken on the edges. You don't need a thorough cooking here since the beef is going to go back on the heat later. Stir the meat around a little so that it cooks evenly. After a couple minutes, use a large slotted spoon or a spider to take the meat out and onto paper towels, then pour the oil out of the wok or skillet. Put the pan back over the heat, dump the meat back into it and simmer for one minute. Add the sauce, cook for one minute while stirring, then add all the green onions. Cook for one more minute, then remove the beef and onions with tongs or a slotted spoon to a serving plate. Leave the excess sauce behind in the pan.

- SERVES 2.

• • • •

P. F. CHANG'S OOLONG MARINATED SEA BASS

MENU DESCRIPTION: *"Broiled and served with sweet ginger soy, baby corn and spinach."*

Grab a couple half-pound sea bass fillets (not too thick), whip up a simple marinade and you're on your way to cloning one of the most beloved dishes at America's fastest growing Chinese bistro chain. The marinade is made with only six ingredients, so you'll have that done in no time. If you can't find oolong tea, you can use green tea. Loose tea is best, but if you can only find bags, that's okay. One teabag contains 1 teaspoon of tea, so you'll just need half of a teabag for this recipe (in fact, the recipe still works even without the tea). You will need to plan ahead for this dish, however, since the fish must marinate for 5 to 7 hours. Once the fish is marinated, fire up the oven to bake it, then finish it off under the broiler. Sauté some spinach, garlic, and tiny corn for an optional bed that makes the dish indistinguishable from the real thing.

MARINADE/SAUCE

2 cups water
⅔ cup soy sauce
¾ cup light brown sugar
2 teaspoons minced fresh ginger

1 teaspoon minced fresh garlic
½ teaspoon oolong tea

Two ½-pound sea bass fillets

OPTIONAL GARNISH

1 tablespoon oil
6 handfuls fresh spinach
½ teaspoon minced fresh garlic

1 5.5-ounce can whole baby sweet
corn (6 to 8 baby corns),
drained

1. Make your sauce and marinade by combining the six ingredients in a medium saucepan over medium heat. Bring to a boil then reduce heat and simmer for 5 minutes. Cool uncovered, then strain out the ginger, garlic, and tea.
2. Put your sea bass fillets in a storage bag or a covered container with 2 cups of the marinade. Let the fish have a nice soak in the marinade for 5 to 7 hours in the fridge. If the sauce doesn't completely cover the fish, be sure to turn the fillets a couple hours in so that all sides get marinated.
3. When you are ready to prepare the fish, preheat your oven to 425 degrees.
4. Arrange the fillets on a baking sheet. Bake the fish for 22 minutes or until the edges of the fillets are starting to turn brown. Crank the oven up to a high broil and broil fish for 2 to 3 minutes or until you get some dark patches around the edge of the fillets. Just don't let them burn.
5. As your fish is baking, heat up a wok or large skillet with one tablespoon of vegetable oil over medium heat. Add the spinach, garlic, and baby sweet corn, and a dash of salt and pepper to the pan. Sauté the veggies just until the spinach is wilted, then arrange half of the spinach and corn on each of two plates.
6. When the sea bass is done broiling, use a spatula to carefully lay each fillet on the bed of spinach and baby corn. Split the remaining sauce and pour it over each of the fillets before serving.

- SERVES 2.

•   •   •   •

P. F. CHANG'S
ORANGE PEEL CHICKEN

MENU DESCRIPTION: *"Tossed with orange peel and chili peppers for a spicy/citrus combination."*

Several of P. F. Chang's top-selling items are similar in preparation technique: Bite-size pieces of meat are lightly breaded and wok-seared in oil, then doused with a secret sauce mixture. That's the basis for this recipe as well, but I have a special fondness for the citrusy sweet and spicy flavors found in this entrée. The heat comes from chili garlic sauce, which you'll find in the aisle with the Asian foods in your supermarket—the rest of the sauce ingredients are common stuff. The orange peel is julienned into thin strips before adding it to the dish. Since the flavor from the peel is so strong, we won't need to add it until the end. Cook up some white or brown rice to serve alongside this dish and get the chopsticks ready.

SAUCE

1 tablespoon vegetable oil
2 tablespoons minced garlic
4 green onions, sliced
1 cup tomato sauce
½ cup water
¼ cup granulated sugar
2 tablespoons chili garlic sauce

1 tablespoon soy sauce

½ cup vegetable oil
4 skinless chicken breast fillets
½ cup cornstarch
peel from ¼ orange, julienned
    (into ⅛-inch-wide strips)

1. Prepare sauce by heating 1 tablespoon of oil in a medium saucepan over medium heat. Add minced garlic and sliced green onions. Add tomato sauce and water quickly before the garlic burns. Add sugar, chili garlic sauce, and soy sauce and bring to a boil. Simmer 5 to 6 minutes or until sauce thickens, then turn off the heat.
2. Prepare the chicken by heating ½ cup oil in a wok over medium heat. Slice chicken breast fillets into bite-size pieces. Coat each piece of chicken with cornstarch. Arrange coated chicken on a plate until all chicken is coated. When oil in the wok is hot, add about half of the chicken to the oil and cook for a couple minutes or until brown on one side, then flip the chicken over. When chicken is golden brown, remove the pieces to a rack or paper towels to drain. Repeat with the remaining chicken. When all of the chicken is cooked rinse the oil out of the wok with water and place it back on the stove to heat up.
3. When wok is hot again add julienned orange peel and chicken. Heat for 20 to 30 seconds or so, stirring gently. Add sauce to the pan and cook for about 2 minutes. Stir the dish a couple times but do it gently so you don't knock the coating off the chicken. Cook until the sauce thickens then serve with white or brown rice on the side.

- SERVES 3 TO 4.

• • • •

P. F. CHANG'S
CHOCOLATE TORTE

MENU DESCRIPTION: *"Served with vanilla bean and raspberry sauce."*

P. F. Chang's contracts with local bakeries to produce these delicious flourless chocolate cakes in each city where the Chinese bistros are based. The restaurants aren't built for baking, and this way the chain can ensure a fresh product every day. Now, if you're a chocolate lover or there's one nearby, this is the recipe for you. The torte is only five ingredients, and the versatile sauces create the perfect gourmet touch. Any leftover torte and sauce can be frozen, then thawed at a later date to effortlessly impress.

½ cup butter (1 stick)
3 cups semi-sweet chocolate chips
   (18-ounces)

4 eggs
½ cup granulated sugar
1 teaspoon vanilla extract

VANILLA SAUCE

2 cups cream
½ cup granulated sugar
½ of a vanilla bean (split down
   the middle)

4 egg yolks

RASPBERRY SAUCE

one 12-ounce bag frozen
raspberries, thawed
3 tablespoons granulated sugar

2 to 4 tablespoons water
2 tablespoons Chambord
raspberry liqueur

1. Preheat oven to 325 degrees.
2. Melt butter in a medium saucepan over low heat. Add chocolate chips and stir occasionally until chocolate is completely melted. Be very careful not to overcook the chocolate or it may burn and taste funny. Not funny ha-ha—funny bad. Remove chocolate from the heat when it's melted.
3. Beat 4 eggs until fluffy in a large bowl, then add sugar and vanilla and mix well until sugar is dissolved.
4. Temper the egg mixture by stirring in just a few tablespoons of the warm chocolate at first. This will keep the eggs from cooking. Slowly add the rest of the chocolate and mix until well combined.
5. Pour the batter into a 9-inch springform pan that has been lined on the bottom and sides with parchment paper (butter the pan before you add the parchment paper—the butter will make the paper stick). Bake for 40 to 50 minutes or until middle of the cake begins to firm up. Remove, cool, cover and chill the cake until you are ready to serve it.
6. As the torte bakes, prepare vanilla sauce by combining cream with ¼ cup sugar in a medium saucepan over medium/low heat. Use a knife to scrape the seeds from inside the vanilla bean half, then add the seeds and the bean pod to the pan. Heat mixture, stirring often, just until boiling then turn off heat. Watch the cream closely so that it does not boil over.
7. In a medium bowl whisk together remaining ¼ cup of sugar and egg yolks until smooth. Temper the egg yolks by stirring in a few tablespoons of the hot cream mixture. Pour the entire mixture back into the saucepan and heat it up again, stirring often until it begins to boil. Immediately pour the sauce into a medium bowl that has been set in a larger bowl filled with ice. This ice bath will help to quickly cool the sauce so

that it doesn't curdle. Cover and chill the sauce until you are ready for it.

8. Make the raspberry sauce by pureeing the thawed raspberries in a blender. Add 2 to 4 tablespoons of water to thin the pureed berries a bit—if your berries have a lot of juice add 2 tablespoons of water; if they have just a little juice, add 4 tablespoons of water. Strain the seeds from the raspberry puree then pour the puree into a medium saucepan over medium heat. Add 3 tablespoons granulated sugar and 2 tablespoons of raspberry liqueur to the pan. Heat until boiling then remove raspberry sauce from heat. Cover and chill it.

9. When you are ready to serve your torte, first spoon some raspberry sauce and vanilla sauce onto a plate. Carefully place the slice of torte on the sauces, but turn it over so that the top of the torte is on the bottom. This is how a flourless chocolate cake is served—topside down. The restaurant zaps the cake for 30 seconds or so in the microwave before serving, so that it is slightly warm. However, you might prefer yours cold.

•   SERVES 8.

•   •   •   •

RED LOBSTER
TARTAR SAUCE

Here's a clone for the dollop of sweet, creamy goodness that comes alongside your fish entree at the world's largest seafood chain. This original kitchen replica gives you a quick and tasty sauce that has the look and flavor of the real thing—and it's only five ingredients! Use the sauce to dress up your next home-cooked fish platter or as a spread on fish sandwiches and fish tacos.

½ cup mayonnaise
1 ½ tablespoons finely minced
   onion
1 tablespoon sweet pickle relish

1 ½ teaspoons shredded and
   chopped carrot (bits the size
   of rice)
1 ½ teaspoons sugar

Combine all ingredients in a small bowl. Cover and chill.

• MAKES 4 SERVINGS.

• • • •

MAYONNAISE,
ONION, RELISH,
CARROT & SUGAR

SERVING SUGGESTION

PROJECT:	RED LOBSTER TARTAR SAUCE	
CATEGORY: *SAUCE*	JOB NO.	*RL6940696-TS*

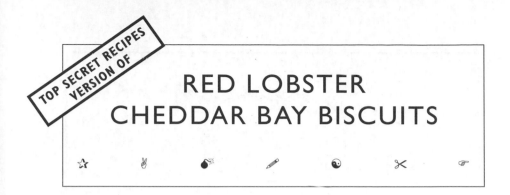

RED LOBSTER
CHEDDAR BAY BISCUITS

Order an entree from America's largest seafood restaurant chain and you'll get a basket of some of the planet's tastiest garlic-cheese biscuits served up on the side. For many years this recipe has been the most-searched-for clone recipe on the Internet, according to Red Lobster. As a result, several versions are floating around, including one that was at one time printed right on the box of Bisquick baking mix.

The problem with making biscuits using Bisquick is that if you follow the directions from the box you don't end up with a very fluffy or flakey finished product, since most of the fat in the recipe comes from the shortening that's included in the mix. On its own, room temperature shortening does a poor job creating the light, airy texture you want from good biscuits, and it contributes little in the way of flavor. So, we'll invite some cold butter along on the trip— with grated Cheddar cheese and a little garlic powder. Now you'll be well on your way to delicious Cheddar Bay. Wherever that is.

2½ cups Bisquick baking mix
4 tablespoons cold butter (½ stick)
1 heaping cup grated Cheddar
    cheese

¾ cup cold whole milk
¼ teaspoon garlic powder

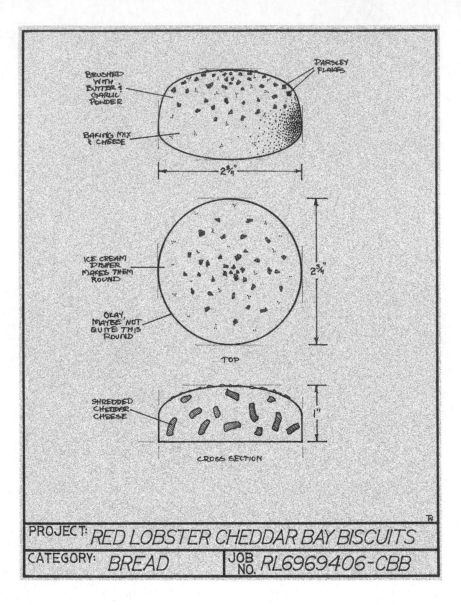

BRUSHED
WITH
BUTTER &
GARLIC
POWDER

PARSLEY
FLAKES

BAKING MIX
& CHEESE

2⅜"

ICE CREAM
DISHER
MAKES THEM
ROUND

OKAY,
MAYBE NOT
QUITE THIS
ROUND

2¾"

TOP

SHREDDED
CHEDDAR
CHEESE

1"

CROSS SECTION

PROJECT: *RED LOBSTER CHEDDAR BAY BISCUITS*

CATEGORY: *BREAD*

JOB NO. *RL6969406-CBB*

BRUSH ON TOP

2 tablespoons butter, melted　　　*¼ teaspoon dried parsley flakes*
½ teaspoon garlic powder　　　　*pinch salt*

1. Preheat your oven to 400 degrees.
2. Combine Bisquick with cold butter in a medium bowl using a pastry cutter or a large fork. You don't want to mix too thoroughly. There should be small chunks of butter in there that are about the size of peas. Add Cheddar cheese, milk, and ¼ teaspoon garlic. Mix by hand until combined, but don't over mix.
3. Drop approximately ¼-cup portions of the dough onto an ungreased cookie sheet using an ice cream scoop. Bake for 15 to 17 minutes or until the tops of the biscuits begin to turn light brown.
4. When you take the biscuits out of the oven, melt 2 table-spoons butter in a small bowl in your microwave. Stir in ½ teaspoon garlic powder and the dried parsley flakes. Use a brush to spread this garlic butter over the tops of all the biscuits. Use up all of the butter.

• MAKES A DOZEN BISCUITS.

•　•　•　•

RED LOBSTER
BACON-WRAPPED
STUFFED SHRIMP

It's shrimp, it's bacon, it's cheese; what's not to like? It's one of the groovy appetizers on the Red Lobster menu, and now you can create it at your crib. Find some large shrimp, a wooden skewer, and cook the bacon about halfway to done before you begin. Mix up a clone of Red Lobster's top secret seasoning and the cilantro-ranch dipping sauce, and you're minutes away from scarfing down a delectable dish that's meant to be a teaser for what's to come. Looks like you'll need to make the main course a real doozy.

SEASONING

¼ teaspoon salt
¼ teaspoon paprika
pinch ground black pepper
pinch garlic powder

pinch onion powder
pinch cayenne pepper
pinch ground allspice

CILANTRO-RANCH DIPPING SAUCE

⅓ cup ranch dressing
1 teaspoon minced fresh cilantro

10 pieces bacon
10 large shrimp

5 fresh jalapeno slices
2 ounces pepper
    Jack cheese

1. Preheat oven to 425 degrees.
2. Make the seasoning blend by combining the ingredients in a small bowl. Set this aside.
3. Make the dipping sauce by combining the ranch dressing with cilantro in another small bowl.
4. Cook the bacon in a frying pan over medium/high heat, but don't cook it all the way to crispy. You want undercooked bacon that, when cool, will easily wrap around the shrimp. Cook the bacon about 3 minutes per side, and don't let it brown. When the bacon is done lay it on paper towels to drain and cool.
5. Shell the shrimp, leaving the last segment of the shell and the tail. Remove the dark vein from the back of the shrimp, and then cut down into the back of the shrimp, without cutting all the way through, so that the shrimp is nearly butterflied open. This will make a pocket for the pepper and cheese.
6. Pour 1 cup of water into a small bowl. Add the shrimp and jalapeno peppers and microwave for 90 seconds or until the shrimp has just cooked through and changed color to white. Immediately pour the water out of the bowl, remove the jalapeno slices and pour cold water over the shrimp. Place the shrimp and jalapeno pepper slices onto paper towels to drain off excess water.
7. Build the appetizer by cutting the jalapeno slices in half and removing the seeds. You should now have 10 jalapeno slices. Place one slice into the slit on the back of a shrimp. Cut an inch-long chunk of cheese (about ¼-inch thick), and place it on the jalapeno slice. Wrap a piece of bacon around the shrimp, starting where the cheese is. Start wrapping with the thinnest end of the bacon. Go 1½ times around the shrimp and then cut off the excess bacon and slide a skewer through the shrimp to hold everything in place. Repeat with the remaining shrimp and slide them onto the skewer with the tails facing the same direction. Make two skewers of 5 shrimp each.
8. Put the skewers onto a baking sheet and sprinkle a light coating of the seasoning blend over the shrimp, then bake for

5 to 7 minutes or until the bacon browns and the cheese begins to ooze. Serve over a bed of rice if desired. Feed the leftover bacon pieces to the dog while you scarf out on the shrimp.

- SERVES 4 AS AN APPETIZER.

• • • •

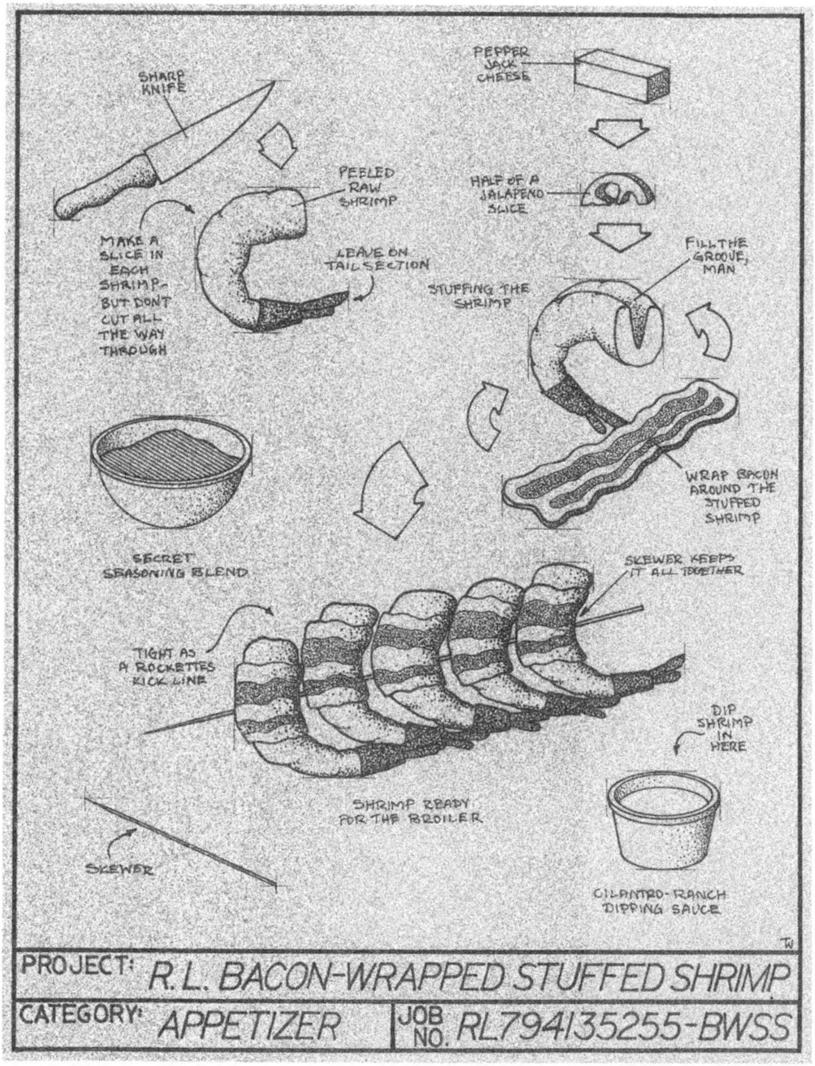

SHARP KNIFE

PEPPER JACK CHEESE

PEELED RAW SHRIMP

HALF OF A JALAPENO SLICE

FILL THE GROOVE, MAN

MAKE A SLICE IN EACH SHRIMP BUT DON'T CUT ALL THE WAY THROUGH

LEAVE ON TAIL SECTION

STUFFING THE SHRIMP

WRAP BACON AROUND THE STUFFED SHRIMP

SECRET SEASONING BLEND

SKEWER KEEPS IT ALL TOGETHER

TIGHT AS A ROCKETTES KICK LINE

DIP SHRIMP IN HERE

SHRIMP READY FOR THE BROILER

SKEWER

CILANTRO-RANCH DIPPING SAUCE

PROJECT: R.L. BACON-WRAPPED STUFFED SHRIMP

CATEGORY: APPETIZER   JOB NO. RL794135255-BWSS

RED LOBSTER
CHEDDAR BAY CRAB BAKE

Ahoy. Banking on the popularity of the chain's Cheddar Bay Biscuits, Red Lobster chefs developed this pizza-shaped appetizer with crust made from the cheesy biscuit dough, and crab and Cheddar cheese baked on top. If you like those tender, cheesy garlic biscuits that come with every meal at Red Lobster, then you'll probably like this. If you don't like it, then you're probably not alone. This item is nowhere to be found on Red Lobster's menu these days, and that should tell you something about how well it sold. But hey, even good dishes get discontinued. If you're up for giving this clone a shot, get yourself some fresh crabmeat. If you want to take a shot a little less expensively, find some quality canned stuff. If you don't want to take a shot at all, try the next recipe.

2 cups Bisquick baking mix
1 ¾ cup finely shredded Cheddar
   cheese
⅔ cups milk
2 tablespoons butter, melted

¼ teaspoon garlic powder
½ teaspoon dried parsley flakes
⅓ cup crabmeat (fresh or canned
   lump)

1. Preheat oven to 450 degrees.
2. Combine baking mix, 1 cup of the Cheddar cheese, milk, and half of the melted butter in a medium bowl. Mix by hand until combined.

3. Pat out the dough into circle approximately 8 inches in diameter, with a slight lip around the edge, like a pizza crust.
4. Sprinkle the parsley over the top of the dough. Be sure the dried parsley flakes are crushed fine. You can easily crush the flakes in a small bowl with your thumb and forefinger.
5. Sprinkle the crab over the top of the dough.
6. Sprinkle the remaining cheese over the crab. Don't go all of the way to the edge of the dough—leave a margin of a half-inch or so around the edge.
7. Bake for 14 to 16 minutes or until the cheese on top begins to brown slightly.
8. Combine the remaining butter with the garlic powder and brush it over the top of the bake as soon as it comes out of the oven. Slice it like a pizza into 8 pieces and serve hot.

• Makes 8 pieces.

• • • •

RED LOBSTER PARROT BAY COCONUT SHRIMP

MENU DESCRIPTION: *"Jumbo butterflied shrimp hand-dipped in batter flavored with Captain Morgan Parrot Bay Rum & coconut flakes. Served with pina colada dipping sauce."*

Fans of this dish say the best part is the pina colada dipping sauce. And it's true; that sauce is so good you could eat it with a spoon. But the coconut shrimp is pretty awesome too, just on its own. Red Lobster's secret formula includes Captain Morgan's Parrot Bay rum, which sweetens the batter and adds a great coconut flavor (plus you can whip up a nice cocktail with it while you're cooking, if that's your thing). Panko breadcrumbs—which give a nice crunch to the batter—can be found in the aisle of your market where all the Asian foods are parked. This secret recipe makes two times the size of a serving you get at the Lobster, so there should be enough for everyone. The real thing comes with salsa on the side in addition to the pina colada sauce, but you may not even want to include it.

PINA COLADA DIPPING SAUCE

½ cup sour cream
¼ cup pina colada mix (liquid)
¼ cup crushed pineapple
   (canned)

2 tablespoons granulated
   sugar

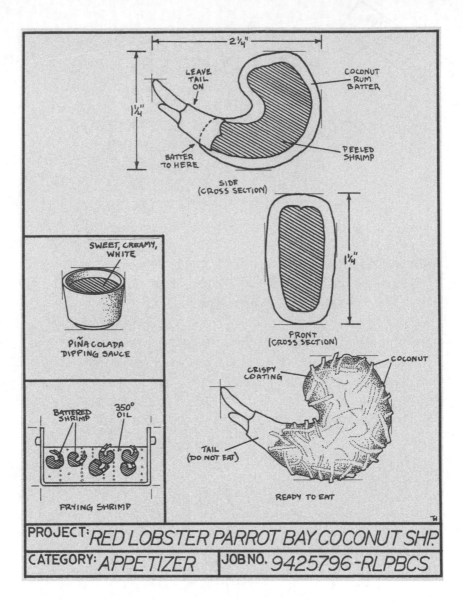

2¼"

1¼"

LEAVE
TAIL
ON

COCONUT
RUM
BATTER

BATTER
TO HERE

PEELED
SHRIMP

SIDE
(CROSS SECTION)

1¼"

FRONT
(CROSS SECTION)

SWEET, CREAMY,
WHITE

PIÑA COLADA
DIPPING SAUCE

CRISPY
COATING

COCONUT

TAIL
(DO NOT EAT)

BATTERED
SHRIMP

350°
OIL

FRYING SHRIMP

READY TO EAT

PROJECT: *RED LOBSTER PARROT BAY COCONUT SHP.*

CATEGORY: *APPETIZER*

JOB NO. *9425796-RLPBCS*

SHRIMP

6 to 10 cups canola oil (amount
    required by fryer)
12 large shrimp, peeled and
    deveined (about ½ pound)
1 ½ cups all-purpose flour
2 tablespoons granulated sugar
¼ teaspoon salt

1 cup milk
2 tablespoons Captain Morgan's
    Parrot Bay coconut rum
1 cup panko (Japanese
    breadcrumbs)
½ cup shredded coconut

ON THE SIDE

salsa

1. Prepare pina colada dipping sauce first by combining all the ingredients. Cover this and let it chill out in the fridge while you make the shrimp.
2. Heat oil to 350 degrees.
3. Measure ¾ cup of flour into a medium bowl. In another medium bowl mix together the remaining ¾ cup flour, sugar, and salt. Stir milk and rum into flour mixture. Let this batter stand for five minutes. While the batter rests, combine panko breadcrumbs and shredded coconut into a third medium bowl.
4. Butterfly cut each shrimp before you start the battering: Use a sharp knife to slice through the top of the shrimp (where the vein was) so that you can spread the shrimp open. Leave the tail intact.
5. To batter the shrimp, dip each one in the flour, then the wet batter, then coat each shrimp with the panko/coconut mixture. Arrange the shrimp on a plate until all of them are battered.
6. Fry the shrimp by dropping six at a time into the hot oil for 2 to 3 minutes or until the shrimp are golden brown. Remove shrimp to a rack or paper towels to drain.
7. Serve shrimp with pina colada dipping sauce on the side, along with a small dish of your favorite salsa, if you like.

• SERVES 3 TO 4 AS AN APPETIZER.

• • • •

TOP SECRET RECIPES VERSION OF

RED LOBSTER NEW ENGLAND CLAM CHOWDER

Considered one of Red Lobster's signature items, this dish has been screaming to be cloned for years now. The tiny screams, which sound like hundreds of little clams being plucked from their shells, could no longer be ignored. What's great about this clone recipe is that we don't have to do any of the plucking ourselves. Rather than going through the tedious (and expensive) task of steaming fresh clams and dicing up all the good parts, we can use the more affordable and convenient canned clams found in any supermarket. Just remember to not toss out the clam juice in the cans when you open them, since you'll need that flavorful liquid in the first step.

2½ cups water
3 6.5-ounce cans minced clams
    (plus liquid)
½ cup all-purpose flour
1 teaspoon minced fresh parsley
½ teaspoon salt
¼ teaspoon ground black pepper

1 bay leaf
dash dried thyme
2 white or red potatoes, peeled
    and diced (not russet or
    yellow potatoes)
1 cup heavy cream

1. Combine water and liquid drained from all 3 cans of clams in a large saucepan. Stir in flour, parsley, salt, pepper, bay leaf and thyme. Turn to medium heat.
2. When water begins to bubble, add the potatoes and simmer for 5 minutes. Stir often to keep the potatoes from sticking to the bottom of the pan.
3. Add the clams to the saucepan and simmer for 10 minutes, stirring often.
4. Add the cream and simmer for an additional 5 minutes. Watch the pan carefully to be sure the chowder doesn't bubble over. Turn down the heat if the soup begins to erupt.

*   MAKES 5 SERVINGS.

TIDBITS

Some brands of canned clams seem to be saltier than others. Depending on the saltiness of the clams you choose, you may want to add a bit more salt. Start with an additional ¼ teaspoon of salt if you find the soup on the bland side.

•   •   •   •

RED LOBSTER
TERIYAKI GLAZED
FRESH FISH

Preheat your grill and put on your sandals for this great clone that's perfect when you've got a hankering for a tropical grilled fish dinner. Red Lobster lets you chose your favorite fish from the menu, then prepares it on the grill with a basting of tangy citrus and ginger teriyaki glaze. The delicious pineapple-mango salsa is the perfect finishing touch. Once you've got your favorite fresh fish from the market, you just need to prepare the sauce and salsa, and light the tiki torches.

TANGY CITRUS & GINGER TERIYAKI SAUCE

½ cup thick teriyaki glaze
   (Kikkoman)
⅓ cup orange juice
2 tablespoons honey

2 teaspoons vegetable oil
1 teaspoon lemon juice
¼ teaspoon fresh minced ginger

COOL PINEAPPLE-MANGO SALSA

½ cup diced canned pineapple
½ cup diced fresh mango
¼ cup diced tomato

1 tablespoon chopped green onion
1 teaspoon diced canned jalapeno
1 teaspoon minced fresh cilantro

4 SERVINGS OF THE FISH OF YOUR CHOICE:
salmon, tilapia, rainbow trout,
  halibut, snapper, or swordfish

1. Prepare teriyaki sauce by combining all the ingredients in a blender until ginger is completely pureed. Chill until needed.
2. Prepare pineapple-mango salsa by combining the ingredients in a medium bowl. Cover and chill until needed.
3. Prepare fish by preheating your grill on high heat. Lightly salt and pepper the fish and grill it until done. Brush the fish with a coating of the teriyaki sauce just before it is removed from the heat. Carefully place each fish serving on the center of the plates. Spoon a garnish of the pineapple-mango salsa on top of each serving. Serve extra garnish and teriyaki on the side, if desired.

• MAKES 4 SERVINGS.

TIDBITS

The P. F. Chang's Mai Tai clone (found on page 294) makes a great companion cocktail for this dish, and the Red Lobster Parrot Bay Coconut Shrimp (on page 335) is the perfect appetizer if you're rolling with the tropical island theme.

•   •   •   •

RED ROBIN
SEASONING

☆ ✌ 💣 ✎ ☯ ✂ ☞

Give yourself some time to make a tough decision when you get to this casual chain because there are nearly two dozen gourmet burgers on the Red Robin menu to pick from, not to mention scores of other fantastic food choices. Red Robin claims the steak fries served with your burger are world-famous. I'm not sure if that's been confirmed, but I do know one thing that makes the fries popular in my book: They come in an all-you-can-eat bottomless portion. Want more fries? Just ask, and you can have as many as your belly can pack in. As you're stuffing yourself, you may notice that the burgers and french fries at Red Robin have something in common that makes them taste so special. That's right, it's the seasoning blend. And I've got a clone for you right here that includes instant tomato soup mix as the secret ingredient. So, next time you make a burger, sprinkle some of this *TSR* version of the seasoning blend on the patty. When you cook up some frozen steak fries or french fries, sprinkle a little of this blend on them as soon as they come out of the oven or fryer. Soon, you'll discover all sorts of uses for this versatile spice blend. And the recipe here makes a portion that fits nicely into an empty spice bottle.

3 tablespoons salt
1 tablespoon instant tomato soup mix (Knorr tomato with basil works great)

2 teaspoons chili powder
¼ teaspoon ground cumin
¼ teaspoon ground black pepper

Combine the ingredients in a small bowl and stir well. Store in a covered container.

• MAKES ⅓ CUP.

• • • •

RED ROBIN
5 ALARM BURGER

MENU DESCRIPTION: *"Crank up the heat with Pepper-Jack cheese, jalapenos, fresh tangy salsa, sliced tomato, crisp lettuce and chipotle mayo."*

According to Red Robin waiters, this spicy production is the second most popular choice from a list of 22 delicious designer burgers on the menu. If you like a peppery punch from your chow, this is the burger recipe to add to your grill-time repertoire. The hamburger patties on Red Robin burgers are huge, weighing in at ⅓ of a pound each, so get out your kitchen scale if you want a good clone. The restaurant chain uses its secret spice blend to season the patty, so whip that up first from the clone recipe on page 342 (or you can substitute seasoned salt, such as Lawry's). Fresh salsa or pico de gallo can usually be found in the deli section at the supermarket, and ground chipotle chile pepper (smoked red jalapenos) can be found next to the chili powder in the spice aisle. It's good stuff to have on hand in your spice cabinet since it's becoming a more popular ingredient these days.

CHIPOTLE MAYO

¼ cup mayonnaise
¼ teaspoon ground chipotle chile pepper
⅛ teaspoon paprika

1 5.5-ounce ground beef patty

¼ teaspoon (approx.) Red Robin Seasoning clone (on page 342)
2 slices pepper Jack cheese
1 sesame seed hamburger bun

4 to 6 bottled jalapeno slices
    (nacho slices)
2 tablespoons fresh salsa or pico
    de gallo

⅓ cup shredded iceberg lettuce

1. Make the chipotle mayo spread by combining the ingredients in a small bowl. Cover and chill until you are ready to use it.
2. Preheat barbecue or indoor grill to medium heat.
3. Since the ground beef will shrink as it cooks, shape it into a round patty that is slightly larger than the sesame seed bun. Sprinkle a bit of the seasoning blend over both sides of the patty. Grill for 3 to 5 minutes per side, or until the patty is cooked the way you like it. About 1 minute before the burger is done place a couple slices of pepper Jack cheese on top of the patty to melt.
4. As the hamburger is grilling toast the face of the top and bottom sesame seed bun on an indoor griddle or skillet over medium heat.
5. Build your burger by first spreading approximately 2 teaspoons of the chipotle mayo on each of the toasted faces of the top and bottom bun.
6. Stack the hamburger patty on the bottom bun.
7. Stack 4 to 6 jalapeno slices on the patty.
8. Spoon 2 tablespoons of salsa or pico de gallo over the jalapeno slices.
9. Add about ⅓ cup of shredded lettuce on next, then finish the burger off with the top bun.

• MAKES 1 BURGER.

•   •   •   •

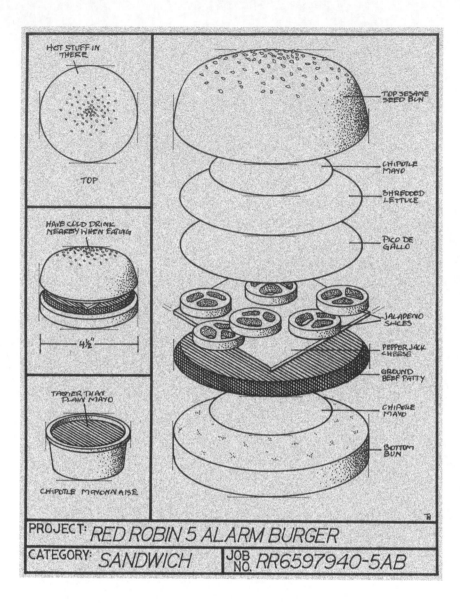

HOT STUFF IN THERE

TOP

HAVE COLD DRINK NEARBY WHEN EATING

4½"

TASTIER THAN PLAIN MAYO

CHIPOTLE MAYONNAISE

TOP SESAME SEED BUN

CHIPOTLE MAYO

SHREDDED LETTUCE

PICO DE GALLO

JALAPENO SLICES

PEPPER JACK CHEESE

GROUND BEEF PATTY

CHIPOTLE MAYO

BOTTOM BUN

PROJECT:	RED ROBIN 5 ALARM BURGER	
CATEGORY: SANDWICH	JOB NO.	RR6597940-5AB

RED ROBIN
BANZAI BURGER

MENU DESCRIPTION: *"Marinated in teriyaki and topped with grilled pineapple, Cheddar cheese, lettuce, tomatoes, and mayo. Dude, you'll be like, ready to ride the pipeline on O'ahu's North Shore after you chomp on this!"*

Here's customer choice number one from Red Robin's huge burger menu. According to Red Robin servers, the beef they use for all their burgers is ground from Angus flank steak. That meat makes for a great burger to be sure, but it's tough to find in the market unless you grind your own. So if you're not up for some good old-fashioned meat-grinding fun, just pick up ground chuck for this recipe. If you can't find chuck, sirloin will have to do. Just make sure the fat content is at least 15 percent, since low-fat ground beef makes burgers that are just too dry and short on flavor. I tested a half-dozen popular teriyaki glazes in the stores and nothing comes close to the stuff they use at the restaurant, so I've included a recipe here to make your own. Be sure to watch your marinated meat and pineapple slices closely on the grill since the sugar in the teriyaki marinade could burn over the open flame. If you're grilling outside, keep the lid open. And don't hit the La-Z-Boy until this puppy's done.

TERIYAKI MARINADE

1¾ cups water
1 cup soy sauce
1 cup light brown sugar

½ teaspoon onion powder
½ teaspoon garlic
   powder

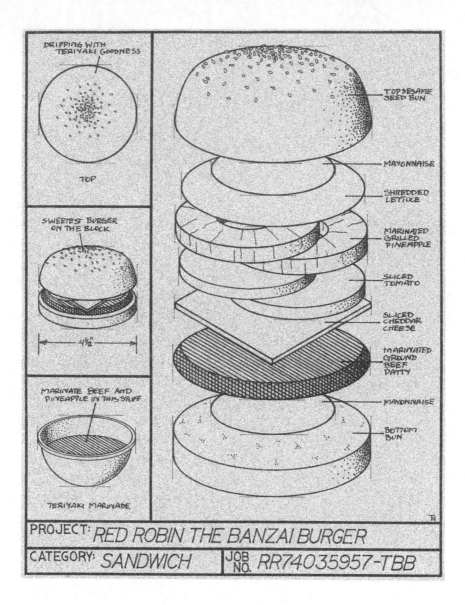

DRIPPING WITH
TERIYAKI GOODNESS

TOP

SWEETEST BURGER
ON THE BLOCK

4½"

MARINATE BEEF AND
PINEAPPLE IN THIS STUFF

TERIYAKI MARINADE

TOP SESAME
SEED BUN

MAYONNAISE

SHREDDED
LETTUCE

MARINATED
GRILLED
PINEAPPLE

SLICED
TOMATO

SLICED
CHEDDAR
CHEESE

MARINATED
GROUND
BEEF
PATTY

MAYONNAISE

BOTTOM
BUN

PROJECT: *RED ROBIN THE BANZAI BURGER*

CATEGORY: *SANDWICH*   **JOB NO.** *RR74035957-TBB*

1 5.5-ounce ground beef patty
2 canned pineapple slices
2 slices Cheddar cheese
1 sesame seed hamburger bun

4 teaspoons mayonnaise
2 tomato slices
⅓ cup shredded iceberg lettuce

1. Make teriyaki marinade by combining all the ingredients in a small saucepan over medium/high heat. Bring mixture to a boil then reduce heat and simmer for 10 minutes or until sauce thickens. Cover and chill marinade in the refrigerator for at least 30 minutes.

2. Form your ground beef into a round patty that is slightly larger in diameter than the sesame seed bun. Pour a little of the teriyaki glaze into a plastic container with a lid (such as Tupperware), then carefully drop in your patty. Add enough teriyaki glaze to cover the patty, then seal up the container and pop it into the fridge for at least 4 hours, but no more than 12 hours. Put the two pineapple slices into another container with a lid, add the remaining teriyaki glaze, cover it and chill the pineapple in the refrigerator for the same time as the burger.

3. When you are ready to make your hamburger, preheat barbecue or indoor grill to medium heat.

4. Start grilling the hamburger patty first. Cook it for 3 to 5 minutes per side or until it reaches your desired doneness. When you flip the burger add the pineapple slices to the grill. The pineapple will take about half as long to cook as the burger. You'll know the pineapple slices are done when they have some nice grill marks on each side. Be careful not to burn the burger or the pineapple. The teriyaki contains sugar, which may char if grilled too long. About 1 minute before the burger is done place 2 slices of Cheddar cheese on top of the patty to melt.

5. As the hamburger is grilling, toast the face of the top and bottom sesame seed bun on an indoor griddle or skillet over medium heat.

6. Build your burger by first spreading approximately 2 teaspoons

of mayo on each of the toasted faces of the top and bottom bun.

7. Stack the hamburger patty on the bottom bun.
8. Arrange the tomato slices on the patty.
9. Stack the grilled pineapple on top of the tomato slices.
10. Add about ⅓ cup of shredded lettuce on next, then finish the burger off with the top bun.

• MAKES 1 BURGER.

•   •   •   •

RED ROBIN
TERIYAKI CHICKEN BURGER

MENU DESCRIPTION: *"A premium charbroiled chicken breast with sweet teriyaki sauce, grilled pineapple, Swiss cheese, lettuce, tomatoes & mayo. Why did the chicken cross the Pacific? Now you know."*

You're out there on the front line hanging over the grill. The smoke's in your eyes, the hair on your forearm is singed, and your sunburn is heading toward 2nd degree. But you don't care, because it's Saturday and you still get all of Sunday to heal. So whip out some chicken and grab the mallet—it's time to pound the flesh for this sweet chicken sandwich. With the kitchen mallet in hand, not only will you have an opportunity for further heroic injury, but you'll also be able to pound the chicken breast to a uniform thickness that works best when building sandwiches. The sweet and salty flavors of the custom secret teriyaki marinade go perfectly with the grilled pineapple and Swiss cheese (this recipe is for one sandwich but you'll have enough teriyaki marinade to make several sandwiches). Just be sure to watch the pineapple and chicken carefully while over the flames, since the teriyaki marinade has sugar in it and could cause charring from nasty flare-ups. Those small fires, while exciting, are just not good for your food.

TERIYAKI MARINADE

1¾ cups water
1 cup soy sauce
1 cup light brown sugar
½ teaspoon onion powder
½ teaspoon garlic powder

1 5-ounce skinless chicken breast
    fillet

2 canned pineapple slices
2 slices Swiss cheese
1 sesame seed hamburger bun
4 teaspoons mayonnaise
2 tomato slices
⅓ cup shredded iceberg
    lettuce

1. Make teriyaki marinade by combining all the ingredients in a small saucepan over medium/high heat. Bring mixture to a boil then reduce heat and simmer for 10 minutes or until sauce thickens. Cover and chill marinade in the refrigerator for at least 30 minutes.
2. Cover the chicken breast fillet with plastic wrap and pound on it with a kitchen mallet so that it is about ½-inch thick. The fillet should be a little larger than the diameter of your sesame seed bun. Pour a little of the teriyaki glaze into a plastic container with a lid (such as Tupperware), then drop the chicken in. Add enough teriyaki glaze to cover the chicken, but make sure you save some to marinate the pineapple slices. Seal up the container and pop it into the fridge for at least 4 hours, but no more than 12 hours. Put the two pineapple slices into another container with a lid, add the remaining teriyaki glaze, cover the container and chill it in the refrigerator for the same time as the chicken.
3. When you are ready to make your sandwich, preheat the barbecue or indoor grill to medium heat.
4. Start grilling the chicken breast first. Cook the chicken for 4 to 6 minutes per side or until it's done. When you flip the chicken add the pineapple slices to the grill. The pineapple will take less time to cook—about 3 or 4 minutes. You'll know the pineapple slices are done when they have some nice grill marks on each side. Be careful not to burn the chicken or the pineapple. The teriyaki contains sugar, which may char if

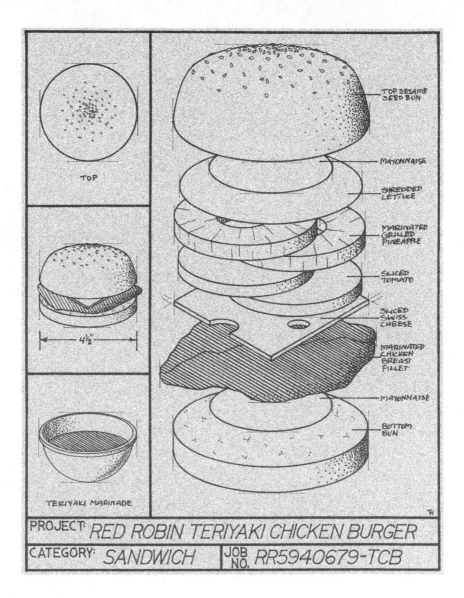

TOP

4½"

TERIYAKI MARINADE

TOP SESAME
SEED BUN

MAYONNAISE

SHREDDED
LETTUCE

MARINATED
GRILLED
PINEAPPLE

SLICED
TOMATO

SLICED
SWISS
CHEESE

MARINATED
CHICKEN
BREAST
FILLET

MAYONNAISE

BOTTOM
BUN

PROJECT: *RED ROBIN TERIYAKI CHICKEN BURGER*

CATEGORY: *SANDWICH*   **JOB NO.** *RR5940679-TCB*

grilled too long. About 1 minute before the chicken is done place 2 slices of Swiss cheese on top of the fillet to melt.

5. As the chicken is grilling toast the face of the top and bottom sesame seed bun on an indoor griddle or skillet over medium heat.

6. Build your sandwich by first spreading approximately 2 teaspoons of the mayo on each of the toasted faces of the top and bottom bun.

7. Stack the chicken breast on the bottom bun.

8. Arrange the tomato slices on the chicken.

9. Stack the grilled pineapple on top of the tomato slices.

10. Add about ⅓ cup of shredded lettuce on next, then finish the sandwich off with the top bun.

- MAKES 1 SANDWICH.

• • • •

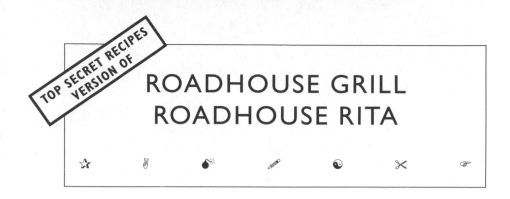

ROADHOUSE GRILL
ROADHOUSE RITA

If you want to keep this cocktail authentic you'll need to rustle up a 32-ounce jar. Bartenders at the Roadhouse Grill mix this delicious yet potent libation in a large mason jar normally used for canning. You say you don't have one of those lying around? You have yet to enter the canning phase of your life? Not to worry. Just wash out a hefty mayonnaise jar—the large size. Those big mayo jars weigh in at exactly 32 ounces and provide you with an excuse for finally ditching the yellow gunk that's been fermenting in the back of the fridge for the last two years. For non-purists, any 32-ounce drinking glass or mug will do. Just be sure to fill your glass nearly to the top with ice before you mix. The salt on the rim is optional, but aspirin after a couple of these babies could prove to be essential.

3 ounces Jose Cuervo Gold Tequila
   (2 shots)
1½ ounces Triple Sec (1 shot)
¾ cup sweet-and-sour mix

¾ cup orange juice
1½ ounces Bud Light (1 shot)
wedge of lime

OPTIONAL
margarita salt (for rim of glass)

1. If you want salt on the rim of your glass, moisten the rim of a 32-ounce mason jar (a cup or glass is fine) and dip it in margarita salt.
2. To make the drink, fill the jar with ice. Add a couple shots of tequila, a shot of Triple Sec, then some sweet-and-sour mix and orange juice (in equal amounts) to within a half-inch of the top of the glass. Stir.
3. Splash a shot of beer over the top of the drink.
4. Add a wedge of lime and serve with a straw.

• MAKES 1 SERVING.

•   •   •   •

ROADHOUSE GRILL
ROADHOUSE
CHEESE WRAPS

MENU DESCRIPTION: *"Our original 'eggrolls' stuffed with Cheddar and Monterey Jack cheese, green onions and a touch of jalapeño peppers. Served with marinara."*

This variation on the popular fried cheese sticks appetizer conceals spicy jalapeno peppers and green onions in the middle, and then it's all wrapped up in large spring roll wrapper before frying. The marinara sauce on the side is perfect for dipping the cheesy tidbit, but you might also try your favorite salsa. To save time—and we all like that—use your favorite bottled marinara sauce for dipping so you won't need to whip up something from scratch.

8 thin slices Monterey Jack cheese
8 thin slices Cheddar cheese
1 jalapeno pepper, seeded and
   diced
1 green onion, diced

4 large spring roll wrappers
1 beaten egg
6 to 10 cups vegetable oil (as
   required by your fryer)

ON THE SIDE
marinara sauce

1. Use a sharp knife to make 8 thin slices each from the end of standard-size hunks of Cheddar and Monterey Jack cheeses.
2. Arrange 2 slices of Cheddar and 2 slices of Jack on your hand, then sprinkle about 1 teaspoon of diced jalapeno on top of the cheese. Sprinkle about ¼ teaspoon of diced green onion on next. Sandwich the peppers and green onion between the cheeses and roll it all up. Fold the cheese and squeeze it all together so that the peppers and green onion are sealed into the middle of the cheeses.
3. Lay a spring roll wrapper with one corner pointing away from you. Arrange the cheese lengthwise on the center of the wrapper.
4. Fold one of the side corners over the cheese filling. Brush a little beaten egg on the tip of the other side corner and fold it over the first corner so that it sticks. Brush some beaten egg on the corner pointing away from you. Fold the bottom corner up and over the filling. Roll the wrapper up, keeping it tight, until it rolls over the top corner with the egg on it. It should stick. Repeat with the remaining ingredients, then cover all the wraps and chill for at least 30 minutes. This will be long enough to heat up the oil in a deep fryer or large saucepan to 350 degrees.
5. When the oil is hot, fry the rolls for 2½ to 3 minutes or until the outside is golden brown. Drain the rolls on a rack or paper towels for 2 minutes before serving with your favorite marinara sauce on the side for dipping.

• SERVES 2 TO 4 AS AN APPETIZER.

• • • •

ROADHOUSE GRILL
BABY BACK RIBS

MENU DESCRIPTION: *"Our award-winning Baby Back Ribs are slow-roasted, then basted with Jim Beam Bourbon BBQ Sauce and finished on our Mesquite grill."*

When your crew bites into these baby backs they'll savor meat so tender and juicy that it slides right off the bone. The slow braising cooks the ribs to perfection, while the quick grilling adds the finishing char and smoky flavor. But the most important component to any decent rack of ribs is a sauce that's filled with flavor, and this version of Roadhouse Grill's award-winning sauce is good stuff. I ordered the ribs naked (without sauce) so that I could see if there was any detectable rub added before cooking and I didn't find anything other than salt and a lot of coarse black pepper. So that's the way I designed the recipe, and it works. You may also wish to add a little sauce to the ribs before they go into the oven as a great variation on the technique.

2 large racks of pork baby back ribs	salt coarse ground black pepper

SAUCE

2 tablespoons vegetable oil	½ cup apple cider vinegar
¼ cup minced fresh onion	½ cup brown sugar
1 ½ cups water	2 tablespoons honey
½ cup tomato paste	1 tablespoon Worcestershire sauce

1 ¾ teaspoon salt
1 teaspoon liquid mesquite smoke
1 teaspoon Jim Beam whiskey
¼ teaspoon coarse ground black
    pepper

⅛ teaspoon garlic powder
⅛ teaspoon paprika

1. To make the ribs, cut each large rack of ribs in half so that you have 4 half-racks. Sprinkle a light coating of salt and a more generous portion of coarse pepper over the top and bottom of each rack. Wrap the ribs in aluminum foil and bake in a preheated 275 degree oven for 2½ hours.
2. As the ribs cook, make the sauce by heating the oil in a medium saucepan over medium/high heat. Sauté the onions for 5 minutes or until they start to brown. Add the remaining ingredients and bring mixture to a boil then reduce heat and simmer for 1¼ hours, uncovered, or until sauce thickens. Remove from heat and set aside until the ribs are ready. Preheat your barbecue grill.
3. When ribs are finished in the oven, the meat should have pull back about ½-inch from the cut ends of the bones. Remove the ribs from the oven, let them sit for 10 minutes or so, then remove the racks from the foil and put them on the grill. Grill the ribs for 3 to 4 minutes per side. They should be slightly charred in a few spots when they're finished. Brush barbecue sauce on the ribs while they're grilling, just before you serve them. Don't add the sauce too early or it may burn.

• SERVES 2 (FULL-RACKS) TO 4 (HALF-RACKS).

•   •   •   •

ROMANO'S MACARONI GRILL CHICKEN PORTOBELLO

☆   ✌   💣   ✏   ☯   ✂   ☞

MENU DESCRIPTION: *"Grilled chicken breast with Portobello mushrooms, smoked mozzarella and demi glace, with a spinach orzo pasta."*

Fire up the grill for this take on one of Romano's most popular entrees. After you grill a couple of portobello mushroom caps, slice them thinly at an extreme angle to make wide slices that fit perfectly on top of grilled chicken breasts that have been rubbed with stone ground mustard (the kind with the whole mustard seeds in it). Romano's delicious demi glace is made from reduced veal stock, but a nice substitute can be made from a combination of canned beef broth and chicken broth. With plenty of garlic, rosemary and thyme in there, you'll have sauce that will get everyone in the house drooling as it simmers on the stove. The fresh julienned spinach tossed into the orzo pasta just before it's served scores extra points.

2 portobello mushroom caps

DEMI GLACE
1 tablespoon extra virgin olive oil   *3 cups beef broth*
6 cloves garlic, crushed   *2 cups chicken broth*

1 tablespoon cornstarch

2 teaspoons chopped fresh
    rosemary

½ teaspoon chopped fresh thyme

¼ teaspoon ground black pepper

ORZO PASTA

1 pound orzo pasta

1 tablespoon extra virgin oil

2 tablespoons minced garlic
    (4 cloves)

¾ cup diced red bell pepper
    (½ pepper)

1 cup chicken broth

4 tablespoons butter (½ stick)

1 teaspoon salt

½ teaspoon ground black pepper

4 cups julienned fresh spinach

4 skinless chicken breast fillets,
    halved (or 8 small fillets)

8 slices smoked mozzarella cheese

8 teaspoons stone ground
    mustard (such as Inglehoffer)

1. Preheat your grill to high. Remove the stems from the porto-
    bello mushrooms and brush the caps with a coating of olive
    oil. Sprinkle salt and pepper on the underside of each cap,
    then grill for about 3 minutes per side. Remove the mush-
    room caps from the grill to cool for about 5 minutes. Slice
    the mushrooms at an extreme angle with a very sharp knife
    so that you get very wide slices. You want the knife almost
    parallel to the cutting surface so that your slices will cover
    the chicken breast. Take 8 of the biggest slices, cover them,
    then chop up the left over mushroom to use in the sauce.

2. Prepare the demi glace sauce by heating 1 tablespoon of extra
    virgin olive oil in a medium saucepan over medium/low heat.
    Crush 6 cloves of garlic with the palm of your hand and toss
    them into the oil along with the chopped mushroom pieces.
    Sweat the garlic and mushroom (slowly cook without
    browning) for 10 minutes. Add beef broth and chicken broth,
    then whisk in cornstarch. Add rosemary, thyme and black
    pepper and simmer for 40 minutes, then remove sauce from
    heat and cover it.

3. Prepare the orzo pasta by boiling it in a large pot of water.
    You want it al dente, which means it should be slightly tough

(we'll be cooking it more later). That should take about 7 minutes. Drain pasta.

4. Heat up 1 tablespoon of oil in a large stockpot or use the same pot you used for cooking the pasta. Add 2 table-spoons of minced garlic and the diced red bell pepper and sauté for 1 minute. Add the drained orzo pasta, 1 cup chicken broth, 4 tablespoons butter, 1 teaspoon salt, and ½ teaspoon ground black pepper. Cook for 10 minutes over medium heat, stirring occasionally.

5. Pound the chicken breasts a bit so that they are uniform in thickness. Rub ½ teaspoon stone ground mustard on each side of each chicken piece, then rub each with some oil. Grill the chicken for 4 to 5 minutes per side or until done. About 2 minutes before the chicken is done lay a slice of portobello mushroom on each piece. Lay a slice of mozzarella on the mushroom on each breast and finish grilling the chicken. When the cheese is melted, remove the chicken from the grill.

6. To serve dish, stir spinach into orzo and immediately spoon an equal helping onto each of four plates. Arrange two chicken pieces on each of the plates, then spoon the demi glace over the chicken and serve.

• MAKES 4 SERVINGS.

• • • •

ROMANO'S MACARONI GRILL CHICKEN SCALOPPINE

MENU DESCRIPTION: *"Chicken breast, mushrooms, artichokes, capers & smoked prosciutto in lemon butter with pasta."*

Mushrooms, artichoke hearts, and prosciutto in a creamy lemon butter sauce surround sautéed chicken breasts and angel hair pasta for this unique and satisfying take on a traditional dish. This clone ranks in the top three most requested recipes on my hit list from the 227-unit Romano's Macaroni Grill. The successful Italian chain is part of the Brinker group of restaurants that controls several other high-profile casual eateries including Border Mexican Grill, Maggiano's, and Chili's.

SAUCE

1 tablespoon white wine
2 teaspoons lemon juice
1 cup salted butter (2 sticks)
⅓ cup heavy cream

1 pound angel hair pasta (or pasta of your choice)
4 skinless chicken breast fillets
½ cup all-purpose flour
3 tablespoons light olive oil

2 tablespoons butter
½ teaspoon lemon juice
2 cups sliced mushrooms
1 ½ cups canned artichoke hearts, sliced (1 14-ounce can)
⅓ cup thick-sliced smoked prosciutto, chopped (about 1 ½ ounces)
2 tablespoons capers

GARNISH

4 teaspoons minced fresh parsley

1. Make the lemon butter sauce by pouring white wine and lemon juice into a saucepan over medium/low heat. Add butter and stir occasionally until it's melted. When the butter is melted, add the cream and whisk thoroughly. Bring mixture to a simmer, stirring frequently. Simmer for 5 to 6 minutes or until the sauce is thick. Remove it from the heat and set it aside.

2. Fold plastic wrap over each chicken breast and pound them with a mallet until the chicken is about ⅛-inch thick. Slice each flattened breast in half, then lightly salt and pepper each piece. Pour flour onto a plate, then coat each chicken piece with a light layer of flour. If you haven't already done it, this is a good time to start boiling your pasta. Follow the directions on the package to cook the pasta al dente, or just slightly tough.

3. Preheat oven to 250 degrees. Heat 2 tablespoons of light olive oil, 2 tablespoons of butter, and ½ teaspoon of lemon juice in a large skillet over medium heat. Add the chicken breast pieces, four at a time, to the skillet and sauté for about 5 minutes per side or until the chicken is light brown. Place finished chicken on a baking sheet and keep it warm in the oven until you are ready to assemble your dish.

4. Rinse out the skillet and place it back over medium heat. Add 1 tablespoon of olive oil to the pan. When the oil is hot add the mushrooms, artichoke hearts, prosciutto, and capers and sauté for 3 to 4 minutes or just until you see some slight browning on the mushrooms and artichoke hearts. Pour the lemon butter sauce into the skillet and remove it from the heat.

5. Prepare each dish by piling pasta on one side of the plate. Sprinkle fresh parsley over the pasta. Arrange 2 chicken pieces on each plate then spoon the mushroom/artichoke sauce over the chicken pieces and serve.

• MAKES 4 SERVINGS.

TIDBITS

If you can't find smoked prosciutto, any prosciutto will do. If you can, have your deli slice it about ⅛-inch thick.

•   •   •   •

ROMANO'S
MACARONI GRILL
PENNE RUSTICA

MENU DESCRIPTION: *"Shrimp, grilled chicken & smoked prosciutto and Parmesan baked in a creamy cheese sauce."*

Romano's top-requested item is so popular they've even trade-marked the name. Grilled chicken, shrimp, prosciutto, and penne pasta bathed in a creamy gratinata sauce is topped with cheese and paprika, and baked until the top is a crispy brown. There's a distinct smoky flavor that comes from the smoked prosciutto used by the chain, and you might have a hard time finding such a unique item at your deli. No big deal. Just use regular prosciutto, and have the deli cut it pretty thick—⅛-inch will do. The dish will still work since you'll get smoky hints from the grilled chicken and shrimp. The chain serves up the entree in a wide, shallow baking dish that comes to you straight from the salamander (overhead oven/broiler). If you don't have any baking dishes like that, try using 9-inch glass pie dishes. These make for a great presentation, especially when served hot right to the table, garnished with a sprig of rosemary and a few sliced pimentos on top. Be sure to get the sliced pimentos, not diced. You want long pieces just like those they use at the restaurant.

GRATINATA SAUCE

3 tablespoons butter
2 tablespoons minced garlic
3 tablespoons Marsala wine
2 cups heavy cream
1 cup grated Parmesan cheese
½ cup milk
½ cup chicken broth
1 tablespoon cornstarch
1 tablespoon Grey Poupon Dijon
    mustard
2 teaspoons minced fresh
    rosemary

½ teaspoon salt
½ teaspoon minced fresh thyme
¼ teaspoon ground cayenne
    pepper

1 pound penne rigate pasta
12 medium shrimp, peeled and
    deveined
2 skinless chicken breast fillets
½ cup (about 2 ounces) thick-
    sliced smoked prosciutto,
    chopped

TOPPING

3 tablespoon grated Parmesan
    cheese

1 ½ teaspoons paprika

GARNISH

12 slices pimentos

4 sprigs rosemary

1. Preheat barbecue grill to high.
2. Prepare gratinata sauce by melting 3 tablespoons of butter over medium/low heat. Add garlic and sweat it for about 5 minutes. Be sure the garlic doesn't brown. Add the Marsala wine and cook for another 5 minutes. Add the remaining ingredients for the sauce and whisk well until smooth. Bring mixture to a simmer and keep it there for 10 minutes or until it's thick. Cover sauce and remove it from the heat.
3. Cook pasta following directions on the package (7 to 9 minutes in boiling water). You want the pasta tender, but not mushy (al dente). Drain pasta and set it aside when it's done.
4. Pound the thick end of your chicken breasts a bit with a kitchen mallet to make them a uniform thickness. Rub chicken

with olive oil, then sprinkle on a bit of salt and pepper. Spear the shrimp on skewers (6 per skewer should work fine), then rub them with oil, and sprinkle with salt and pepper.

5. Grill chicken for 5 to 6 minutes per side. Grill shrimp for 2 minutes per side. When chicken is done, slice each breast into strips.

6. Preheat oven to 500 degrees. Build each dish in a large, shallow baking dish. Or you can use a 9-inch glass or ceramic pie plate. Load 3 cups of pasta into each baking dish. Add one-quarter of the chicken, 3 shrimp and 2 tablespoons of prosciutto onto each serving. Spoon ¾ of a cup of gratinata sauce on each serving and toss to coat. Combine 3 tablespoons of grated Parmesan cheese with 1½ teaspoons paprika, then sprinkle about 1 tablespoon of this mixture over the top of each serving. Bake the dishes for 10 to 12 minutes, or until tops begin to brown. Arrange three pimento slices on the top of each serving, then jab a sprig of rosemary into the center and serve.

• MAKES 4 SERVINGS.

• • • •

RUBY TUESDAY CREAMY MASHED CAULIFLOWER

The low-carb craze is influencing menus of America's restaurant chains, but no chain has embraced the trend as enthusiastically as Ruby Tuesday. *Nation's Restaurant News* awarded the chain "Best Healthy Choice Menu Selection for 2004," based on more than 30 new low-carb dishes added to the menu, including low-carb cheesecake, burgers in high-fiber tortilla wraps, and other low-carb stand-ins such as Creamy Mashed Cauliflower. This most talked-about of the new selections is a side dish stunt double for mashed potatoes, with a carb count coming in at a measly 9 net carbs per ¾-cup serving, according to the menu. The spices and cream that are added to steamed and pureed cauliflower give this dish the taste, texture and appearance of America's favorite side. Serve this up with any entrée that goes well with mashed potatoes, and you'll never miss the spuds.

1 head cauliflower
¾ cup water
1 tablespoon cornstarch
⅓ cup heavy cream
1 teaspoon granulated sugar

¾ teaspoon salt
¼ teaspoon ground white pepper
⅛ teaspoon garlic powder
⅛ teaspoon onion powder

1. Divide a head of cauliflower into florets that are all roughly the same size. Steam cauliflower pieces over boiling water for 15 to 20 minutes, or until the cauliflower is tender. Drain the cauliflower and toss it in a bowl of ice water to bring the cooking process to a screeching halt.
2. When the cauliflower has cooled, put the florets in a food processor along with ½ cup of water. Puree the cauliflower on high speed until smooth, but with some very small pieces of cauliflower remaining in the mix for just a bit of texture.
3. Pour all of the pureed cauliflower into a medium saucepan. Dissolve the cornstarch in the remaining ¼ cup of water and add the solution to the cauliflower.
4. Add the cream, salt, white pepper, garlic powder and onion powder to the cauliflower and stir. Set the saucepan over medium heat and cook, stirring often, for 5 to 10 minutes, or until thick.

• MAKES THREE ¾-CUP SERVINGS.

• • • •

TGI FRIDAY'S
BLACK BEAN SOUP

If you start making black bean soup in the morning using other recipes out there, you're lucky to be slurping soup by lunchtime. That's because most recipes require dry beans that have to re-hydrate for at least a couple hours, and many recipes say "over-night." But you know, tomorrow's just too far away when you're craving soup right now. So, for this often requested clone recipe, I sped up the process by incorporating canned black beans, rather than the dry ones. That way, once you get all the veggies chopped, you'll be souped up in less than an hour. Friday's version of this soup has a slightly smoky flavor that's easily duplicated here with just a little bit of concentrated liquid smoke flavoring found in most markets. Just be sure to get the kind that says "hickory flavor."

2 tablespoons vegetable oil
¾ cup diced white onion
¾ cup diced celery
½ cup diced carrot
¼ cup diced green bell pepper
2 tablespoons minced garlic
4 15-ounce cans black beans

4 cups chicken broth
2 tablespoons apple cider vinegar
2 teaspoons chili powder
½ teaspoon cayenne pepper
½ teaspoon ground cumin
½ teaspoon salt
¼ teaspoon liquid hickory smoke

GARNISH

shredded Cheddar/Monterey   chopped green onion
   Jack cheese blend

1. Heat 2 tablespoons of oil in a large saucepan over medium/
    low heat. Add onion, celery, carrot, bell pepper, and garlic to
    the oil and simmer slowly (sweat) for 15 minutes or until the
    onions are practically clear. Keep the heat low enough that
    the veggies don't brown.
2. While you cook the veggies, pour the canned beans into a
    strainer and rinse them under cold water.
3. Measure 3 cups of the drained and rinsed beans into a food
    processor with 1 cup of chicken broth. Puree on high speed
    until smooth.
4. When the veggies are ready, pour the pureed beans, the
    whole beans, the rest of the chicken broth, and every other
    ingredient in the list (down to the liquid smoke), to the pot.
    Bring mixture to a boil, then reduce heat and simmer uncov-
    ered for 50 to 60 minutes or until soup has thickened and all
    the ingredients are tender. Serve the soup topped with a
    couple tablespoons of the cheese blend and a teaspoon or
    so of chopped green onion.

• MAKES SIX 1-CUP SERVINGS.

•   •   •   •

T.G.I. FRIDAY'S BROCCOLI CHEESE SOUP

So good, and yet so easy. Now you can re-create this one at home just by tossing a few ingredients into a saucepan. Try to find one of the large 32-ounce cartons of chicken broth from Swanson—there's four cups in there, so it's perfect for this recipe. One big head of broccoli should provide enough florets to get you set. Use only the florets and ditch the stem, but be sure to cut the florets into bite-size pieces before dropping them in.

4 cups chicken broth
1 cup water
1 cup half-and-half
4 slices Kraft Cheddar Singles
½ cup all-purpose flour

½ teaspoon dried minced onion
¼ teaspoon ground black pepper
4 cups broccoli florets (bite-size pieces)

GARNISH
½ cup shredded Cheddar cheese

2 teaspoons minced fresh parsley

1. Combine chicken broth, water, half-and-half, cheese, flour, onion and pepper in a large saucepan. Whisk to combine and to break up any lumps of flour, then turn heat to medium/high.
2. Bring soup to a boil, then reduce heat to low.

3. Add broccoli to soup and simmer for 15 to 20 minutes or until broccoli is tender but not soft.
4. For each serving spoon one cup of soup into a bowl and garnish with a tablespoon of shredded cheese and a pinch of parsley.

- MAKES 6 SERVINGS.

• •• • •

T.G.I. FRIDAY'S PECAN-CRUSTED CHICKEN SALAD

MENU DESCRIPTION: *"Pecan-crusted chicken, served sliced and chilled on salad greens tossed with Balsamic Vinaigrette dressing, topped with mandarin oranges, sweet-glazed pecans, celery, dried cranberries and Bleu cheese."*

With dried cranberries, mandarin orange wedges, bleu cheese, pecan-crusted chicken breast, and a delicious sweet and sour balsamic vinaigrette, it's no wonder this salad is the top pick at one of America's first casual dining chains. And don't be intimidated by all the ingredients here. The dressing is a cakewalk since you just pour everything (except the garlic) into a blender. The pecan-crusted chicken is a simple breading procedure, and the chicken cooks up in a snap. You'll be spending most of your time at the chopping block as you hack pecans into little pieces and get the lettuce, garlic and celery ready. I've made this recipe to serve four, but if there are only two of you, you can easily cut it in half.

PECAN-CRUSTED CHICKEN

4 skinless chicken breast fillets
½ cup finely chopped pecans
½ cup corn flake crumbs
¾ teaspoon salt

1 cup milk
2 eggs, beaten
1 cup all-purpose flour
½ cup canola oil

BALSAMIC VINAIGRETTE

1 cup canola oil
1/3 cup balsamic vinegar
4 teaspoons Grey Poupon Dijon
    mustard

4 teaspoons granulated sugar
1/2 teaspoons salt
2 teaspoons minced garlic
    (2 cloves)

1 cup dried cranberries
3 tablespoons dark brown sugar
1/2 cup finely chopped pecans
12 cups chopped romaine lettuce
    (2 heads)

1 cup sliced celery (2 stalks)
2 11-ounce cans mandarin
    orange segments, drained
1/2 cup crumbled bleu cheese

1. We'll make the pecan-crusted chicken first since it is served cold. Pound each chicken fillet to about 1/2-inch thick. You can do this easily by covering each chicken breast in plastic wrap, and pounding away with a kitchen mallet. Combine 1/2 cup finely chopped pecans, corn flake crumbs, and 3/4 teaspoon salt in a shallow bowl. Combine milk with beaten eggs in another shallow bowl. Dump the flour into another shallow bowl. Bread each chicken breast by coating each with flour. Dip the flour-dusted chicken into the egg mixture, and then coat the chicken with a thick coating of the pecans and corn flake crumbs. Preheat 1/2 cup of canola oil in a large skillet over medium/low heat. When the oil is hot, sauté the chicken fillets for 3 to 4 minutes per side or until golden brown. Cool chicken on a rack or paper towels. When you can handle the chicken, cover it and refrigerate for at least two hours.

2. As the chicken chills, you can make the balsamic vinaigrette by combining 1 cup canola oil, balsamic vinegar, mustard, granulated sugar and 1/2 teaspoon salt in a blender. Blend on low speed for just a few seconds, or until the dressing begins to thicken. Don't blend too long or your vinaigrette will get too thick, like mayonnaise. Pour vinaigrette into a small bowl and mix in minced garlic. Chill this until you're ready to use it.

3. When you're ready to build your salads, toss lettuce and celery with about ¾ cup of the balsamic vinaigrette.
4. Arrange the lettuce on four plates, then sprinkle the cranberries over the lettuce (about ¼ cup per serving).
5. Combine the 3 tablespoons of brown sugar with ½ cup finely chopped pecans. Sprinkle 2 tablespoons of this mixture on each salad.
6. Sprinkle about ½ can of drained mandarin segments over each salad, followed by about 2 tablespoons of crumbled bleu cheese.
7. Sliced each chicken fillet into thin strips. Arrange one sliced chicken fillet on top of each salad and serve.

• MAKES 4 SERVINGS.

•   •   •   •

T.G.I. FRIDAY'S
SIZZLING SHRIMP

☆　✌　💣　✏　☯　✂　☞

The T.G.I. Friday's chain engineered a system-wide rejuvenation by upgrading the look of the restaurants and replacing many old menu items with new, creative dishes including several Atkins-approved low-carb selections. Though not low-carb (because of the potatoes) this new menu addition is still a healthy entree choice, and the presentation is very cool with the dish coming to your table in a sizzling iron skillet just like fajitas. This clone re-creates that same sizzling presentation in a large serving for two (if you want to serve more, simply add another 8 to 10 shrimp to the dish—there are plenty of peppers and other stuff in there so the recipe still works). All you have to do is pop an oven-safe skillet into the oven as the potatoes are baking. This way, when the dish is ready to serve, you simply transfer it to this blazing hot pan before bringing it to the table. Ah, nice sizzle. Since this pan will be heating up in a very hot oven, be sure not to use a skillet with a plastic handle that could melt. A large cast-iron skillet is the best choice, if you've got one. If you don't have an oven-safe pan, you can always heat up your skillet on the stovetop.

POTATOES

2 medium red potatoes
2 teaspoons light olive oil
2 pinches salt

2 pinches ground black pepper
2 pinches minced fresh parsley

1 tablespoon light olive oil
1 green bell pepper, sliced
1 red bell pepper, sliced
½ Spanish onion, sliced
1 teaspoon ground cumin
¾ teaspoon Italian seasoning
  (herb blend)
¾ teaspoon salt
¾ teaspoon ground black pepper

¼ teaspoon cayenne pepper
1 14.5-ounce can diced
  tomatoes
24 to 28 medium shrimp, peeled
  and deveined
4 cloves garlic, minced
  (2 tablespoons)
1 tablespoon lime juice

GARNISH

½ cup crumbled ranchero or cotija
  cheese

1 tablespoon minced fresh parsley

1. Preheat oven to 475 degrees. Make sure your oven has two racks so that you have room to heat up the serving skillet. Place a large cast-iron skillet or an oven-safe skillet (that does not have plastic handles) on the lower rack of the oven. This is the pan that will make the shrimp sizzling hot. Slice each of the potatoes lengthwise into 8 wedges. Toss the potatoes in a bowl with 2 teaspoons olive oil, plus a couple pinches each of salt, ground black pepper and minced parsley. Arrange the potato wedges in a nonstick baking pan (or in a pan lined with parchment paper), and bake for 25 to 30 minutes or until potatoes turn golden brown. When the potatoes are done, take them out and turn off the oven. Keep the empty skillet in there on the lower rack. We'll use that at the end.
2. Heat 1 tablespoon of olive oil in a large skillet over medium heat. When the oil is hot, add the red and green bell peppers, and onion. Stir in the cumin, ¾ teaspoon salt, ¾ teaspoon ground black pepper, Italian seasoning, and cayenne pepper. Sauté the vegetables for 8 minutes, stirring often.
3. When peppers and onion have sautéed for 8 minutes, add the can of diced tomatoes, including the liquid to the skillet.

Add the shrimp, garlic and lime juice. Cook for another 5 minutes, stirring often.

4. Use a thick hot pad to carefully remove the hot skillet from the oven. Pour the entire contents of the dish into the hot skillet, then arrange the potato wedges around the edge of the dish. Quickly sprinkle crumbled ranchero or cotija cheese over the center of the dish, followed by about a tablespoon of minced fresh parsley. Serve it up immediately—while it's still sizzling.

• SERVES 2.

• • • •

TONY ROMA'S BLUE RIDGE SMOKIES SAUCE

☆   ✌   💣   ✏   ☯   ✂   ☞

Of the four famous barbecue sauces served on those delicious, tender ribs at Tony Roma's, this is the only one that wasn't cloned in the first restaurant book, *Top Secret Restaurant Recipes*. This sweet, smoky sauce is great on pork spareribs cooked with the Tony Roma's clone recipe in that book, or you can use either of the techniques found in this book: for Chili's Baby Backs on page 123, and for Roadhouse Grill Baby Backs on page 359. Or you can use the sauce on a recipe of your own for pork or beef ribs, even chicken. Now Tony Roma's sells each of its four sauces at the restaurant chain, separately, or in gift sets. But if you don't have a Tony Roma's close by, or you just like to dabble, this is a good way to get that one-of-a-kind barbecue taste at home.

1 cup ketchup
1 cup red wine vinegar
½ cup brown sugar
¼ cup molasses
1½ teaspoons liquid hickory
    smoke

½ teaspoon salt
rounded ¼ teaspoon ground black
    pepper
¼ teaspoon garlic powder
¼ teaspoon onion powder

1. Combine all of the ingredients in a medium saucepan over high heat, and whisk until smooth.
2. Bring sauce to a boil, then reduce heat and simmer uncovered for 30 to 40 minutes or until sauce has thickened.

- MAKES 1½ CUPS.

• • • •

TONY ROMA'S
BAKED POTATO SOUP

MENU DESCRIPTION: *"A house specialty full of baked potatoes and topped with cheddar cheese, bacon and green onions."*

The thick-and-creamy texture and rich taste of Tony Roma's best-selling soup is duplicated with a little flour, some half-and-half, and most notably, instant mashed potatoes. Give yourself an hour to bake the potatoes and around 30 minutes to prepare the soup. Garnish each serving with shredded cheese, crumbled bacon and green onions, and then humbly await your due praise.

2 medium russet potatoes
3 tablespoons butter
1 cup diced white onion
2 tablespoons all-purpose flour
4 cups chicken broth
2 cups water
¼ cup cornstarch

1 ½ cups instant mashed
   potatoes, dry
1 teaspoon salt
¾ teaspoon ground black pepper
½ teaspoon dried basil
⅛ teaspoon dried thyme
1 cup half-and-half

GARNISH

½ cup shredded Cheddar cheese
¼ cup crumbled cooked bacon

2 green onions, chopped
   (green part only)

1. Preheat oven to 400 degrees and bake the potatoes for 1 hour or until done. When potatoes have cooked remove them from the oven to cool.
2. As potatoes cool, prepare soup by melting butter in a large saucepan, and sauté onion until light brown. Add the flour to the onion and stir to make a roux.
3. Add broth, water, cornstarch, mashed potato flakes, and spices to the pot and bring to a boil. Reduce heat and simmer for 5 minutes.
4. Cut potatoes in half lengthwise and scoop out contents with a large spoon. Discard skin. Chop baked potato with a large knife to make chunks that are about ½-inch in size.
5. Add chopped baked potato and half-and-half to the saucepan, bring soup back to a boil, then reduce heat and simmer the soup for another 15 minutes or until it is thick.
6. Spoon about 1½ cups of soup into a bowl and top with about a tablespoon of shredded Cheddar cheese, a half tablespoon of crumbled bacon and a teaspoon or so of chopped green onion. Repeat for remaining servings.

- SERVES 6 TO 8.

• • • •

TONY ROMA'S
MAPLE SWEET POTATOES

Here's a clone for a new menu item at Tony Roma's that's served alongside the Carolina Honeys BBQ Salmon (cloned in the following recipe on page 387). With maple syrup, cinnamon and pecans in there, this is a great new way for you to easily prepare sweet potatoes that everyone at the table will surely scarf down with unbridled glee.

I large sweet potato
I tablespoon butter
¼ of a white onion, chopped
   (about ½ cup)

3 tablespoons finely chopped
   pecans
3 tablespoons maple syrup
¼ teaspoon cinnamon

1. Bake sweet potato for 40 to 45 minutes at 400 degrees. This will bake the potato nearly all the way through, while still leaving it firm enough to slice when cool. Remove the sweet potato from the oven and let it cool so that you can handle it. When the sweet potato has cooled, remove the skin and slice it into 1-inch bite-size cubes.
2. Melt 1 tablespoon of butter in a large skillet. Add onion and pecans and sauté for a couple minutes or until onion begins to brown.
3. Add cubed sweet potato, maple syrup and cinnamon and sauté for 3 to 5 minutes, stirring often, or until the sweet potato pieces are hot and tender.

• SERVES 2 TO 4.

• • • •

TONY ROMA'S CAROLINA HONEYS BBQ SALMON

Take one of Tony Roma's famous sauces, brush it over some grilled salmon and you've got a bravo moment. But it's not just about saucing up the fish. The salmon is first rubbed with a secret seasoning blend before it's grilled. The sauce doesn't appear in the show until the end. For your encore, serve this dish along with the preceding recipe for Maple Sweet Potatoes (page 386) on the side just like in the restaurant, and absorb the applause.

SAUCE

1 cup ketchup
1 cup white vinegar
½ cup molasses
½ cup honey
1 teaspoon liquid hickory smoke

½ teaspoon salt
¼ teaspoon garlic powder
¼ teaspoon onion powder
¼ teaspoon Tabasco pepper
   sauce

SEASONING

1 teaspoon salt
½ teaspoon ground black pepper
¼ teaspoon paprika
¼ teaspoon garlic powder

¼ teaspoon cayenne pepper
4 6-ounce salmon fillets (without
   skin)
canola or olive oil nonstick spray

1. Combine all ingredients for the sauce in a saucepan over medium/high heat. Blend the ingredients with a whisk until smooth. When the mixture comes to a boil, reduce heat and simmer uncovered for 30 minutes or until mixture thickens. Remove from heat.
2. Combine all ingredients for seasoning in a small bowl. Preheat barbecue or indoor grill to high heat.
3. Sprinkle seasoning lightly over both sides of the salmon, spray each fillet lightly with olive or canola oil nonstick spray. Grill the salmon for about 3 minutes then rotate it 90 degrees to make criss-crossing grill marks. Grill for another 3 minutes then turn the salmon over for 3 minutes and rotate it again to make criss-crossing grill marks on that side. Grill until done. Remove salmon fillets from the grill, brush with the sauce and serve.

• SERVES 4.

•   •   •   •

WAFFLE HOUSE WAFFLES

It was two friendly Atlanta, Georgia, neighbors who got together in 1955 to build the first Waffle House in their eventual 1,479-restaurant chain. With the dimpled breakfast hotcake as a signature item (and this is 3 years before IHOP was founded!), the privately held chain grew into 20 Southern U.S. states. Today tasty food at rock-bottom prices, plus 24-hour-a-day service, makes Waffle House a regular stop for devoted customers any time of the day or night. And don't even think about referring to your server as a waitress; they're called "associates."

For the best clone of the 50-year-old secret formula for these waffles you really should chill this batter overnight in the fridge as they do in each of the restaurants. But hey, sometimes you just can't wait. If you need instant gratification, the recipe still works fine if you cook up the waffles the same day. At least wait for 15 to 20 minutes after you make the batter so that it can rest and thicken a bit. That'll give you time to dust off the waffle iron and heat it up.

1 ½ cups all-purpose flour
1 teaspoon salt
½ teaspoon baking soda
1 egg
½ cup plus 1 tablespoon
   granulated sugar
2 tablespoons butter, softened

2 tablespoons vegetable
   shortening
½ cup half-and-half
½ cup milk
¼ cup buttermilk
¼ teaspoon vanilla extract

1. Combine flour, salt and baking soda in a medium bowl. Stir to combine.
2. Lightly beat the egg in another medium bowl. Add the sugar, butter, and shortening and mix well with an electric mixer until smooth. Add the half-and-half, milk, buttermilk and vanilla. Mix well.
3. Add the wet mixture to the dry mixture while beating. Mix only briefly. It's okay if there are small lumps in the batter since over beating could produce waffles that are too tough.
4. Cover and chill overnight. (You can use batter right away if you like, but a good 12-hour chill makes a better batter.)
5. Rub a light coating of vegetable oil on your waffle iron or use a non-stick oil spray. Preheat the waffle iron. Leave the batter out of the refrigerator to warm up a bit as your waffle iron is preheating.
6. Spoon ⅓ to ½ cup of batter into the waffle iron and cook for 3 to 4 minutes or until the waffles are brown.

- MAKES 6 WAFFLES.

• • • •

TRADEMARKS

Applebee's is a registered trademark of Applebee's International, Inc.

Benihana is a registered trademark of Benihana, Inc.

Bennigan's is a registered trademark of S&A Restaurant Corp.

Best Foods and Hellman's are registered trademarks of Unilever.

Buffalo Wild Wings is a registered trademark of Buffalo Wild Wings Grill & Bar

California Pizza Kitchen is a registered trademark of California Pizza Kitchen, Inc.

Carrabba's is a registered trademark of Carrabba's Italian Grill, Inc.

The Cheesecake Factory, Sweet Corn Tamale Cakes, Bang-Bang Chicken & Shrimp, and White Chocolate Raspberry Truffle are registered trademarks of The Cheesecake Factory, Inc.

Chevys is a registered trademark of Chevys, Inc.

Chili's, Romano's Macaroni Grill, and Penne Rustica are registered trademarks of Brinker International.

Claim Jumper is a registered trademark of Claim Jumper Restaurants LLC.

Denny's is a registered trademark of DFO, Inc.

Hard Rock Cafe is a registered trademark of Hard Rock Cafe International, Inc.

Houston's is a registered trademark of Hillstone Restaurant Group.

IHOP, Country Griddle Cakes, and Harvest Grain 'N Nut are registered trademarks of IHOP Corp.

Islands is a registered trademark of Islands Restaurants.

Joe's Crab Shack is a registered trademark of Landry's Restaurants, Inc.

Lone Star Steakhouse is a registered trademark of Lone Star Steakhouse & Saloon, Inc.

Margaritaville is a registered trademark of Margaritaville Restaurants.

Marie Callender's is a registered trademark of Marie Callender Pie Shops, Inc.

Mimi's Cafe is a registered trademark of SWH Corporation.

Olive Garden and Red Lobster are registered trademarks of Darden Concepts, Inc.

Original Pancake House is a registered trademark of Original Pancake House Franchising, Inc.

Outback Steakhouse, Kookaburra Wings, Cinnamon Apple Oblivion, and Sydney's Sinful Sundae are registered trademarks of Outback Steakhouse, Inc.

P. F. Chang's is a registered trademark of P. F. Chang's China Bistro, Inc.

Red Robin and Banzai Burger are registered trademarks of Red Robin International, Inc.

INDEX